LIBERTY STYLE

STYLE   MARTIN WOOD

LIBERTY
STYLE MARTIN WOOD

F

FRANCES LINCOLN LIMITED
PUBLISHERS

CONTENTS

For one who had a verdant heart

A MAN WITH
A VISION

Amid the Edwardian Baroque splendour of London's Regent Street, the
Elizabethan-style building of Liberty's department store strikes a delightfully
discordant note. For more than a century this shop has been a magnet for all those
with an interest in design, fashion and interior decoration – just as its founder
intended. A man of enormous talent and boundless energy, Arthur Liberty set out
with a vision. Remarkably, he achieved it.

Arthur Lasenby Liberty was born on 13 August 1843 at Chesham in Buckinghamshire.
His father, also called Arthur, was a draper with a small shop at 16 High Street, next door to
the George Inn (now the George and Dragon). The Liberty family were long established in
Buckinghamshire, Hertfordshire and Surrey. However, in later life Arthur Liberty became
intrigued by the notion that the family might have been descended from one Baglioni, a Corsican
who in around the year 1400 prevented the Spanish from taking control of his native Calvi on
Corsica. In recognition the town gave him the name Libertà, which passed down the generations.
The family subsequently migrated to Marseilles, where Pierre de Libertat (1550–97) defended
the city against the Spanish on behalf of Henry, King of Navarre 1572–1610 and King of France
1589–1610.[1] Some accounts say that the Liberty family fled to England following the French
Revolution in 1789. There appears to be no evidence at all for this. It is just possible that the
family came to England following the revocation of the Edict of Nantes by Louis XIV in October
1685. However, this is also unlikely.[2]

A rather more mundane, but more probable, explanation of the Liberty family's origin is that
they were native to England. The name Liberty is said to derive from that given to people who
worked in lead; various other English surnames, such as Leadbetter and Ledbitter, have a similar
derivation.[3] We know that Arthur Liberty's great-great-grandfather, Daniel Liberty, lived
at Kensworth, then in Hertfordshire, in the early eighteenth century, and his great-grandfather,
also Daniel Liberty, was born there in 1731. He apparently did not travel far, for he was married
at Ivinghoe in Buckinghamshire in 1756 and died at Dunstable in Bedfordshire in 1815.[4]

The second Daniel's son, Thomas Liberty, who was Arthur Liberty's grandfather, was born
in 1772 (or 1773) and married Margaret Edwards on 3 June 1802 in Chesham. Thomas and
Margaret Liberty settled at Weybridge in Surrey and had at least nine children, one of whom,

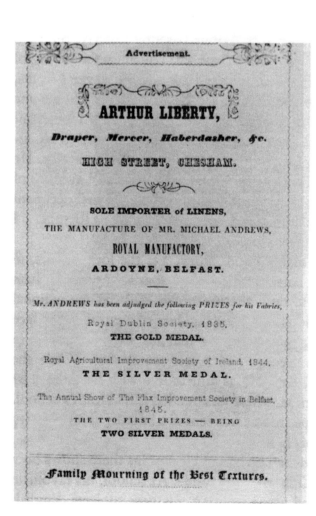

named Arthur, died in infancy.[5] Their next child was a boy
who was also christened Arthur, on 25 December 1814.

We know nothing more of the second Arthur's life until
1842, when he married Rebecca Lasenby in Chesham.[6]
The Lasenby family were an old Buckinghamshire family of
yeoman farmers living in the village of Chartridge, a couple
of miles from Chesham. By the time of the marriage Arthur
Liberty owned a draper's shop in Chesham High Street
and it was here that Arthur Lasenby Liberty was born on
13 August 1843.

It seems that the drapery business was not a success, for
we know that when the young Arthur was eight (in 1852)
the family moved to Nottingham, where his uncle, George
Liberty, had a lace warehouse.[7] Arthur's father went into the
same business, manufacturing lace and hosiery. In the early
days after the move to Nottingham the family's finances
were in a perilous state, and Arthur was sent to stay with
his aunt, Mrs Robert Vernon (his father's sister Margaret).
While he was living with her he attended Miss Heath's
school in High Wycombe. He later went to the University
School at 5 Waverley Street, Nottingham, as a boarder.
Arthur was a clever and artistic child – he loved 'amateur
theatricals, scene painting and butterfly collecting' – but
the school was a mediocre establishment and he always
felt his education had been 'superficial'.[8] He was entered
for a university scholarship, which he failed to win, and it
seems that without the scholarship there were simply not
the funds available to allow him a university education.
His father's business affairs must have continued to be
somewhat erratic, for when he was sixteen, in 1859, he was
obliged to leave school and start work in his uncle George's
lace warehouse. This arrangement did not last very long and
he was sent to London to be a clerk for another uncle, John
Liberty, who had a wine merchant's at 21 Spring Gardens,
a street which is now bisected by Admiralty Arch. We
know Arthur was working for his uncle in May 1859 and
a letter to his mother reveals that his uncle's business was
'really dreadful and it makes him so miserable and without
any spirit that I don't think he can take any interest or use
his influence in getting me into any situation'.[9] His uncle
was indeed unable to help him and shortly after writing

this letter Arthur was apprenticed to John Weeks, a linen
draper of 54 Baker Street, Portland Square.[10] Apparently
'he soon found the place very uncongenial. He did not like
the trade, to begin with, nor the class of customers he had
to attend to, while he was far too excitable in temperament
to be of the slightest use as a cashier.'[11] He also found both
Mr Weeks and his customers dreadfully old-fashioned. It
is hardly surprising that the apprenticeship was terminated
(by mutual agreement) after only two years.[12]

In 1862, after a short holiday at home in Nottingham,
Arthur was able to use the experience he had gained at
Weeks's to take a position at Farmer & Rogers's Great Shawl
and Cloak Emporium at 171–175 Regent Street. He was
eighteen. Designed by John Nash, completed in 1825 and
named in honour of the Prince Regent, Regent Street was
the most fashionable street in London. Forming part of the
Crown Estate, the street was intended for 'luxury trades'
and a ban on butchers, bakers and candlestick makers was
strictly enforced. Indeed it is said that no fewer than half
the shops had royal warrants, including Farmer & Rogers.
Their emporium was among the most celebrated in
Europe, matching anything to be found in Paris, Berlin
or St Petersburg.

We know little of Arthur Liberty's life at this time,
but in an interview published in the *Daily Chronicle* on
21 February 1913 he mentioned that in 1862 Farmer &
Rogers expanded their business into premises next door,
where they opened the Oriental Warehouse. This was the
year of the Great London Exposition, where there had been
an exhibit of Japanese goods that had caused a sensation,
and Farmer & Rogers were presumably cashing in on the
vogue for all things oriental. They put the new department
into the care of two of their younger employees, the junior
of whom was Arthur Liberty. He very soon became its
manager and he held the position for twelve years.

It soon spread around London artistic circles that this
young man had flair, enthusiasm and an interest in the arts.
Among the aesthetes who would drop in to look at goods that
had recently arrived were the artists Dante Gabriel Rossetti,
Frederic Leighton, John Everett Millais, Edward Burne-Jones,
George Frederic Watts and James McNeill Whistler.

Liberty Style

BELOW An engraving
of Farmer & Rogers's
Great Shawl and Cloak
Emporium in Regent Street.

ELIZABETH, N. J.

William Morris was a frequent caller, purchasing items for his own studio; Thomas Carlyle would call, and so would John Ruskin. The architect Norman Shaw came often, as did the sculptor Thomas Woolner. They all found Arthur friendly and engaging, and in the *Daily Chronicle* interview he mentioned that among his closest friends at the time was the actress Dame Ellen Terry (1847–1928). Her elder sister, Kate Terry (1844–1924), then regarded as an even finer actress, had married Arthur Lewis, a partner in Lewis & Allerby, silk mercers of 195 Regent Street, and it may have been he who introduced Arthur Liberty to Dame Ellen.

On 8 June 1865, when he was twenty-one, Arthur Liberty married Martha Cottam at St Pancras Church. How he met her no one knows, but as she was described as an 'actress' (a description that could hide a multitude of sins) it could have been through the Terrys and Arthur Lewis. Martha Cottam seems to have been a colourful character. She had been 'married before', to Henry Wells, whom she married at the church of St John the Baptist, Shoreditch, in 1861. The marriage was a disaster and in 1863 she petitioned for divorce on the grounds of adultery and her husband's cruelty: he had, apparently, held a loaded gun to her head and on another occasion assaulted her with a lobster. Before the petition could be heard, her father-in-law, William Henry Wells, lodged a suit for a decree of nullity, alleging that his son was only eighteen at the time of the marriage and thus unable to marry without parental consent, which he had neither sought nor gained and which would in any case never have been forthcoming. He also alleged that the banns had been called using his son's middle name in an effort to avoid detection (a ruse that had evidently worked). He won the case and the marriage was declared null. George Henry Wells was subsequently packed off to Madrid.[13]

Liberty family folklore is vague on the subject of Martha Cottam. Years later a cousin (Muriel Collie, granddaughter of Margaret Vernon) remarked: 'All I know is, that in his early days, before he started Regent Street, he lodged with a tobacconist, married the daughter – she went off with another man.'[14] The other man was Augustus Glover, also an actor, and Arthur sued for divorce, on the grounds of his wife's adultery, on August 1868.

Free from this unwise entanglement, Arthur determined to find a new wife. Muriel Collie recalled, 'I know he proposed to my Mother three times and, as he had no prospects and no money, she said no!'[15] Recognizing defeat, Arthur pursued other avenues and eventually he married Emma Louise Blackmore at All Souls, South Hampstead, on 25 September 1875. A wedding breakfast was held at the home of his new father-in-law, Henry Blackmore, at 7 Fairfax Road, Hampstead. Emma was two years younger than her new husband. How they met we don't know, but the marriage was to be a long and happy one.

At the time of his engagement to Emma Blackmore, Arthur, now aged thirty, felt he could reasonably expect some form of advancement at Farmer & Rogers – such as being taken on as a partner. This was not an unreasonable request, as the Oriental Warehouse, for which he was responsible, had become the most profitable part of the entire business. The partners refused, however, on the grounds 'that the state of their general business would not justify any further division of the profits'.[16] Arthur's artistic friends all urged him to open his own shop, promising to follow him from Farmer & Rogers, but there was a minor problem: he didn't have the capital with which to do it, and nor, it seems, did they.

Emma decided to persuade her father to support Arthur, even though they were not yet married. Her father might have taken some persuading, for, as Henry Blackmore's grandson wrote, 'Two men more opposite in their general ideas, as my grandfather and Arthur Liberty would have been difficult to find, as my grandfather was a very correct early Victorian', while Arthur Liberty was something of a bohemian: he seems to have engaged in a certain flamboyance of dress, with 'velvet jackets, low turned-over collars, and informal necktie' – he must have cut a rather dandyish, almost Oscar Wilde-like figure.[17] There is a Blackmore family legend that at this time Henry Blackmore was gradually losing his mind and that his daughter stood over him and made him sign a cheque in the sum of £1,500.

However, Henry Blackmore (1808–83) was a fine Christian gentleman and he may have been moved to help young Liberty because he saw in him something of himself. Blackmore had been born in Littleham in Devon and was the son of a plumber. His elder brothers had migrated to London, or more correctly to Putney, where they had set up in the tailoring business. It is likely that Henry was apprenticed to them, but we don't really know. He was living in Clapham when he married in 1837, but in 1840 he and his wife, Mary, were living over his tailoring shop at 33½ Strand, then one of the most fashionable shopping streets in London (though not quite as grand as Regent Street). It seems they did not remain there very long, for by 1847 he was at 55 Brook Street, Mayfair, which now forms part of the site of Claridge's Hotel. This was an even more fashionable location. He may have been helped to start out in business by his wife's family, the Pinsents, who seem to have been tenant farmers at Teigngrace near Exeter in Devon. The business, 'Henry Blackmore & Son, Tailors', remained at 55 Brook Street until the lease came to an end in about 1872, when it moved to 31 Brook Street. Henry died in 1883, but the business carried on, run by Emma until the mid-1890s; in the 1898 Trade Directories it had become 'Spark & Co., Tailors', suggesting that Emma had sold out.

As well as loaning Liberty that intitial £1,500, Blackmore also backed a bill (acted as the guarantor for a loan) of a further £1,000 with Henry Hill, a tailor of 3 Old Bond Street. Liberty's opening balance was £2,800, which suggests that Arthur Liberty had only £300 of his own money to put in. That represented everything he had.[18]

Now with capital behind him, Arthur Liberty began to search for suitable premises. He eventually spotted a vacant shop (actually it was half a shop) in an excellent location. He had to pay a hefty premium of £1,800, and a substantial rent, to acquire the lease to 218A Regent Street, which he (a bit pompously) rechristened East India House. He opened for business on 15 May 1875. There were four employees: William Judd, who followed him from Farmer and Rogers; Mr Carty; Hannah Browning, a girl of sixteen; and Hara Kerossaki (or Kitsui), a Japanese boy. Speaking years later, Arthur Liberty recalled: 'On the morning my business was started, I had arranged for a staff of two assistants when lo! to my surprise three instead of two were busy at work . . .

CLOCKWISE FROM TOP LEFT
Emma Blackmore and
Arthur Liberty on their
engagement; Arthur Liberty
on his twenty-first birthday
in 1864; Henry Blackmore,
who funded Liberty to
found the shop.

BELOW, CLOCKWISE FROM TOP A postcard showing East India House, c.1890; William Judd, who worked with Arthur Liberty at Farmer and Rogers and follwed him to Liberty's; Arthur Liberty in c.1875.

I found that the third [William Judd] was a volunteer who declared he had resolved to follow my fortunes, "Yea or nay, pay or no pay".'[19]

In setting up the business, which was to focus on apparel and interior decoration, Arthur aimed 'not to follow existing fashion but to create new ones'.[20] Before opening, he had 'dressed' the shop windows in a distinctive style, framing them 'with the Arabic tracery in white that has since become so familiar, and filled them with a lavish display of the most beautiful products from the Far East'.[21] The ploy worked: his became one of 'the' shops in London. William Judd recalled those early days fifty years later: 'I remember when there were only four of us – the Master [meaning Arthur], two others and myself . . . We just sold coloured silks from the East – nothing else. The sort of thing William Morris, Alma-Tadema and Burne-Jones and Rossetti used to come in and turn over and rave about.'[22] It seems half of London raved with them, and many also spent, for the £1,500 loan from Henry Blackmore was paid off out of the first year's profits, or at least very soon thereafter, as was the £1,000 bill – a remarkable achievement.

Perhaps Liberty was helped by the fact that soon after he opened his modest shop Farmer & Rogers closed down. It transpired that the Oriental Warehouse had been the only profitable part of the business, shawls having gone out of fashion. What fools they had been not to make Arthur a partner!

The coloured silks proved to be very popular and Liberty soon diversified into selling cashmere and other types of fabric, together with lacquerware, cloisonné enamel, porcelain and indeed all manner of oriental goods. As space allowed, they began to sell oriental carpets and small items of furniture (especially bamboo). This led on to supplying panelling and other fitments and general interior decoration work. The business expanded quickly and very soon Arthur Liberty was in a position to acquire the other half of the shop. By retaining the profits within the business the firm was able to fund expansion and the acquisition of further premises until, in 1884, ony nine years after opening in half a shop, Liberty occupied 218, 220, 230, 142 and 144 Regent Street; 42 and 43 King Street; and 29, 30 and 31 Warwick Street.[23]

Clearly a born retailer, Arthur Liberty was also a good businessman. One employee, Mr Elsom, recalled that in the early years Arthur would stop the first employee he met and ask, 'How much cash have you taken today?' 'I had been busy serving, how on earth was I to know, so I would say, "Well, Sir, I think about–". He would say, "I don't want you to think, but to know, and not how many wells or rivers you have, but how much cash you have taken". So I would say, "I will find out" and he would say, "I don't want you to find out, of course it's left to me to do that, why don't you say you don't know?"'[24] Hard taskmaster he may have been, but he is also remembered as a fair and generous employer,

a reputation borne out by the length of service of many of the firm's employees. He was also popular with customers, who liked his knowledge of the goods he stocked, his easy manner and that he paid them careful attention. On one occasion he 'had the honour of escorting [a lady] down the street to the adjoining premises, in blissful ignorance that the gracious lady to whom he was acting as guide was none other than the most popular Princess of Wales', later Queen Alexandra.[25] (As Liberty advanced in years he came to bear a striking resemblance to the Prince of Wales, later Edward VII, and was often mistaken for him.)

In 1883 Arthur's father-in-law died, leaving his tailoring business to Emma and his house to Arthur. The house may have been an unwelcome legacy, for it seems it took a little trouble, and a lot of cash, to get out of the lease. The entire contents of the house were sold at auction by J.W. Boden of Finchley New Road on 30 October 1883. The Libertys soon moved to a larger house at 13 Cornwall Terrace in Regent's Park, which the company entirely redecorated over the winter of 1887 while the Libertys were away in North Africa.[26] Unfortunately, according to Emma Liberty's journal, the house was not ready upon their return, necessitating a stay in a hotel.[27]

As the business expanded rapidly in London, it also established outlets in other major cities. An early outpost, opened in 1887, was at 117–119 Corporation Street in Birmingham, and many other towns, from Aberdeen to Torquay, had Liberty agents.[28] A store in Paris opened in 1890 at 38 avenue de l'Opéra. The same year that the Birmingham shop opened Arthur Liberty took on a partner, Frank Brunton Goodyer, but this does not seem to have been a fruitful arrangement, for the partnership was dissolved in 1888.[29] Arthur and Emma Liberty had no children. He obviously needed to give thought to the shop's future, and in 1894 Liberty's became a public company.[30] The share capital was £200,000 in £10 shares, which opened with a 10*s*. premium. Arthur Liberty was, of course, the chairman, with William Street and John W. Howe, who had been his secretary since 1884, the other directors, while Emma Liberty held 10 per cent of the shares in her own right.

The success and containing expansion of the business brought Arthur a substantial income. In the year 1893 his monthly income was £200 and for the entire year it came to £3,627.[31] This was a 'gentleman's income', so it is hardly surprising that he aspired to live like a gentleman and began to contemplate a country house. He decided to rent the Manor House at The Lee in Buckinghamshire, four miles from Chesham, where he had been born. The Plaistowe family had owned the estate for centuries but, following the agricultural depression, had fallen on hard times[32] and needed to let; so Arthur Liberty took a 21-year lease on the property.[33] We do not know what the rent was, but it would have been several hundred guineas per annum. In about 1900 the Plaistowes sold the house to Arthur Vernon, an auctioneer of High Wycombe and Arthur Liberty's cousin, who in turn sold the property to Arthur Liberty in 1902. Over the succeeding years Arthur added to the estate until it was more than three thousand acres in extent, including numerous farms, cottages and even the Lee Gate Inn. Arthur gradually settled into the role of a country squire. He instigated the building of two transepts to the parish church and also extended its nave, providing a large proportion of the funds required. In front of the Manor House, by rerouting a road through the village, he created a village green, and he was also a great planter of trees.

When he found that the village pub, the Cock and Rabbit, interrupted his view, like many an eighteenth-century squire before him he had it moved to a less obtrusive position on the corner of the village green. In the same year, 1907, a huge sarsen stone was discovered in a field, and he had this erected on a brick plinth in pride of place on the green, where it remains. When the parishes in the locality were rearranged and the parish of The Lee more than quadrupled in size, Arthur re-established the ancient tradition of 'beating the bounds' of the parish.

The Manor House is not particularly grand or imposing, and though much of it dates from the eighteenth century it is not architecturally distinguished in any way. Rather it is a pleasant, rambling house –

it eventually rambled to five reception rooms, sixteen bedrooms and four bathrooms, set within seven acres of gardens. Bits of it are brick, bits are stucco, and bits are tile-hung, and it is surmounted by a mini bell tower. Basically it is a house that had simply grown, and it appears that Arthur added to it in turn by building a number of additions in the Arts and Crafts style.[34] Certainly he raised a roof on a central section of the building to create attic bedrooms, probably for servants.

One Liberty relative remembers it as a comfortable house, 'where there was so much of interest to look at – stuffed tigers on the floor as rugs, huge butterfly collections, a collection of birds' eggs', and numerous objects that the Libertys had gathered on their foreign travels.[35] However, a servant who worked at the Manor after Arthur's time was not impressed: 'The Lee Manor in itself, as far as I can see, consists of more passages, short steps, dark hidey holes and lobbies than I have seen elsewhere.' She spoke more favourably of the garden, which had 'many fish pools and water lily ponds, rose gardens, tennis lawns'.[36] There were touches of the Orient, including a large Japanese temple vase and a pair of Chinese lions that guarded the garden door. There was also a large conservatory or 'winter garden', which was a source of great pleasure to Emma Liberty, who created much of the garden.

We also have a brief description from Denise Wren, a friend of the designer Archibald Knox, who did a lot of work for Liberty's. She vividly recalled visiting Sir Arthur at The Lee and being shown into his study: 'My mother [the account is written by her daughter, Rosemary] was shown into a huge room with a beautiful white carpet, an elegant white Persian cat sat in front of a great wood fire, a huge and elegant desk with a distinguished-looking man behind it and on the desk a wonderful silver cigar box enriched with opals, obviously designed by Archibald Knox.' Many years later (in 1953) Mrs Wren was passing Liberty's on her way to buy a new bed, for which she had saved £40. To her astonishment there in the window was the silver cigar box she had seen all those years before: she rushed in and bought it for the princely sum of £30.[37]

The Libertys were comfortably off almost from the foundation of the business, and their good income enabled them to travel a great deal. In 1884 they seem to have gone to the Levant for a month, and as early as 1888 they undertook a round-the-world trip.[38] They recorded some of these travels in various books, many of which are scarce in the second-hand book market today (but if there is anything more dull than another people's holiday photographs it must surely be their travel journals). These holidays were also an opportunity to search out products for the shop. The searches didn't always go according to plan. Following the Young Turk Revolution in 1908–1909 Arthur Liberty raced to Constantinople (now Istanbul), having received a message that many treasures were to be had from the Sultan's Palace (probably the Topkapi Palace). Apparently he was instructed to meet a royal prince at the Porte, who escorted him to the Yildiz Kiosk, where he was charged a franc for admission. He said later, when recounting the story at dinner parties, 'It was the charming oriental way of informing us we had been humbugged.'[39] The little book Arthur Liberty produced, *The Treasure Hunt: The Conspirators in Constantinople*, in 1915, is today the rarest of all his travel writings.[40]

Arthur Liberty was not a great one for the pen. He wrote an article for the first issue of *The Studio* magazine in 1893 on 'Spitalfields Brocades', but the style is rather heavy and ponderous. He gave papers at the Society of Arts and received its Silver Medal for a paper on 'The Industrial Arts and Manufacturers of Japan', and again in 1900 for a paper on 'English Furniture'. He also wrote a small booklet on pewter, produced by the Smithsonian in the United States, which was based on a paper he had given to the Institution and published in their journal in June 1904.

On the eve of the First World War the company had a thousand employees in London, a hundred in Paris and another hundred in Birmingham. There were shops in Bristol and Manchester, and where Liberty's themselves had no shop they had agents. Among their earliest Continental agents were Metz & Co. in The Netherlands, but there were agents across the United States, in Tasmania and Shanghai, and in Japan. The Japanese agent issued a poorly produced

BELOW The drawing room, looking towards the fireplace.

BOTTOM The entrance, showing the jumble of gables.

THE LEE MANOR, GREAT MISSENDEN.   Coles, Photographer, Watford.

BELOW LEFT A silver cigar box designed by Archibald Knox which stood on Arthur Liberty's desk in his study at Lee Manor.

BELOW RIGHT Arthur Liberty at his desk in East India House.

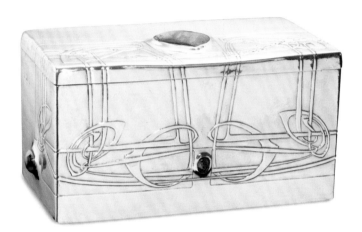

catalogue proudly proclaiming 'Liberty's of London, Paris, and Yokohama'.

In 1913 Arthur Liberty was knighted for his services to the applied and decorative arts. To mark the occasion, the employees presented him with a portrait by Arthur Hacker, RA. Looking back over the thirty-eight years since he first opened his shop must have given Sir Arthur considerable satisfaction. His policy of seeking out good and innovative design – be it in fabrics, wallpapers, costume, furniture and interior design – had made Liberty's a byword for design and quality. In contrast to Morris, whose 'products were so costly that they could be acquired only by the wealthy', Sir Arthur had set out to 'bring art into the homes of the great mass of people'.[41]

Sir Arthur made his nephew, Ivor Stewart, his heir, on the condition that he hyphenate his name to Stewart-Liberty, a name the family retains to this day.[42] Less than a year later Ivor was in France as an officer in the Oxfordshire

and Buckinghamshire Light Infantry. Although he lost a leg and was invalided out, he survived the war, becoming a director of Liberty's in 1916. By then Sir Arthur was semi-retired and in poor health, but with so many younger men off at the front he, like many of his older employees, rallied to keep the business running. He did not live to see peace: after a short illness he died at the Manor on 11 May 1917.

His funeral at The Lee a few days later attracted a congregation of over five hundred people, and it was said that 150 members of staff made the journey from Regent Street. The coffin, the design of which was carefully discussed at Liberty's, rested overnight in the village church, with estate workers keeping vigil. Aside from his family, and the mourners from Liberty's led by William Judd, there were representatives of the many organizations – some local, such as the Buckinghamshire Archaeological Society, and some national like the Japan Society – with which he was associated. The lesson was read by the Bishop

BELOW Arthur and Emma
Liberty at the Alhambra
in Granada in 1910.

of Buckinghamshire, who also gave the benediction. The
congregation sang the hymn 'Now the labourer's task is
o'er' at the graveside and Sir Arthur was laid to rest in a plot
he had himself selected beneath the spreading branches of
some fine old trees. A beautiful granite cross in a distinctive
Celtic style, designed by Archibald Knox, stands today in
memorial. Lady Liberty did not long outlive her husband:
she died suddenly in 1920.

In his will, published later in the year, Arthur left the
bulk of his fortune – almost £350,000, a considerable
sum – in trust for his nephew, Captain Ivor Stewart-
Liberty, and his children. Sir Arthur's controlling interest in
Liberty & Co. Ltd was an inheritance well worth having.
The company results for the year ending in January 1918,
which show a net profit of over £61,000, with a 16 per cent
dividend and a 4 per cent bonus on the ordinary shares,
clearly show not only how successful the business was
but also how solid its foundations were, thanks to Arthur
Liberty's prudence.

Arthur Liberty took an enormous gamble in 1875 when
he opened his modest shop in one of the most fashionable
and expensive shopping streets in London. That gamble,
and the wisdom of Henry Blackmore in backing his
prospective son-in-law, paid off. It did so not just because
Arthur Liberty was a talented retailer, but also because he
had an eye for good design and a deep appreciation for the
products he sold. What was most significant about him
was his ability to spot talented designers. He lived through
many phases in artistic taste: the Aesthetic Movement, the
medievalism of William Morris and the Arts and Crafts
Movement, Art Nouveau with its free-flowing lines and
the birth of Art Deco, which blossomed just after his death
– and from the mid-1880s, partly through his extensive
social life, he knew, and was on good terms with, virtually
everyone of importance in the design world in England.
His shop became an outlet for many of these people, even
if anonymously so. Many of the figures who worked for
Liberty's are now enormously important in design history –
Voysey, Baillie Scott, Knox, Butterfield, to name but a few.
It was Arthur Liberty's patronage of these people that made
Liberty's such a remarkable place.

LEFT Lady Liberty in the winter garden at Lee Manor, c.1920.

RIGHT *Sir Arthur Lasenby Liberty*, by Arthur Hacker RA, 1910. The painting was commissioned by the staff of Liberty's and presented to Sir Arthur in 1914.

FROM A FARAWAY COUNTRY TO REGENT STREET

Japan's Meiji Restoration in 1868 was one of those events 'in a far away country' concerning 'people of whom we know nothing' which had far-reaching consequences.[1] For more than two centuries Japan, under the Tokugawa Shoguns, had effectively been a closed society. Trading with the outside world was limited and, such as it was, conducted almost entirely though the Dutch East India Company, based in the port of Nagasaki. Then, in 1853, the American Commodore Matthew Perry sailed into Edo Bay (now Tokyo Bay) and demanded trading concessions from the Shogun, who had his seat at Edo Castle. This was gunboat diplomacy with a vengeance. In the face of overwhelming force, the Shogun had little choice but to concede. The Shogun's prestige – and his power – were eroded. In 1866 Shogun Tokugawa Lemochi died and Tokugawa Yoshinobu was chosen to succeed him. The following January the Emperor Kmei died and was succeeded by his son, the Emperor Meiji. Realizing, presumably, that the game was up, Shogun Yoshinobu effectively resigned, handing back power to the Emperor, who in short order moved the Imperial court from Kyoto to Edo Castle (now the Imperial Palace, Tokyo), where it remains to this day. Emperor Meiji and his advisers recognized the necessity of opening Japan to the world, and the world to Japan. Trade with the West began to boom.

In England, the architect E.W. Godwin (1833–86) was a particular devotee of all things Japanese.[2] On hearing that a delivery of Japanese fans was to be unpacked at Liberty's in Regent Street, he went along to have a look; and in December 1876 he published a long review in *The Architect* which includes a vivid description of the excitement at this event: 'There was quite a crowd when we arrived. A distinguished traveller had buttonholed the obliging proprietor in one corner; a well-known baronet, waiting to do the same, was trifling with some feather dusting brushes; two architects of well-known names were posing an attendant in another corner with awkward questions; three distinguished painters with their wives blocked up the staircase; whilst a bevy of ladies filled up the rest of the floor space.'[3]

It is perhaps difficult for us today to understand the mania for Japanese goods which was one of the defining characteristics of what came to be known as the Aesthetic Movement, but Godwin – whom Oscar Wilde once described as 'the greatest aesthete of them all' – gives us an idea: 'There is one inexpensive article, however, the little lacquer ash tray selling for sixpence, that bears the unmistakable impress of that artistic nation to which so many of us are directly or indirectly

LEFT Unpacking oriental goods at Liberty's.

BELOW The architect and aesthete E.W. Godwin.

RIGHT A mid-nineteeth-century Japanese woodblock print.

indebted. On one are a bit of old weather-beaten bamboo and a butterfly; on another, one plant of the iris, with two blossoms and three buds; on a third, a few naked branches; on a fourth, a baby bamboo shooting up like an arrow, each and all designed with a freedom, and withal a delicacy, that is unmatchable by any other nation.'[4]

Waxing lyrically about so small an object as an ashtray inevitably invited satire, and aesthetes like Godwin were treated to that in spades. The satirical magazine *Punch* was only too delighted to puncture their pomposity, and the cartoonist George du Maurier took particular pleasure in making many of the aesthetes appear absurd. *Punch*'s editor, F.C. Burnard, wrote a popular farce called *The Colonel*, first performed in April 1881, which contained the memorable line 'There is so much to be learned from a teapot', which neatly encapsulates the arid pretensions of some aesthetes.[5]

Liberty's was very much the aesthetes' shop. Although it had started by selling coloured silks and nothing else, it soon diversified into stocking other goods. Fans were very popular, as were Japanese drawings and prints, bronzes, porcelains and lacquer ware. An article explained: 'Liberty's have people working for them all over the Oriental world. Quaint, parchment-skinned pedlars are wandering throughout the length and breadth of China gathering together ancient embroideries of wonderful colourings, and throughout Persia and among the temples of India the same thing is going on.'[6]

In reality Liberty had a network of agents sourcing products. They were occasionally put to work in other ways. It seems that for the first production of Gilbert and Sullivan's *Mikado* in 1885 at the Savoy Theatre, Liberty's not only used contacts in Japan to source suitable fabrics for the costumes but also did detailed research to ensure that they were factually correct. (Both *The Colonel* and Gilbert and Sullivan's *Patience* also used Liberty fabrics, some of which were specially printed. Arthur Liberty always had a box for the first night of any new Gilbert and Sullivan offering.)

Initially Japanese goods were held in high regard, but following the Meiji Restoration and the opening of trade links with the West, there was a swift and marked deterioration in the quality and style of goods. Godwin lamented this in the same review: 'Either the European market is ruining Japanese art or the Japanese have taken our measure and found it wanting; perhaps there is a little of both. Take for example the common paper fan of today and compare it with some imported here ten or even eight years ago. Those are for the most part lovely in delicate colour and exquisite in drawing, but most of today's fans are impregnated with a crudeness of the European's sense of colour, and are immeasurably beneath the older examples.'[7] In December 1897 Liberty's sent a Japanese dressing gown to Edward Burne-Jones on approval and he promptly returned it, with a note expressing 'regret at the decadence in colour which it shows'.[8]

LEFT A small cupboard designed by E.W. Godwin in 1877, very much under the influence of Japanese designs.

BELOW 'Felicitous Quotations', a cartoon published in *Punch* on 20 October 1894.

BOTTOM 'The Six-Mark Tea-Pot', a cartoon by George du Maurier published in *Punch* on 30 October 1880.

RIGHT 'Bamboo', a wallpaper designed by E.W. Godwin for Liberty's in around 1872. This paper was found in a house in Hartford, Connecticut.

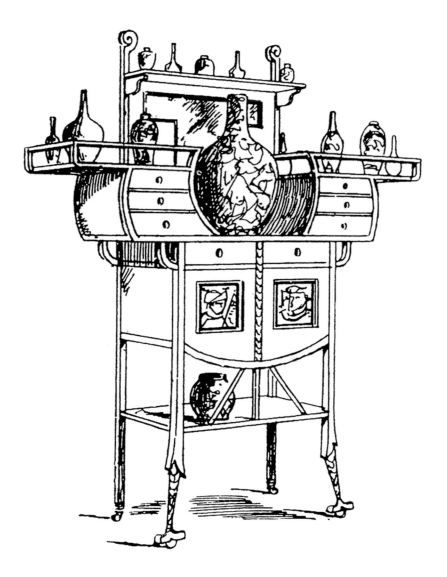

FELICITOUS QUOTATIONS.

Hostess (of Upper Tooting, showing new house to Friend). "WE'RE VERY PROUD OF THIS ROOM, MRS. HOMMY. OUR OWN LITTLE UPHOLSTERER DID IT UP JUST AS YOU SEE IT, AND ALL OUR FRIENDS THINK IT WAS *LIBERTY*!" *Visitor (sotto voce).* "'OH, LIBERTY, LIBERTY, HOW MANY CRIMES ARE COMMITTED IN THY NAME!'"

Punch, October 20, 1894

THE SIX-MARK TEA-POT.

Æsthetic Bridegroom. "IT IS QUITE CONSUMMATE, IS IT NOT?"
Intense Bride. "IT IS, INDEED! OH, ALGERNON, LET US LIVE UP TO IT!"

ABOVE AND OPPOSITE
A jug and teapot in glazed
Parian 'Sgrafitto Ware',
designed by F.W. Rhead of
the Foley Art Pottery and
retailed by Liberty's, c.1905.

30

BELOW Work by the Guild of Handicrafts displayed at the eighth exhibition of the Viennese Secession in 1900.

BOTTOM LEFT An early advertisement for Umritzur cashmere.

BOTTOM RIGHT Liberty's first Registered Trade Mark, registered on 17 June 1882.

A New Material for Autumn and Winter Costumes.

UMRITZUR CASHMERE.

Manufactured specially for Messrs. LIBERTY & CO., from pure Indian Wool, and woven in this country, by which means the softness, lightness, and warmth of the Indian Cashmere is combined with the regular texture and durability of European fabrics.

As the present is only a sample delivery which cannot be repeated in time for the Winter Season, it is respectfully requested that all applications for patterns be made as early as possible.

IN ARTISTIC SHADES OF RED, BLUE, OLIVE, GREEN, GOLD, ETC.

Price 21s. and 25s. per piece of 9 yards, 27 inches wide.

PATTERNS POST FREE.

The Aesthetic Movement was a cult long before it became a 'movement', but it really emerged from the shadows with the foundation of the Grosvenor Gallery in Bond Street in July 1877.[9] Like the later Art Nouveau, it had its roots in the Arts and Crafts Movement and was basically a stylistic development emphasizing art in the production of furniture, metalwork, ceramics, etc. The guiding mantra was 'art for art's sake'. Many of the Pre-Raphaelites were part of the movement. Burne-Jones was a leading light and the first exhibition held at the gallery included works by G.F. Watts, Rossetti, William Holman Hunt and Whistler.

Oscar Wilde was inextricably linked with the Aesthetic Movement. With his flamboyant clothes (which Arthur Liberty tried to copy) and his long floppy hair (which Arthur did not copy), Wilde was a perfect subject for a magazine like *Punch*. He was also a godsend for Liberty's, as he lectured extensively and one of his topics was 'House Decoration' and another 'Art and the Handicraftsman'. Wilde married Constance Lloyd in 1884 and, requiring some sort of regular income to support his family, he accepted a job as editor of *Woman's World* magazine, a position he held from 1887 to 1889. (It is difficult to imagine Wilde as editor of a women's magazine.) His plays came in rapid succession, starting with *Lady Windermere's Fan*, which opened in February 1892. The opening of *The Importance of Being Earnest*, in February 1895, proved to be the zenith of Wilde's success, for when, most unwisely, he sued the Marquess of Queensberry (father of Wilde's lover, Lord Alfred Douglas) for criminal libel, evidence produced at the trial led to Wilde's being charged and convicted of gross indecency, and he went to prison for two years. Upon his release – his reputation ruined, his health broken – he went to live in Paris, where he died on 30 November 1900, aged forty-six.

Arthur Liberty was in the thick of the Aesthetic Movement, for he knew them all. He recalled: 'From first to last I was closely associated with that tendency which unfortunately overreached itself, mainly owing to the eccentricities of those who took it up.' He went on, 'The Aesthetic Movement was frightfully ridiculed, of course;

but I stuck to my own position of what I regarded as the trunk lines – as distinct from the freaks.'[10] Gradually the movement degenerated and became 'decadent' – the extremists took over – and it is hardly surprising that as a movement its duration was relatively brief. The Grosvenor Gallery closed in 1890, and by then a number of the major figures were no longer around. Whistler, following his pyrrhic libel victory in the High Court over John Ruskin, had left London to live in Paris; Rossetti had died in 1882; E.W. Godwin had died in 1886; and Oscar Wilde was enjoying Her Majesty's hospitality in Reading Gaol.

There is no doubt that Wilde was a huge help to Liberty's, and indeed Arthur Liberty acknowledged as much in an interview in 1884: 'My art fabrics were produced before he became a celebrity. I gave him his opportunity and he helped me mightily with mine through the publicity he commanded.'[11] But by the time Wilde fell from grace, Liberty's had moved on and was no longer so closely associated with him, and the scandal of Wilde's fall had no lasting consequences for the business.

'Art fabrics', as Arthur Liberty described them, were what Liberty's was built on. Although initially he imported and sold coloured silks, demand soon began to outstrip the available supply, and the nature of some fabrics and their dyes was not conducive to the uses being made of them. With the opening of the Japanese markets producers began to change the colours so that they would be more in tune with perceived Western tastes. While Liberty's continued to import goods from Japan, China, Persia, India and elsewhere (it was noted, for example, for its imported cashmere fabrics, especially for its very successful introduction of the better-wearing Umritzur cashmere),[12] but there was a gradual shift to sourcing goods of British design and manufacture: it was, after all, far easier to control production when the source was a short train journey away rather than halfway around the world. There was also a shift in the type of goods sold. 'Art silk' gave way to patterned fabrics, which were better produced locally. This quest to find local manufacturers was how Liberty's began working with Thomas Wardle, a dyer and printer from Leek in Staffordshire.

Thomas Wardle (1831–1909), although perhaps not widely known or appreciated today, was an important figure in the Arts and Crafts Movement (of which more in the next chapter). Born in Macclesfield, he was the son of Joshua Wardle, who established the Leekbrook Dyeworks in Leek in 1831 and became a leading silk dyer and finisher. From an early age Thomas Wardle was fascinated by colour and by silk. He became a dye chemist and acquired the Hencroft Dyeworks in Leek in 1872, slightly later founding the Churnet Dyeworks there. The town became a centre for dyeing because of the purity of the water in the River Churnet. Soft and with special chemical constituents, the water was particularly suitable for raven-black dye, which produced a blue-black when treated with iron salts and tannic acid. Wardle rapidly became a leading authority on dyeing and printing, and when William Morris began creating textiles it was Wardle who printed his first fourteen designs on silk and cotton in 1878. By this time aniline dyes, introduced in 1856, had largely replaced vegetable dyes, but Morris was keen to use the older vegetable dyes – especially madder, woad and indigo – so Wardle employed old dyers who were skilled in working with these. Between 1875 and 1877 Morris came to Leek frequently to experiment and to learn about the processes of dyeing and finishing.

At Liberty's, stocking coloured silks gradually gave way to importing 'grey pieces' – undyed and unfinished fabric straight from the loom, which the shop would dye and finish itself. (This is exactly what Laura and Bernard Ashley were to do almost a century later, with remarkably similar results.) Liberty's had begun an association with Wardle very shortly after the shop was established, and it was Wardle who experimented and was able to produce the subtle colours of dyed silk that Arthur Liberty sought; it was these that became known as 'art colours' or, on the Continent and in America, 'Liberty colours'. Colour was one factor, texture another. Many of these early fabrics that Liberty's imported were hand-woven, which gave an uneven texture to the weave when compared to a machine-woven fabric, which is far more regular and uniform.[13]

In 1872 Wardle developed a process for finishing Tussar silk – something that had eluded everyone else. Unlike the wild silkworm (*Bombyx mandarina*) and the domestic silkworm (*B. mori*), which will only dine on mulberry leaves (and only certain types of mulberry, as James I discovered to his cost when he planted the wrong sort), Tussar worms are happy to feed on a variety of leaves.[14] The Tussar filament is coarser and flatter than that produced by the domestic silkworm, which is rounder and thinner in form. The Tussar silk was more textured and also cheaper than ordinary silk, but it was a dull beige-gold colour and notoriously resistant to dyeing, the nub of the problem being the protective coating of the filament. Wardle developed a method of bleaching the Tussar silk which made it receptive to dyes, and it became possible to produce a wide range of rich, subtle colours.

At the time Tussar silk was hand-woven in India, on narrow-width looms (27 inches/70 centimetres wide). Liberty's agents in India persuaded the weavers to use broader-width looms, making the fabric more practical and useful. The Indian silks which Liberty's imported and Wardle printed were exhibited in the British India Pavilion at the Paris International Exhibition held in 1878. They were a huge success.

The relationship between Liberty's and Wardle continued and deepened. In 1880 Wardle registered for two years six block-print designs on behalf of Liberty's.[15] However, he did not register any designs between 1882 and 1885 for Liberty's, probably because he had opened his own shop at 71 New Bond Street (although the shop was only open briefly, from 1883 until 1888). Thereafter Wardle marketed fabrics under his own name, with Liberty's being one of the retailers. A few of the designs were Wardle's own, and a few by his son, but the majority were bought in from the leading designers of the day.

Liberty silks were quite different from the stiff, over-finished fabrics that were then generally available. Everyone raved about them: 'The texture of them is so pure and fine that they adapt themselves particularly to the present style of dress.' There were, apparently, 'Indian silks in reds so soft that not even the most rubicund wearer could vulgarize them; greens and blues so indefinite that it is difficult to class them as greens and blues'; the texture was such that 'They wash like a silk handkerchief.'[16] Despite such enthusiasm for the subtlety of the colours and the soft texture, Arthur Liberty recalled: 'In those days we were in a difficulty with regard to soft fabrics, because the British dressmaker was deadly opposed to them. She was accustomed to work on hard, stiff lines, and the new material gave her more trouble. Everything then was on harsh lines and in crude colourings. It was a great drawback from a commercial point of view, because when our artistic friends bought material they generally came back and said "My dressmaker will not touch it." The only way out of this difficulty seemed to be to turn dressmaker myself.'[17]

At first Liberty's was not in the business of apparel manufacture and retailed only a variety of fabrics and *objets d'art*. But when the firm acquired Chesham House (132–154 Regent Street) in 1883, Arthur Liberty decided to use some of the space there to open a costume department. He was probably encouraged to do so by E.W. Godwin, whom he engaged as a consultant.

The texture of the Liberty's Indian silks was ideal for the type of dress Godwin advocated. As well as being an architect, Godwin had studied historical dress and he became secretary of the Costume Society. Theatre reviews he wrote for a newspaper in Bristol in the 1860s made at least as much comment on the costumes and decoration as on the actual performance. In 1863 he designed the costumes for a performance of Shakespeare's *A Midsummer Night's Dream* at the Theatre Royal in Bath. (Titania was played by Ellen Terry, aged sixteen. After her short marriage to G.F. Watts, Ellen went to live with Godwin in Hertfordshire – a scandalous thing to do at the time. In 1874 they moved to Taviton Street in Bloomsbury, London, but the relationship foundered the following year.) Godwin also produced a handbook for the National Health Society Exhibition in which he advocated dress based upon classical Greek costume. Some modifications were obviously required and, recognizing the climatic differences between Athens and Accrington, Godwin advised that the dress be worn 'over a sub-stratum of pure wool, such as supplied by Dr Jaeger under the modern German system'. The object was for the dress to fall off the shoulders and 'rely for beauty not on the stiff, ready-made ornaments of the modern milliner, bows where there should be no bows, flounces where there should be no flounces, but on the exquisite play of light and line that one gets from rich and rippling folds'.[18]

ABOVE LEFT A tea gown in silk brocade, c.1887.

ABOVE RIGHT A blue shantung day dress, c.1905.

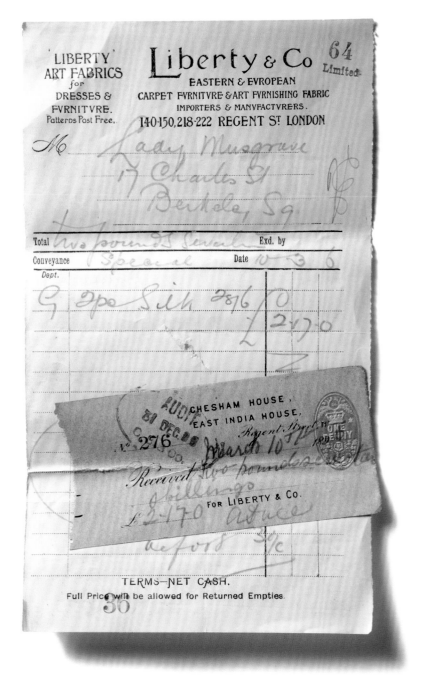

ABOVE A Liberty & Co. receipted account from 1906.

TOP The couture salon of Maison Liberty at 3 boulevard des Capucines.

ABOVE Maison Liberty's first Paris shop at 38 avenue de l' Opera, in 1889.

Liberty Style

A series of sketches from *A History of Feminine Costume*, a booklet of historical dress designs, and patterns based on them, produced by Liberty's.

TOP ROW Historical styles. From left: 'Grecian'; 'Charles I'; 'Eton Jacket 1813'.

BOTTOM ROW Liberty designs based on historical styles. From left, a satin evening dress in Empire mode; a soft silk evening dress inspired by a Reynolds painting; a tea gown.

Godwin's letter of appointment from Liberty's, dated 17 January 1884, gives him a fee of one guinea an hour for his time spent in the studio, but imposes a cap on his hours per week at six. Still, these were generous terms. Quite what influence Godwin had on the costume department can now only be a matter of conjecture, although we have one observation from the time: 'The reception room of itself is a study. To enter this room rests one instantly, it looks so sweet and quiet and full of harmony. Several young ladies spend their entire time in getting up new designs adopted from classic models. For the taste of today there must be a clinging under-dress, fitted perfectly, of silk, velvet or cashmere. About this, soft drapings are arranged, suited to the figures of the wearer.' This was in marked contrast to what one normally found: 'The everlasting and monotonous rows of frills and pleats are thus done away, and garments substituted which have a meaning and subtlety of their own.'[19] Godwin did not, alas, live long to enjoy his appointment, for he died in October 1886, but some of the dresses in the catalogue 'Liberty Art Fabrics and Personal Specialities' produced in late 1886 or early 1887 reveal his influence. The classical Greek gown 'Athene' was undoubtedly designed or at least inspired by him, and the three pages of advice upon what colours and shades should be selected by women with various skin tones and hair colourings were certainly his.

The costume department was to be one of Liberty's many successes. Years later Arthur Liberty recalled: 'Smocking was one of the things we brought to the fore – the revival of an old English fashion – and it has been a wonderful revival, for it has spread all over the world.'[20] The department's success was founded not merely on the dress designs used but also upon the fabrics, which remained the core of the business. As well as using Thomas Wardle & Co. in Leek as their main dyer and printer, Liberty's began very early on also to use Edmund Littler & Co. at Merton Abbey in south-west London. Merton Abbey is, of course, famous for its association with William Morris, and it is often assumed that Liberty's began to use printers there because of him.[21] In reality it was the other way round. Morris did not establish himself at Merton until 1881, when he bought

BELOW A carved wood
wallpaper printing block.

the calico printing business of the Welch family, probably at the suggestion of Arthur Liberty,[22] while Liberty's probably began to use Littler's in about 1877 (although the exact date is unknown). Littler's works were slightly upstream of Welch's, and on the opposite bank of the river, leading Liberty's staff to joke 'we sent our dirty water down to Morris'.[23] Certainly by the 1890s Liberty's had taken all Littler's production and in 1904 they bought him out. The firm continued to produce hand-blocked fabrics there until 1972, when the works were sold to Vita-tex Ltd.

The increased space available at Chesham House could hardly just be given over to rolls of fabric and a few dresses. Liberty's had already begun to retail furniture, so this business was expanded and the shop established a furniture and decoration department. Chesham House (between Beak Street and Leicester Street) gradually expanded from a single shop until Liberty's occupied almost the whole block, but with the jewellers Rowlands & Frazer in between; eventually they acquired the jewellers' premises too. In the basement they created an 'Eastern Bazaar', while other delights included the curios department, full of oriental antiques, and the Arab tea rooms, which aside from selling tea and cream cakes to fortify weary shoppers retailed all manner of condiments such as chutney, curry powder, various sorts of peppers, speciality teas from India and China, and jars of preserved Chinese ginger. These, used 'to make up the weight' in the silk shipments, were eagerly sought after.

The mania for all things Japanese led to a demand for bamboo furniture. Liberty's imported some, but soon began to buy locally manufactured items. From 1881 most of Liberty's bamboo furniture was made by a Monsieur Ursin Fortier, an expat Frenchman (he had been a soldier in Algeria) whose hilarious English endeared him to the staff. Barely five feet tall, and as broad, with white hair, moustache and 'imperial' (sideburns), he had a workshop in Soho, at one point in Lisle Street and later in Dean Street.[24]

TOP John Llewellyn watching over a printer at work at Merton Abbey, 1890.

BOTTOM LEFT A printer about to tamp a block after positioning.

BOTTOM RIGHT Printers working on commemorative scarves.

BELOW An advertisement from *The Studio Yearbook* of 1906.

RIGHT A bamboo writing bureau with lacquer shelves and panels, probably designed by Ursin Fortier.

As the 1880s gave way to the last decade of the century there was a new spirit in the air. A significant event in artistic circles was the publication of a new quarterly magazine dedicated to the promotion of 'new art', new artists, designers and architects: *The Studio*, first published in April 1893 at a price of 6*d*. The cover of the first issue was designed by Aubrey Beardsley, who went on to be a major contributor.[25] And, as mentioned earlier, that first issue included an article by Arthur Liberty on Spitalfields brocades. The magazine was the brainchild of Gleeson White and Charles Holme, the latter a very important figure in late nineteenth-century artistic circles.[26]

Born in Derby, Charles Holme (1848–1923) was the younger son of a successful silk manufacturer. When he was twenty his father sent him to Bradford to act as his agent, but he soon established his own woollens business. In 1873 he attended a lecture on East Turkestan given by traveller Robert Barkley Shaw at the Bradford Chamber of Commerce. This inspired him to establish the Central Asia Trading Company in 1874 to import carpets, embroideries and silks, from India, China and Turkestan, while

exporting to them Bradford woollen goods. The company did not last all that long: Holme closed it in 1879 and moved to London.

Holme must have met Arthur Liberty soon after he arrived in London. They became good friends, and were to remain so for the rest of their lives. The Libertys visited Japan with Holme in 1888–9, together with the painter Sir Alfred East – a trip Holme chronicled in a book with photographs by Emma Liberty.[27] Holme was an enthusiast for all things Japanese and it is striking, turning the pages of *The Studio* today, to notice that virtually every issue contains an article with a Japanese connection. Holme himself penned one on the 'Artistic Garden in Japan' for the first issue.

The Studio became a hugely influential journal in both Britain and Continental Europe. Both the magazine and *The Studio Yearbook of Decorative Art*, launched in 1906, regularly featured the work of architects Charles Voysey, Mackay Hugh Baillie Scott and Charles Rennie Mackintosh, and designers such as Lindsay P. Butterfield, Archibald Knox and the Silver Studio. The products featured were often sold by Liberty's.

Liberty Style

BELOW LEFT Charles
Holme, founder of *The
Studio* magazine.

BOTTOM LEFT Christopher
Dresser, perhaps the
most influential designer
of the late nineteenth
century.

BELOW RIGHT Aubrey
Beardsley's draft for the
cover of the first issue of
The Studio. The finished
cover did not include the
faun on the left

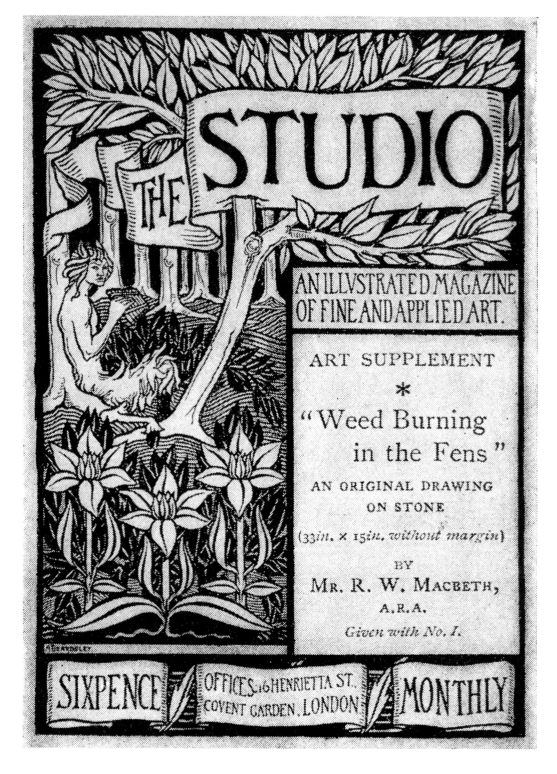

BELOW William Morris, photographed by Frederick Hollyer in 1887.

BOTTOM Edward Burne-Jones and William Morris, again by Hollyer, 1874.

Charles Holme also had a long-standing relationship with someone else who was to become important to Liberty's, the designer Christopher Dresser (1834–1904). Born in Glasgow, Dresser was a contemporary of William Morris (Morris was the elder by four months), but the two men could hardly have been more different. Dresser's father was an Excise Officer and Collector of Taxes, while Morris's father was a city broker, and a wealthy one. Morris Senior left a fortune of over £60,000 when he died in 1847, placing him among the 1,500 wealthiest people in the land. Dresser's family had no such means. At the age of thirteen Dresser was enrolled at the Government School of Design at Somerset House, and while still a student he won a prize for 'Garment Fabrics'. He became a textile designer, and also probably the leading industrial designer of his day. Whereas Morris rejected industrialization and yearned for a return to the ways of medieval craftsmen, Dresser embraced industrial processes and sought to harness their power to bring well-designed mass-produced products to as wide a public as possible.

Christopher Dresser has quietly slipped into obscurity, yet he was a designer of great originality and the most interesting design theorist of his day. Unlike Morris, 'gentleman amateur' and champagne socialist, Dresser was a professional designer. In design terms Dresser is probably more important than Morris, for he was far more innovative and far less dogmatic and reactionary. However, a proper appreciation of his work is hampered by the fact that as a professional designer he would sell a design and the product produced would not be attributed to him; as a result his name would never be associated with it. In 1853, while still a student, he registered his first fabric design, 'Ladies Smock', which was produced by Liddiard & Co.[28] He designed a plate (a geometrical arrangement of flowers) for Owen Jones's famous book *The Grammar of Ornament*, published in 1856, and two years later he designed his first carpet and his first known wallpaper. From then on his output was prodigious. For example, in 1869 he sold 158 silk damask patterns to Ward's of Halifax and in 1871 he supplied 142 carpet designs to Crossley's, also in Halifax, for a fee of between three and ten guineas apiece.

A selection of
Christopher Dresser's
designs reproduced by
the Italian manufacturer
Alessi in the 1990s.

Dresser was also a prominent figure in the cult of all things Japanese. He had visited Japan in 1876–7 as a guest of the Japanese government, and this visit led to the establishment of Dresser & Holme – in partnership with Charles Holme – in 1878, primarily for the import of Japanese products to the United Kingdom. Furniture companies like Gillow and Maple were customers, and the business had two agencies in Japan, in Kobe and in Yokohama, the Kobe office being run by Dresser's sons Louis and Christopher. Dresser retired from the partnership because of ill health in August 1882, after which the company became Holme & Co.

In 1880 the Art Furnishers Alliance was established at 157 New Bond Street, and Dresser was appointed as art superintendent.[29] The shop, staffed with attendants suitably attired in aesthetic costume in tasteful 'art colours', predominantly sold furniture, metalwork, glass and ceramics, many of the items designed by Dresser.[30] The absence of things Japanese might have been due to the rapid decline in quality and the perceived 'Westernization' of Japanese goods. The Art Furnishers Alliance was not a financial success and it went into liquidation in 1883. Arthur Liberty had been one of the investors (he is said to have invested £300), and on the liquidation bought a considerable amount of the remaining stock.[31]

Dresser's connection with Liberty's began with textile designs. He may have been their art advisor, but no firm documentary evidence survives to confirm this. A reversible printed cotton fabric depicting dragons on a fretted background, which was produced in 1882, is certainly by him.[32] He designed many other fabrics for Liberty's, and the Liberty's *Art Fabrics* catalogue of *c.*1883 surely contains a number of his designs, but we cannot be absolutely sure. Liberty's retailed some of Dresser's metalwork designs, many of which were revived by the Italian manufacturer Alessi in the 1990s, and it is by these designs that Christopher Dresser is known to the public today. Some of these designs were far in advance of their times, such as his take on the humble toast rack or his whimsical on-end square teapot; by comparison his cruet

design seems sedate, almost conventional, as does his soup tureen. These designs were mostly done in electroplate rather than solid silver, which made them more affordable by the middle classes, who were the bulk of Liberty's customers.

At Liberty's Dresser was better known for his glass designs, which were produced by James Couper & Sons and marketed under the name of 'Clutha', derived from the Gaelic word for the River Clyde.[33] 'Clutha' glass came mostly in delicate shades of green, pink and russet, yellow and amber; but occasionally it was turquoise and even black. It often had numerous air bubbles and irregular cloudy streaks and aventurine (metallic particles).

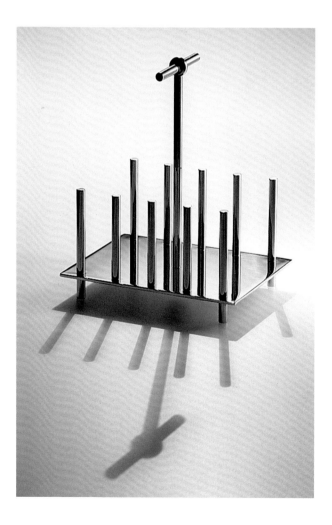

These imperfections were a part of the character and charm of the product, as Liberty's promotional material pointed out, describing the glass as 'a rich translucent substance interspersed with air bubbles and brilliant flakings and whorls forming a very "Kosmos" of impressionist design'.[34] The shapes created were also impressionistic and even today, more than century on, they look radical and modernist. Dresser seems to have understood the glass blower's art, for he often employed wide rims and tall, thin necks, or cylinders that were given a twist. Occasionally glass threads would be applied, coiling and twisting. The effect of the overall end product owed as much to the glass blower's skill as it did to Dresser's imagination – if anything more so. Unusually for Liberty's, 'Clutha' glass would often be marked as 'Clutha/Designed by C.D./Registered'. Some pieces were illustrated in an article published in *The Studio* in 1899.

Just after the turn of the century Liberty's was also stocking more conventional glassware produced by James Powell & Sons. One range, known as 'Mediaeval Decorative Glass' was illustrated in a catalogue issued about 1900. The shapes, although more conventional than those of the 'Clutha' range, were derived from glass made across Europe between the fourteenth and eighteenth centuries.

Dresser had produced designs for Minton, the ceramics manufacturing company, from the 1860s, and also for the Coalbrookdale foundry from about 1867 to 1872. The latter produced cast-iron furniture, particularly garden furniture, and many of their designs from that time, which are now highly sought after, were by Dresser. He also produced designs for domestic furniture. The style was always distinctive. There was, for instance, an 'Egyptian Chair' in ebonized wood with gilt decoration, which was manufactured in the early 1880s and retailed through the Art Furniture Alliance. One of these chairs, probably made by Chubb & Sons, is now in the Victoria & Albert Museum. Similar designs were illustrated in the *Furniture Gazette* on 3 July 1880.

Perhaps Liberty's most famous pieces of furniture from the early 1880s were the two 'Thebes' stools. Based on pieces in the British Museum, the designs, possibly by Dresser, were both patented by Liberty's in 1884.[35]

BELOW Also designed by Christopher Dresser. From left to right: a ceramic vase made by the Ault pottery, c.1890; a copper ewer manufactured by Benham & Froud in 1885.

LEFT Sketch for 'A Saracenic smoking room', from Liberty's *Handbook of Sketches*, 1890.

RIGHT ABOVE A design in watercolour by Leonard Wyburd for 'A Living Room in a Country House', published in *The Studio Yearbook* of 1906.

RIGHT BELOW Another watercolour design by Wyburd, this one for 'A Drawing Room', published in *The Studio Yearbook* of 1907.

Until the discovery of the tomb of the pharaoh Tutankhamen in 1922, very little ancient Egyptian furniture had been discovered, although there were representations in tomb paintings. One of Liberty's 'Thebes' stool designs is a rather ungainly looking three-legged stool, which was produced in oak; it could be adapted and was also made as a wine table or plant stand. A second design, which also had a number of different permutations, is basically a trellis construction with a curved seat. It is light and elegant and was produced in a variety of different woods, including oak and mahogany, and also with a painted finish. The two stools remained in production for well over twenty years.

Arthur Liberty had established the furniture and decoration department in 1883 under the direction of Leonard Wyburd; the manager was a Mr Robinson, about whom we know virtually nothing. Leonard Wyburd (1866–1960), the son of the artist Francis John Wyburd, was a skilful and talented designer who exhibited at the Royal Academy between 1888 and 1904. The development of Liberty's furniture retailing owes a great deal to Wyburd,

who worked for Liberty's for twenty-two years. He left in 1905 to establish his own interior decorating business at 1 Cambridge Street near Hyde Park (just off the Edgware Road). An advertisement for his business appeared in *The Studio Yearbook of Decorative Art* for 1907, but the venture seems to have been short-lived – he was certainly not at the same premises in 1915.

Quite often furniture and *objets d'art* would be displayed at Liberty's in specially designed room sets, so that they might have a context. The first such room set, in 1883, was 'Indian Furniture and Decoration', cashing in on the vogue for all things Indian (Queen Victoria had become Empress of India in 1876, celebrating the fact by building the Durbar Hall at Osborne House on the Isle of Wight). Wyburd was adept at creating themed sets and he designed a great many, including a Chinese set, a Japanese set and an Arabian set. He had made a special study of Arab design. There was a fashion in nineteenth-century design for 'Moorish interiors', which evoked the romance of the Alhambra Palace in Spain: the Moorish-style tea rooms in Chesham House followed this trend.

The fashion for the Moorish look was short-lived, and neither this nor the Japanese phase was much lamented by Liberty's staff, particularly Guy Bentley, who ran the contracts department. Bentley was a classical scholar and his particular passion was for book illustration; some of his illustrations were exhibited at the Royal Academy. He also had a huge knowledge of interior decoration, and it was he who would prepare the drafts of papers Arthur Liberty gave to the Royal Society of Arts. Bentley recalled years later that both the Japanese and Arab styles 'had their run for a time and a very considerable trade was done in them, but . . . "Arab" sideboards, wardrobes and writing tables . . . were hopelessly incongruous.'[36] He had a point.

ABOVE An armchair from William Morris's 'Sussex' range, together with two side chairs in Liberty's rival 'Argyll' range.

LEFT A three-legged 'Thebes' stool. This design was patented by Liberty's in 1884.

It was probably Wyburd who designed the 'Argyll' range of simple country-style furniture, which could be made in oak, mahogany or walnut with rush seats. It could also be in black wood. It was intended as a direct competitor to Morris's 'Sussex' range, which the firm had introduced in 1864 and which was possibly a design of Ford Madox Brown's. Rather surprisingly it seems that an 'Argyll' settee at £3 18s. 6d. (if painted black; £4 12s. 6d. if supplied in oak, walnut or mahogany) cost twice as much as the Morris version.[37]

At first Liberty's furniture department bought in stock from people like James Thallon, who owned a cabinetmaker's. Eventually Liberty's bought Thallon's business and he became an employee.[38] (James Thallon retired in 1898 and was succeeded by his son Thomas Thallon, and later by his old foreman, George Wolfe. Apparently Thallon and Wolfe were old friends and had been apprentices together at the upholsterers Howard's in Berners Street.) The desire for 'integration' may have been driven by the fact that the fabric and furniture trade had a very hard time in the 1880s (as William Morris remarked).

In an interview in *The Citizen* in 1898, J.W. Howe (Arthur Liberty's secretary) explained that although Liberty's was first and foremost a silk and dress house, 'In our four factories and workrooms . . . we make our own costumes, do our own upholstery, and make our own furniture.' The exact chronology is not clear, but the article refers to 'the establishment of upholstery workshops at the rear of East India House, which again was further enlarged in 1885 by the addition of 222 Regent Street'. It would seem logical if you were doing upholstery also to make furniture, and 'in 1889 a furniture and cabinetmaking factory was started in Newman Street'.[39] However, it was only in about 1905 that Liberty's described themselves as 'Furniture Manufacturers' in the trade directories of the period. At this time they had a works in Dufours Place, Soho, which could have been Thallon's old premises; the works moved to larger premises in Highgate in 1912.

The Aesthetic Movement had presented Liberty's with a great opportunity, and they had exploited it with skill and achieved tremendous success. But nothing lasts forever. None of the various movements in artistic taste have ever had a definite beginning or a final end. They just appear and then they just seem to fade away, usually subsumed into another movement or trend. Aestheticism was no different. Many of its leading figures died in quick succession, and with the disgrace, vilification and untimely death of Oscar Wilde the Aesthetic Movement lost its most eloquent champion. But by then the wheel of taste had already moved on towards new horizons and new artistic movements – and Liberty's had moved with it.

OPPOSITE, ABOVE A craftsman at Aller Vale Pottery applying under-glaze decoration

OPPOSITE, BELOW Throwers at work at Aller Vale.

RIGHT, ABOVE 'Eygptian Ware', from Watcombe Pottery.

RIGHT, CENTRE 'Crocus Ware', a new introduction by Aller Vale in 1900.

RIGHT, BELOW 'Green- and Straw Ware', from Watcombe.

THE ARCHITECTS
AND THE
DESIGNERS

The Arts and Crafts Movement was the dominant artistic movement throughout most of the latter part of the nineteenth century and into the twentieth century. Although the term 'Arts and Crafts' was not coined until 1887, when it was used by T.J. Cobden-Sanderson, the movement can trace its origins back at least to the early 1860s, if not even earlier.[1] It grew out of the Gothic revival, improbable as that may sound, just as the Georgian revival in the early years of the twentieth century was born of the Arts and Crafts Movement. The movement was dominated by architects, most of whom - rather ironically - were inspired, and enraptured, by buildings that had not been designed by architects: vernacular architecture, the pretty cottages in country villages, and the wonderful old tithe barns, which in the nineteenth century were still very much in use.

The Arts and Crafts Movement was all about craftsmanship and the use of simple forms, often inspired by medieval and folk art styles. It is sometimes said that the movement was also anti-industrial, which is some ways it was; this can be seen in some of the obsessions of William Morris (whose work was, of course, usually most attractive to the rich: after all, they were the only people who could afford his grand tapestries, hand-knotted carpets and other luxury goods). This hostility to industry had deep roots. In the early nineteenth century in the textile towns in northern England, as various manufacturing processes were mechanized, there was a political reaction to the rapid pace of change. Gangs of Luddites would storm the new mills and smash the machines, hoping to preserve their jobs and livelihoods. It was a futile battle.[2] Thomas Carlyle crystallized this anti-industry sentiment in his *Edinburgh Review* treatise 'Signs of the Times' in 1829, lamenting what he saw as the dehumanizing effects of machines. This attitude is a thread that runs throughout the Arts and Crafts Movement and the emerging socialist movements.

In popular perception it is often assumed that the Arts and Crafts Movement was created by William Morris. There is no denying that he was a leading figure; but the movement pre-dated Morris, drawing inspiration from the writings of John Ruskin, and also from those of Augustus Welby Pugin, among others. The architect Richard Norman Shaw, who designed many modest houses in Bedford Park in London (E.W. Godwin designed the first eighteen houses) and who influenced much of this type of work, thought William Morris a dreadful old humbug.[3] It is true that Morris suffered from a bad case of reactionary nostalgia. Even his socialism, for which he is still fêted today, was of the 'champagne' variety: he inherited a large fortune from his father, and spent £4,000 of it on building the Red House in Bexleyheath, Kent, designed by Philip Webb and later owned by Charles Holme.[4] There is no denying Morris's talent as a pattern-maker and he remains an influential figure. He could, however, have been far more influential had he been less dogmatic in his opposition to industry.

Arthur Liberty served a different market, that of the aspiring middle classes. The balance within society was gradually shifting – particularly after the passage of the Second Reform Bill in 1867– away from the old landed aristocracy and gentry towards the new middle classes, who derived their income from trade, industry and the professions. Liberty's catered for such people by stocking products by designers such as Christopher Dresser, who did not reject industrial production, as Morris did, but positively embraced it. Dresser's designs – of toast racks, teapots and the like, usually made in electroplate rather than sterling silver – were aimed quite plainly at the middle-class market, at those who had bought a home in the newly created suburbs of the ever-expanding cities.

In 1887 a number of those prominent in the artistic professions, among them the artist Walter Crane, the designer Lewis F. Day and the architect J.D. Sedding, founded the Arts and Crafts Exhibition Society. Arthur Liberty may have been a founder member; he was at the very least a prominent supporter. Of course with the success of the shop Arthur, who was already well known in London artistic circles, became a much more significant figure. The society was founded in reaction to the fact that the Royal Academy had refused even to consider including a decorative arts section in its summer exhibition. The objective, as Walter Crane, the founding president, wrote, was 'to give opportunity to the designers and craftsmen to exhibit their work to the public for its artistic interest' and to demonstrate that art was also to be found beyond the canvas. He went on, 'Ignoring the artificial distinction between Fine and Decorative art, we felt that the real distinction was what we conceived to be between good and bad art, or false and true taste and methods in handicraft, considering it of little value to endeavour to classify art according to its commercial value or social importance.'[5]

Some of the founding or early members of the Arts and Crafts Exhibition Society were also members of the Art Workers Guild.[6] This pre-dated the Arts and Crafts Exhibition Society, but only by three years. Its co-founder was William Lethaby (1857–1931), an architect and architectural historian who was very influential in the later Arts and Crafts Movement and in the emerging Modern Movement. He was born and brought up in Devon but, after apprenticeship to a local architect, he came to London in 1879 and became chief clerk to Richard Norman Shaw. He made major contributions to Shaw's projects, particularly Scotland Yard (the old headquarters of the Metropolitan Police) and Cragside, the magnificent house built for Lord Armstrong in Northumberland. After he left Shaw, Lethaby went on in 1906 to become Surveyor of Westminster Abbey, an appointment that had been held in previous times by Christopher Wren, Nicholas Hawksmoor and George Gilbert Scott.

Most notable among those who were members of both the Society and the Guild was the artist Walter Crane (1845–1915). He was a prolific illustrator of children's books and also produced designs for an array of different products including textiles, wallpaper and ceramic tiles. He was heavily influenced by William Morris, and was closely associated with the emerging socialist movement. Crane was born in Liverpool, the second son of the portrait painter and miniaturist Thomas Crane. He studied, and had a deep appreciation of, the Pre-Raphaelite Brotherhood, and was also a student of John Ruskin. Fired by Morris-like zeal, he produced many textile and wallpaper designs for the masses, some of which seem to have been bought by Liberty's, while many others were destined for Thomas Wardle's collection and thus sold in Liberty's. Crane differed from many of his contemporaries in his use of human figures in his designs; this characteristic obviously derived from his work in book illustration, and often his designs, which are full of symbolic meaning, appear to be book illustrations writ large. Crane was also vice-president of the Healthy and Artistic Dress Union, which had been founded in 1890. He even illustrated one of their pamphlets, *How to Dress*

BELOW LEFT Walter
Crane, photographed by
Frederick Hollyer in 1886.

BOTTOM LEFT William
Lethaby, co-founder
of the Arts and Crafts
Exhibition Society.

BELOW RIGHT A poster for
a lecture given by Crane
in Budapest in 1900.

PUBLISHED BY LIBERTY & CO., LONDON & PARIS

Without a Corset. This was very much the style of dress sold at Liberty's.

A major influence on children's dress (and subsequently that of adults), had been Kate Greenaway's book *Under the Window*, published in 1878. It was engraved and printed by Edmund Evans, who was to do much work for Liberty's and who also printed work by Walter Crane. Greenaway (1846–1901) soon became something of a cottage industry and in 1883 the first *Kate Greenaway Almanac* appeared. It sold over 90,000 copies. Arthur Liberty was a huge fan, as, rather surprisingly, was John Ruskin. Greenway's children dressed in her interpretations of late eighteenth-

century and Regency fashions; the fashions shown in portraits by John Hoppner (1758–1810) were possibly an inspiration. The style – high-waisted Regency dresses, smocks, skeleton suits for boys and straw bonnets, all sold by Liberty's – was hugely popular with the liberal-minded middle classes, and also among more aristocratic circles, most notably with the group known as the Souls.

Another founder member of the Art Workers Guild – he was also its Master in 1888 – who designed for Liberty's was Lewis F. Day (1845–1910). Born in London, the son of a Quaker wine merchant, Day began his career working in the offices of the stained-glass manufacturers Lavers and Barraud. He stayed with them for a few years before moving to Heaton, Butler & Bayne, where he worked on the decoration of Eaton Hall in Cheshire, the seat of the Duke of Westminster. He started to do freelance designs himself and in 1881 he joined Turnbull & Stockdale, a firm of textile printers near Ramsbottom in Lancashire, as their artistic director. Turnbull & Stockdale became the main supplier to Liberty's of printed cretonnes (printed cotton fabrics of a heavier weight than chintz and usually unglazed), which they produced by hand blocking and roller printing.[7] It is probable that many of the cretonne fabrics sold by Liberty's during the period were Day designs.

Lewis Day was not only a skilled designer but also a scholar of design and design history. He published extensively, both contributing to magazines and writing a number of books, most notably *Nature in Ornament*, published in 1909. His books were enormously successful and went into many editions, and they were to influence succeeding generations of designers. Day was perhaps more worldly than many of his contemporaries, and his designs were more commercially orientated. He did not like the use of human figures, nor birds and beasts in repeating patterns, although he conceded that Walter Crane was one of the very few designers who were capable of manipulating these forms into repeating patterns.

As Liberty's business grew and expanded, so did the variety and nature of the goods sold, and in 1888 Liberty's started its wallpaper department. William Judd recalled: 'Our Mr Fletcher designed the Damasque Wallpaper in single prints. They sold in thousands of pieces . . .'[8] One of the most significant figures to design wallpaper, and textiles, for Liberty's – and one of the most important designers of the 1890s and early twentieth century – was the architect Charles Voysey.

The son of a clergyman, Voysey (1857–1941) was born at Hessle in Yorkshire. What might have been an idyllic childhood was shattered when his father was tried before an ecclesiastical court for heresy, having denied the doctrine of everlasting hell. He was found guilty. In 1871 he appealed, but lost and was declared a heretic by the Privy Council, deprived of his living and defrocked. Mostly educated by his father, Voysey briefly attended Dulwich College before being articled to the architect J.P. Seddon and then going

on to establish his own practice in 1882. It was his friend A.H. Mackmurdo who suggested, in 1883, that he begin to design wallpapers for Jeffrey & Co. At the first exhibition held by the newly formed Arts and Crafts Exhibition Society, at the New Gallery in 1888, Voysey exhibited wallpapers and also printed textiles.

In the very first issue of *The Studio* in 1893 there was a long interview with Voysey, possibly by Charles Holme, although it was unsigned. At the time most of what Voysey produced was wallpaper, so the interviewer asked what he thought was a good design. Voysey answered: 'a wall-paper should be always essentially a pattern, the repeat of which is recognised as one of its chief characteristics, rather than a pattern disguising the repeat and presenting in detail

BELOW An unnamed two-tone Voysey design of c.1911.

BOTTOM 'Fool's Parsley', an elegant Voysey composition of stylized floral forms incorporating charmingly drawn birds. The design dates from c.1907.

OPPOSITE 'Seagulls', an early Voysey design of gulls on a rolling sea. This was manufactured both as a wallpaper and as a woven textile.

interwoven pretty bits known to the trade as "all-over pattern".[9] Wallpaper, Voysey went on to say, was merely a background and as most modern furniture was 'vulgar or bad in every way', bold-patterned colour would distract the eye. However, if your furniture was good, then Voysey said, 'wooden panelling, whether polished or hand-stained, is best of all; next to that comes painted panelling, but as papers wear better than the plain wall, we must permit them to exist on this ground.'[10] In 1893 he began to design for Essex & Co., for whom he ultimately produced hundreds of patterns. He also continued to design for Jeffrey & Co.

Voysey's association with Liberty's began in the 1890s, when they produced a few of his textile patterns. Sometimes a design intended as a wallpaper would be turned into a printed fabric, or occasionally into a woven fabric. 'Stag Design', for instance, was a wallpaper pattern, but was turned into a weave by Alexander Morton & Co., who were one of Liberty's major suppliers.

Alexander Morton & Co. Ltd was founded in 1867 in Darvel in Ayrshire, where they began weaving leno, a type of gauze.[11] In 1881 they started to weave lace curtaining and later they moved on to producing chenille. These products are mostly speciality weaving, but they also went into producing heavyweight woollen upholstery fabrics that were known at the time (rather confusingly) as tapestries. These were woven on jacquard looms. Morton's had also established a carpet division, a carpet-weaving workshop at Killybegs in County Donegal in 1898, having been encouraged to do so by government development grants. The objective was to produce hand-tufted carpets of comparable quality to those produced in Turkey, but in Arts and Crafts designs rather than traditional patterns. Liberty's were Morton's English agents and Morton's produced a great deal of merchandise that was sold exclusively through Liberty's as well as producing work commissioned by them. Carpets were an important part of Liberty's business and they sold a lot of Oriental rugs. The carpets produced by Morton's in Donegal were hand-made, but Liberty's also stocked conventional machine-produced carpet by manufacturers such as James Templeton, based in Glasgow, and Tomkinson & Adam, who were based in Kidderminster in Worcestershire.

Weaving sheds at
Alexander Morton Ltd.

TOP LEFT The handloom
weaving shed, used for
weaving chenille curtains.

BELOW LEFT The jacquard
machine weaving shed,
where muslin or 'Madras'
curtains were woven.

BELOW RIGHT Another
view of the jacquard
shed. Note the jacquard
cards: the holes are the
pattern code indicating
where the warp thread is
'lifted' and will be on top
of the weft thread.

Today, aside from his architecture, Voysey is chiefly remembered for his textile and wallpaper designs. He signed a contract with Morton's in 1897 to supply them with ten fabric designs a year for five years, and he had a similar contract with Tomkinson & Adam to supply designs. He was to supply Liberty's with many designs, some exclusive to them and others through the manufacturers mentioned. Some designs were prints but others were weaves. The complexity of his designs meant that they were jacquard designs (produced on jacquard looms) and occasionally 'double cloths'.[12]

Voysey's textile designs (and his wallpapers for that matter) were heavily influenced by the style of William Morris (who of course influenced all the designers of the period). However, a comparison of Voysey's work with that of Morris (who designed his last print, 'Daffodils', in 1891 and died in 1896) shows that in many of Voysey's best designs, particularly those created after Morris had died, the flowers and foliage tend to be stylized in form rather than botanically correct, as they would have been in Morris's work. Voysey believed that three-dimensional realism was not suitable in decoration – a view he also expressed in his 1893 interview in *The Studio* – but he thought such motifs could be used if reduced to mere symbols: in other words, if they became stylized representations. There was also another difference. Voysey, who often worked on a slightly smaller scale than Morris, was more economical with his ornament, so more of the background was visible. In this way he allowed the design more space in which to 'breathe', while Morris tended to favour a stiflingly oppressive design. This freer style, really a reflection of the times, also characterized the work of other designers, such as Lewis F. Day and Lindsay P. Butterfield.

As well as producing textiles for Liberty's, Voysey designed a great deal of furniture and other objects, some of which Liberty's sold. Architecturally Voysey's most prolific years were the late 1890s and the Edwardian period: he designed no houses after 1918. Even so, many of the housing estates constructed in the 1930s and after the Second World War quite clearly show his influence and that of Baillie Scott. This is hardly surprising, given that their work was published extensively in the pages of both *The Builder* and *The Studio*. Like many architects working at the time, Voysey was inspired by the English vernacular tradition, from which he drew heavily, as can be seen in the great sweeping pitched roofs, the rough render and the horizontal ribbon windows that are all characteristics of his work. (Sir Edwin Lutyens, under the tutelage of the indomitable Gertrude Jekyll, also drew on the vernacular tradition of Old West Surrey and Sussex, but even if there were superficial similarities his work was in reality quite different, and he soon moved on into the classical revival.) Voysey built a number of houses in the Lake District, including what is considered – certainly by Nikolaus Pevsner – his masterpiece, Broadleys, now the home of the Windermere Motor Boat Racing Club.

THE DISCOMFITURE OF THE PHILISTINES.

ON BEING PRESENTED WITH ARTFUL AND CRAFTY PUZZLE BY ARTISTIC FRIEND. (QUERY—IS IT THE RIGHT WAY UP? AND, IF SO, WHAT IS IT?)

CLOCKWISE FROM TOP LEFT A 'Tudric' pewter clock, probably designed by Voysey, c.1905; a Punch cartoon showing perplexing Voysey furniture; a gate-leg table and chair designed by Voysey and made by F.C. Nielsen.

FROM TOP TO BOTTOM
M.H. Baillie Scott as a
young man; the dining
room at Broadleys,
showing Voysey's original
furniture; the drawing
room at Broadleys.

By a quirk of fate, not far distant from Broadleys is Blackwell, built by Mackay Hugh (M.H.) Baillie Scott, who also designed for Liberty's. Blackwell is considered to be Baillie Scott's finest house, and it is certainly his largest. Unlike Blackwell, which sits end on to the lake, Broadleys overlooks the water. Its three beautifully elegant semicircular full-height bay windows look on to the lake, and flood the house with light. Broadleys was built as a holiday home for the son of a Yorkshire coal owner, Arthur Currer Briggs, in 1898. Voysey also designed some of the furniture used in the house.

Both Broadleys and Blackwell, neither of which are now family homes, are beautiful houses in wonderful settings, but some architectural critics regard Blackwell as the finer house.[13] It is slightly larger than Broadleys and draws more clearly on the Westmoreland vernacular tradition, but it also has the look and air of an Elizabethan manor house of the type typically found in the West Country. Interestingly, the plan seems more fluid and settled than Voysey's work, where there are discordant notes. Blackwell, which was built for the Manchester brewer Sir Edward Holt, might be a large, even grand house, but it is a fine example of Arts and Crafts architecture. It is also a good example of the type of house envisaged as the setting for the textiles, wallpapers, ceramics, and other artefacts designed by Baillie Scott, Voysey and other designers of the period. Part of the inspiration was Tudor and Jacobean architecture, as is plain from the exterior elevations. In their interiors these designers often created very deep friezes, which would be decorated with specifically designed frieze papers. This was a common feature in Tudor buildings, as can be seen in houses like Hardwick Hall in Derbyshire, where many of the rooms have deep decorative plaster friezes. The wall colours would often be strong, perhaps even dark, as can be seen in the dining room at Blackwell. (Of course at Blackwell Baillie Scott created a white drawing room, with a window overlooking the lake, but he was following a familiar Arts and Crafts idea: Philip Webb had created a white drawing room at Clouds in Wiltshire, built in 1886 for the Wyndhams.)

ABOVE Broadleys and
Blackwell, two great
Arts and Crafts houses.

LEFT, CLOCKWISE FROM TOP The Great Hall at Blackwell; a detail of the carved Great Hall frieze with stylized rowan leaves and berries; the upstairs corridor; the peacock frieze above a doorway in the Great Hall.

TOP RIGHT The White Drawing Room at Blackwell.

BOTTOM RIGHT The ceiling plasterwork using the same stylized rowan leaves and berries as appear in the carved frieze in the Great Hall.

Baillie Scott's work for Liberty's is not as easy to identify as Voysey's; nor is the full extent of his work known. Unfortunately, a disastrous fire in 1912 destroyed all his early papers, and his later papers (recording his work after he went into partnership with Edgar Beresford) were lost in the London Blitz during the Second World War. Though stuck in the relative backwater of the Isle of Man, where he had an architectural practice in Athol Street, Douglas (years later he was to joke, 'I went to the Isle of Man for a holiday. I was so seasick I couldn't face the journey back, so I set up practice there),[14] Baillie Scott was adept at publicizing his work. He first appeared in the pages of *The Studio* in December 1894 as a competitor in a competition to design the 'Ideal Coal Scuttle'. He didn't win. In the following issue (January 1895) he published an article entitled 'The Ideal Suburban House'. Baillie Scott hated the dull headline, which in no way reflects the interest of the article. He was a romantic, with a vision: 'On crossing the threshold we pass into charmed territory, where everything we possess shall be in harmony.'[15] He was as skilled with a watercolour brush as he was with the pen, and *The Studio* published many of his renditions. These and the articles established his reputation as an architectural theorist of great originality and brought him many commissions, including one from the Grand Duke of Hesse to design a suite of rooms in his palace in Darmstadt in Germany.

Darmstadt was to become to lovers of Arts and Crafts and Jugendstil (as the Art Nouveau style was known in Germany) what Bayreuth is to lovers of Wagner. The Grand Duke, Ernst Ludwig, commissioned Baillie Scott to redecorate a dining room and sitting room. The designer C.R. Ashbee and the Guild and School of Handicraft (described in Chapter 4) were also engaged, and it seems Baillie Scott did the design work while all the furniture, metalwork, etc., was made by the guild. When Baillie Scott visited Darmstadt he was, according to John Betjeman, met at the station by two coaches, with liveried coachmen and footmen – one to convey him and another to convey his luggage. He arrived dressed in tweeds, carrying one small bag. In September 1897 the telegrams seem to have been flowing thick and fast, for it transpired that the Grand Duke was expecting a visit in the first week of October from the Tsar of Russia (Nicholas II, who was married to the Grand Duke's sister) and the apartments were required for the Tsar's visit. Alas, the two rooms Baillie Scott and the guild created were destroyed, together with the ducal archives, during the Second World War.[16]

Baillie Scott gave up his practice in Douglas and moved to Bedford in about 1901. He had been producing furniture designs for a number of years, and since 1898 he had been working especially for John P. White. In 1901 White produced a catalogue of over 120 pieces designed by Baillie Scott, which were manufactured in his Pyghtle Works, Bromham Road, Bedford. He sold pieces to Liberty's, but also had a showroom at 134 New Bond Street.[17] The catalogue – *Furniture Made at The Pyghtle Works, Bedford by J. P. White Designed by M.H. Baillie Scott* (copies of which are now very rare) – clearly reveals Baillie Scott's style. In *The Studio* in 1897 Baillie Scott wrote an article 'On the Choice of Simple Furniture', which featured many of his designs, and these later appeared in White's catalogue. They were perhaps more traditional and conservative, but certainly less austere than Voysey's. Much of White's furniture was sold into the trade, to German and American dealers, and this may explain why J.P. White seems to be unknown on the Continent. Baillie Scott's furniture intended for his other German commissions was usually made by Deutsche Werkstätten in Munich or Dresden.

Voysey drew heavily on the simple forms of country furniture, the sort of things found in cottage homes and small manor houses. This was in accordance with fashionable artistic taste, as seen in the sort of products sold by Morris & Co. The 'Sussex' range, which Liberty's imitated with their 'Argyll' range (see page 54), is a classic example. People like Voysey and Baillie Scott developed the style in new and at the time exciting ways. Voysey's chairs, for example, follow the style but, perhaps revealing the puritan in his soul, pieces was often quite stiff, with lots of straight lines, and they seldom had much decoration, aside from the characteristic pierced heart shape or some other cut-out motif – often used to decorate chairs – or occasionally some inlay. However,

although in many ways his furniture seems slightly austere, Voysey's style was enormously influential and many architects and designers followed in his wake. He certainly influenced the work of Leonard Wyburd. In period photographs of the interiors Wyburd designed the austerity is quite evident, and even his sitting rooms appear uninviting today. What is lacking is any modicum of comfort: faced with the formality of a Voysey settle one longs for the generous ease of an upholstered sofa.

Aside from simple country furniture, another major influence on Voysey was the architect A.H. Mackmurdo (1851–1942), who had formed the Century Guild in 1882. The guild's aims were to 'render all branches [of design] the sphere no longer of the tradesman but of the artist'.[18] The guild propagated its ideas through a magazine, the *Hobby Horse* (which inspired William Morris to set up the Kelmscott Press).

CLOCKWISE FROM ABOVE
An armchair, a corner chair and a cradle, all designed by Baillie Scott; a sideboard designed by Voysey for Hurtmore in Sussex, c.1897; a music cabinet designed by Baillie Scott and made by the Guild of Handicraft for the drawing room at the New Palace, Darmstadt, c.1898; a barrel chair designed by Baillie Scott and made by John White.

Most of the early members – with the exception of William de Morgan – were young and unknown. The Century Guild was relatively short-lived (1883–92), but it provided inspiration for the founding of the Art and Crafts Exhibition Society. Voysey and Mackmurdo were great friends and in a letter in 1930 Voysey acknowledged his debt: 'You were a very great influence in those days and set me going on wallpapers and fabrics.'[19] Mackmurdo also influenced Voysey's furniture designs. For instance, Voysey adopted Mackmurdo's habit of forming a wooden pillar, which he terminated by a flat piece of wood as a 'capital'. Voysey refined and developed the idea, and it became very much part of the Art Nouveau style.

As well as fabrics and wallpapers Voysey designed carpets. In 1903 Liberty's held an exhibition at the Grafton Galleries in Bond Street of 'Irish Carpets', all made in the Donegal workshops owned by Alexander Morton & Co. There were seventeen exhibits and although the designs are unsigned, it is probable that six of them are the work of Voysey.[20] He often adapted his carpet designs from those produced for fabrics.

Some, such as 'The Lisburn', which was in the 1903 exhibition, had a central pattern in the body of the carpet, which is quite clearly adapted from a fabric design, surrounded by a border pattern. Such adaptations allow us to identify Voysey's work more easily.

Although Liberty's would buy in designs from prominent designers of the time such as Voysey, they also stocked exclusive designs from manufacturers. John Llewellyn – who started as the silk buyer, became a director in 1898, and after Sir Arthur's death in 1917 became a sort of design director – fostered and developed many of these contacts and relationships. He explained in an interview published in *The Citizen* in 1898, 'we flatter ourselves that we have created a new "English" period', ousting French designs.' John W. Howe, in the same article, when asked where the designs came from, remarked, 'It is no matter to us where the design comes from so long as it possesses merits worthy to be put before the public by the House of Liberty. We collect designs from all quarters, and our manufacturing friends are only too pleased for us to suggest the designs which should be taken up.'[21] In this way Liberty's was in the vanguard, creating a style that was admired widely at home and abroad.

BELOW The Donegal carpet factory established by Alexander Morton & Co.

BOTTOM The 'Irish Carpets' exhibition held by Liberty's at the Grafton Galleries in Bond Street in 1903.

STILE LIBERTY: THE ART NOUVEAU MOVEMENT

'Squirrel and Blackbird', a wallpaper designed by Charles Voysey in the late 1890s as 'Squirrel and Dove' and adapted c. 1907.

Art Nouveau had its origins in the Arts and Crafts Movement. As a style it was at its most popular from the 1890s to 1914 (although by the beginning of the First World War its popularity had already begun to wane). An early example can be seen in Arthur Mackmurdo's book cover design for *Wren's City Churches*, which was published in 1883: its free-flowing pattern was a surprise and a daring departure (and had no particular relationship with the book's contents). The style was also heavily influenced by Japanese woodblock prints with their flat perspective and strong colours. These influences can be clearly seen in the work of Aubrey Beardsley, who designed the cover for the very first issue of *The Studio* magazine in 1893 (see page 44).

The style was named after a shop. In 1895 the German art dealer Siegfried Bing (1838–1905) opened at 22 rue de Provence in Paris a shop selling modern art, which he called Maison de l'Art Nouveau.[1] The shop gave its name to the style in France and Britain, while in Germany the style came to be known as Jugendstil. Liberty's were in the vanguard of Art Nouveau in Britain, and also in France through their Paris shop, which they opened at 38 avenue de l'Opéra in 1890, following the success of the aesthetic gowns they exhibited at the Exposition Universelle in 1889. Liberty's developed links with other companies across the Continent – in 1902, for instance, Metz & Co. of Amsterdam and The Hague, the leading store for Art Nouveau furnishings in Holland, became their sole agents in The Netherlands – and in Italy Art Nouveau became known as Stile Liberty.

Art Nouveau did not develop as a uniform style, but had marked local differences. In Britain it was more restrained, more sober, more conservative and more austere than it was on the Continent. By contrast, in France, Germany, Austria and Hungary it was freer, more flamboyant, even more decadent. This Continental Art Nouveau can be seen today in some of the entrances to the Paris Métro, which were designed by Hector Guimard (1867–1942) and gave rise to the term Style Métro.[2] The free-flowing curves so characteristic of Style Métro are often described as 'whiplash' because they were seen as reminiscent of the sudden violent curves generated by the cracking of a whip.[3] Arthur Liberty disapproved of these Continental excesses, as did a number of the designers who worked for him, and gradually the British public grew to dislike the vulgarities of the style seen on the Continent. This spawned a desire for something more restrained, which was the seed of various revival movements.

In Britain the Art Nouveau style became particularly associated with the Glasgow School of Art and the name of Charles Rennie Mackintosh (1868–1928).[4] The Glasgow School received a great deal of publicity from *The Studio*, which featured their work. A close associate of Mackintosh was George Walton (1867–1933), who collaborated with him on the Cranston Tea Rooms in Glasgow in 1897. Walton had close links with the Arts and Crafts Movement, but his style had a distinctive touch of the Scottish Art Nouveau. Scottish Art Nouveau was more extreme than the relatively restrained and sober English form. In Scotland Art Nouveau was quite heavily infused with the Celtic revival – although in the work of Mackintosh you see a strong linear emphasis that is almost modernist in tone.

There is no evidence that Mackintosh ever designed for Liberty's (which seems rather a pity), but Walton began designing furniture for the store in the mid- to late 1890s. It was probably Liberty's who recommended him to James Couper & Sons when they wanted to update their 'Clutha' range of glass, originally created by Christopher Dresser. Walton's efforts were more sober, more restrained than Dresser's, and were usually produced in pale green glass, often decorated with white enamel and/or flecked with gold.

Liberty's also secured the services of a remarkable designer whose work has come to characterize the period: Archibald Knox. Knox's work, like that of Dresser, has acquired something approching cult status. It is redolent of Art Nouveau, but he was also greatly influenced by, and a great exponent of, the Celtic revival, or what might be termed Insular art.[5] Celtic design is characterized by intricate geometric designs, interlacing patterns and stylized animal decoration, and was regarded as an art form indigenous to these islands. Beginning sometime in the late seventeenth century, the Celtic revival was spurred on by the discovery in 1850 of the Tara brooch (a Celtic brooch of about AD 750), which is now in the National Museum of Ireland in Dublin. As early as 1861 Morris, Faulkner & Co. (William Morris's company at the time, which was succeeded by Morris & Co.) produced a cabinet with Celtic-inspired inlay work.

Liberty's also did a huge amount to revive it. However, the influence of the Celtic revival on the Art Nouveau movement basically remained firmly within Britain and in Scandinavia, and it seems to have been only in Norway and Sweden that it had any real influence on architecture and interior design; it never really caught on in these fields in Britain.

Archibald Knox (1864–1933) was born at Cronkbourne on the Isle of Man in April 1864. His father was an engineer and both his parents were originally from Scotland. It seems that from an early age he was never without a pencil in his hand, which prompted his father to remark, perhaps in exasperation, 'Why, he doesn't even know how to hold a hammer.'[6] A pencil can be as useful as a hammer, so his parents, embracing defeat, enrolled him at the Douglas School of Art in 1879. At the end of five years of study Knox sat his final examination on 'Historic Ornament', for which he had chosen to specialize in Celtic design – a form that was to characterize much of his work.

By 1893, possibly slightly earlier, Knox had begun to do work for M.H. Baillie Scott, who at that time had his architectural practice in Douglas. As Baillie Scott was producing designs for Liberty's (see Chapter 3), in all probability it was he who introduced Knox to Arthur Liberty. This introduction was to establish Knox's career. One problem in tracing Knox's work for Liberty's – and indeed that of other designers too – is that Liberty's had a policy of anonymity for its designs (the aim being to protect the Liberty brand). Another is that unfortunately all the records from this early period, notably the cost books, which would have revealed who designed particular items, were lost in a fire. This means that most attributions can be made only on stylistic grounds and are thus open to interpretation and error. However, Guy Bentley recalled that Knox produced more than four hundred designs for Liberty's, mostly for jewellery and 'Cymric' silver, some of which were reproduced in their 'Tudric' pewter range, aimed at the mass market.

Liberty's metalwork venture was the brainchild of Arthur Liberty and John Llewellyn, who joined Liberty's in 1889, in the silk department. Llewellyn came from the silk mercers and wine merchants Howell & Jones in Lower Regent Street. They had originally had a shop in Pall Mall, which later became the War Office, and later still the Royal Automobile Club. When Llewellyn joined Liberty's he brought with him the rights to sell Royal Barum Ware, a range of pottery made by C.H. Brannam of Barnstaple in Devon. Llewellyn's talent was soon spotted. Mr Nelrood, the silk department buyer, went to Arthur Liberty and told him that he had a brilliant young man working under him and he should retire so that Llewellyn could take his job. Nelrood did retire and after being appointed as the silk buyer Llewellyn would commission and purchase designs from studios and work directly with manufacturers such as Morton's, in the process developing the relationship with the manufacturer. Within nine years Llewellyn was a director, remaining so until he retired in 1935.

The jewellery department had been established in 1883. It sold Eastern silverware and Indian items in gold and precious stones, but among all the rare and expensive

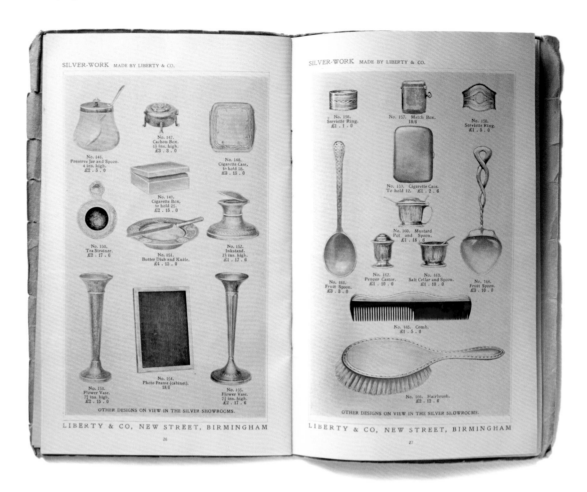

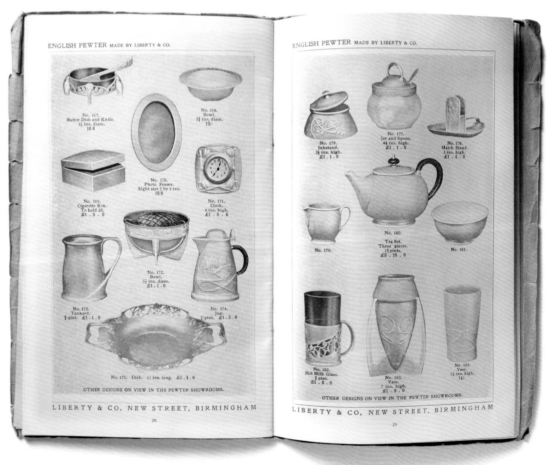

antique work it also sold quite inexpensive pieces. Later the department became famous for its jade and amber; it even published a booklet, *Jade Amulets*, in 1925.[7] It went on to sell Dutch and Greek jewellery, before establishing its own workshops in order to produce Renaissance revival pieces. In 1899 it launched its 'Cymric' silver and this, together with 'Tudric' pewter, which was introduced in 1902, proved to be Liberty's greatest contribution to the Art Nouveau movement. 'Cymric' silver was a joint venture with the old Birmingham firm of W.H. Haseler, who had a shareholding in a new company, Liberty & Co. (Cymric) Ltd.

In the mid-1890s Arthur Liberty had seen modern German domestic metalwork, particularly the products of J.P. Kayser & Son of Krefeld. When he stocked these they sold well, which prompted him to look at producing his own ranges, manufactured in England. It was part an exercise in producing new designs, but also a revivalist endeavour: what could better evoke the seventeenth century than pewter?

The revival of pewter manufacture seems to have been a theme in artistic circles in the 1890s. J. Starkie-Gardener gave a lecture on the topic at the Royal Society of Arts in 1894. At the time the trade was dominated by Britannia metal, a type of pewter which is an alloy of 92 per cent tin, 6 per cent antimony and 2 per cent copper. It had been introduced in 1770 by Ebenezer Hancock and Richard Jessop from Sheffield and was initially marketed as 'Vickers White Metal'. This alloy is rather soft, so products made from it are not particularly robust or durable. It was, however, cheaper than Sheffield plate,[8] far cheaper than silver, and cheaper and a more honest product than electroplate. In their own production Liberty's developed a more durable product – German alloys tended, as Arthur Liberty observed, to be rather brittle. After some experimentation, Haseler developed an alloy of 90 per cent tin, 8 per cent copper and 2 per cent antimony.[9] Thus the 'Tudric' pewter range was born.

There is no doubt that 'Tudric' drew heavily on Art Nouveau style, but in the restrained English manner and fusing it with the Celtic revival. Arthur Liberty gave a lecture on pewter in 1904 and illustrated it with examples of German manufacture and examples drawn from Liberty's

'Tudric' range. As he pointed out, 'Tudric' – the name, with its allusion to the Tudors, has a comforting ring – was simply decorated with simplified Celtic motifs, sometimes augmented by botanical motifs. Sometimes the objects were entirely plain. This was in marked contrast to French and German examples, with 'the fantastic motif which pleases our Continental friends to worship as l'art nouveau'.[10]

Knox designed extensively for the range, although he contributed no new designs after 1912, and his most prolific period was in the early years of the century, up to about 1905. The range continued after the First World War, but often simplified, bereft of decoration and with a hammered surface. Production ceased in 1939.

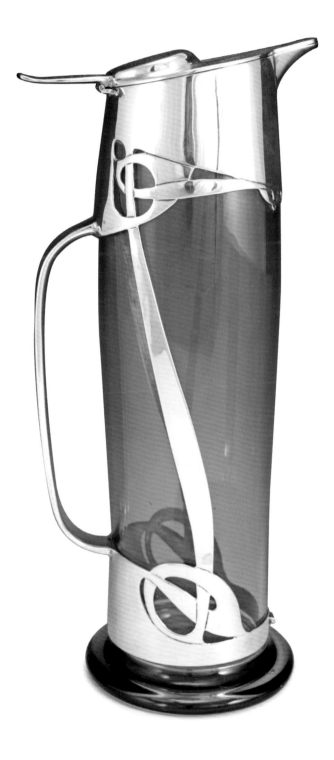

A 'Cymric' silver and
glass claret jug designed
by Archibald Knox,
hallmarked 1902.

A fine silver vase with
Celtic-inspired designs
in enamel, c. 1902.

A ceramic jardinière
with polished pewter
decoration by Orivit,
c.1902.

A silver belt buckle
designed by Archibald
Knox, London 1909.

Both 'Cymric' and 'Tudric' were very much a part of the prevailing Arts and Crafts Movement, but they also drew heavily on Art Nouveau style. 'Cymric' was moreover greatly influenced by Charles Robert Ashbee and his Guild and School of Handicraft. Ashbee was born in Isleworth, the son of a wealthy merchant (who had an unfortunate predilection for pornography – he assembled the largest Victorian collection of erotic literature and porn). Charles Robert grew up to detest his father and adore his mother. On leaving university (King's College, Cambridge) he was articled to the architect G.F. Bodley (1827–1907), the leading ecclesiastical architect of the day and famous for designing the Washington National Cathedral. While working for Bodley, Ashbee lived at the Universities Settlement at Toynbee Hall in Whitechapel, where students could undertake social work in deprived areas in the East End and perhaps gain an understanding of the grinding poverty found there.[11] The artist Roger Fry lived there too and was a great friend of Ashbee.

Toynbee Hall, though well intentioned, did not impress Ashbee. It was, as he remarked, 'neither a college, convent nor a club',[12] and smacked too much of tea and sympathy. He conceived the more practical idea of teaching drawing and decoration, and found an enthusiastic audience. This led on to the idea of forming a co-operative of skilled craftsmen and, despite discouragement from William Morris, whom he consulted about it, he founded the Guild and School of Handicraft in June 1888. It was an instant success, and soon moved from Toynbee Hall into Essex House, a Georgian mansion on the Mile End Road, also opening a shop at 16a Brook Street, just off Bond Street in the heart of Mayfair.

The 'Fintona' carpet, designed by the Silver Studio and made in Donegal in 1902.

In 1900, when the lease on Essex House had barely two years left to run, the search began for new premises. This was how the idea of a move to Chipping Campden came about: they arrived by bicycle in 1902. There is a certain romance in this doomed utopian venture – of living and working in an enchantingly pretty country village untouched by the Industrial Revolution. Fifty families, a total of 150 people in all, made the move, which had been democratically decided.[13] The agricultural depression had hit the area very hard, so there was plenty of property to renovate, but it soon became apparent that the village was too remote and the transport links too fragile (even though it was on the railway) for it to be economically viable (which was just what Morris and William de Morgan had discovered before them). Utopia proved to be of brief duration and the guild went into liquidation in 1908.

Although Ashbee was very different from Morris – he was never a socialist – he too was a romantic who lamented the passing of the old crafts, the old rural communities (as did many others, including Gertrude Jekyll, who chronicled some of the old ways of life in her books *Old West Surrey* and *Old English Household Life*). Eventually he came to the conclusion that the Arts and Crafts 'war' against industry was basically futile, for, as he observed in *Should We Stop Teaching Art*, published in 1911, 'Modern civilisation rests on machinery, and no system of endowment, or the encouragement, or the teaching of art can be sound that does not recognise this.'[14] Industry won.

Unfortunately Liberty's 'Cymric' and 'Tudric' ranges infuriated Ashbee, because he felt that his own work was being plagiarized and ultimately degraded. He was particularly irritated by the addition of 'hand wrought' distressing or patination on to what was actually a machine-manufactured piece. He felt it betrayed the ethos of the Arts and Crafts Movement.

One of the most significant design companies in the development of the Art Nouveau style in Britain was the Silver Studio. Founded by Arthur Silver (1853–1896) in 1880, the Silver Studio became one of the most important textile and wallpaper design studios. After Arthur Silver died in 1896, the Studio continued under his sons, Reginald 'Rex' Silver (1879–1965) and Harry Silver (1882–1972). Its archive is now at the Museum of Domestic Design and Architecture at the University of Middlesex. There are over 20,000 designs in the archive, some 4,000 textiles, 2,000 wallpapers and 50 wallpaper pattern books, as well as some furniture and metalwork designs. Because the Studio was active from 1880 until it finally closed in 1963, it saw many phases in artistic taste and these phases are represented in the archive. The studio also maintained meticulous records, so it is possible to date designs accurately (something which is all too rarely the case).

The Silver Studio produced designs that companies like Liberty's would buy and have produced by manufacturers.

LEFT A charcoal and gouche design for a Liberty's printed velvet, by Harry Napper.

BELOW A watercolour and gouache design for a Liberty's chintz, probably produced by Stead McAlpin in 1891.

ABOVE A design for printed cretonne, sold to Liberty's in April 1891.

OPPOSITE, ABOVE Stylized anemones on a cotton furnishing fabric, c.1905.

OPPOSITE, BELOW Indigo-discharge design for cotton, by Arthur Silver, 1891.

Most textile manufacturers did not maintain a design studio of their own, but would – then as now – buy in designs. These were sold in a variety of forms, from sketches at various stages to fully worked-up designs. These were mostly made for textile printers, although some designs were woven, in which case it was the manufacturer who would create the point-paper design for a weave, as this was a more technical process. In the studio a pattern started out as a 'miniature' drawing, usually on a one-eighth scale. The design was in full repeat so would give an impression of the overall effect. Manufacturers could buy a miniature and do the rest of the work themselves, or they could allow the design to be developed. Sometimes a design proves unsatisfactory when drawn up at full scale: reduced scale can distort proportions. A sketch design, produced on thin copy paper in black and white, usually in charcoal, showed the pattern layout (designs are usually created on what are known as pattern bases) and its repeat, but it was not coloured or fully worked up. A sketch design was more expensive than a miniature, costing, at the turn of the century £1 10*s*. A fully worked-up design, which was coloured, took a lot of time to produce, and would cost £12 12*s*., which equated to two weeks' wages for a provincial bank manager; however, for that a manufacturer not only got a finished product that he could immediately put into production, he also acquired the copyright to the design and could do what he liked with it.

We know from the Silver Studio's day book that Liberty's were buying designs from the studio as early as 1891. A design which has almost become Liberty's emblem, 'Peacock Feathers', was exhibited by Arthur Silver at at the Manchester Royal Jubilee Exhibition in 1887 and subsequently printed by the Rossendale Printing Co. and sold at Liberty's. It was so successful that Liberty's revived the pattern in 1975 for their centenary. However, in this case it seems likely that Arthur Silver actually adapted the pattern from a design for woven silk called 'Hera' that was registered in 1876 by William Fry of Dublin, who manufactured designs by Christopher Dresser.[15]

Arthur Silver was, like so many of his generation, hugely influenced by Japanese art; indeed in an interview

he gave to *The Studio* the interviewer mentioned that the design studio had for inspiration 'photographs after Botticelli and other old masters, panels of lustrous enamels and gesso work, scraps of fine fabrics, and books of Japanese drawings'.[16] The article was copiously illustrated, with one pattern called 'A Japanese Leather Paper' and many other designs that clearly show a Japanese influence. Arthur Silver was a regular exhibitor at Arts and Crafts Society exhibitions and he also became a member of the Royal Society of Arts. Having studied at the Reading School of Art Silver had been an apprentice to the freelance designer H.W. Batley and it may well be that Silver's interest in Japanese design was fostered by Batley, who quite often incorporated Japanese motifs into his designs. Silver's work was regularly featured in *The Studio*, which helped to burnish his reputation.

The records are not complete, so we do not know exactly how many staff Silver employed. He certainly had two assistants in the 1890s: Harry Napper and John Illingworth Kay. After Arthur Silver died in 1896, aged forty-three, Napper stayed on to manage the studio for Silver's widow while the two sons learned the business. It may have been a small studio but nevertheless in the 1890s it produced something like five hundred designs a year.

The Silver Studio also produced some metalwork designs for the 'Cymric' silver range. A pair of candlesticks, 'Conister', was certainly designed by Rex Silver in about 1900 and published in *The Studio*. Some of the metalwork designs which Liberty's bought from the Silver Studio were the work of Archibald Knox, who had probably met Silver through the Arts and Crafts Exhibition Society or the Art Workers Guild, of which they were both members. However, like Liberty's, the Silver Studio did not credit individual designers, which makes unravelling who designed what very difficult. Towards the end of his life Rex Silver gave an interview in which he maintained that all the metalwork designs sold to Liberty's were his. This may have been the case, but it seems improbable.

John Illingworth Kay (1870–1950) was one of the designers who worked for Silver between 1892 and 1900, producing a variety of designs for metalwork, textiles and wallpapers. (In 1900 he left to become the manager of the stencilling department of the wallpaper manufacturers Essex & Co, where he stayed for over twenty years before leaving to take up a part-time teaching post at the Central School of Arts and Crafts.) However, after Arthur Silver died it was Harry Napper (1860–1930) who kept the studio alive. Napper went to work for Silver, it is believed, in 1893 and probably left in about 1898 to work freelance, still selling designs through the studio. He was also a talented watercolour artist and his works occasionally come up at auction. After he left the Silver Studio Napper supplied Liberty's with designs on a freelance basis. As Mario Amaya observed in his study of the Art Nouveau movement, 'Around 1900 the strongest personality at Liberty's appears to have been Harry Napper, whose fabrics depended less on undulating curves than drifting geometrized motifs, strident with angular petals and thorny leaves.'[17] Napper may have been influenced by the graphic designs of Aubrey Beardsley and also by the work of Archibald Knox.

In 1902 Lindsay Butterfield (1869–1948) signed a contract with Alexander Morton & Co. to supply ten designs a year for five years. A contemporary of the Silver brothers, Butterfield was an important textile designer, in relation both to Arts and Crafts and to Art Nouveau, but he is a rather obscure figure. He trained at the Lambeth School of Art in 1887, taking evening classes. He was later to teach textile design at Kingston and Camberwell Art Schools, and after 1905 at the National Art Training School in South Kensington. He was also a founder member of the Society of Industrial Designers in 1930, just as in 1909 he had been a driving force in founding the Design Club, which sought to bring together designers and manufacturers. In his early designs he was, like everyone else, much influenced by William Morris, but he progressed and developed, so it is not really possible to typecast him in design history terms. Butterfield made use of devices favoured by Morris, such as a recessive background pattern on to which he superimposed his main pattern. In his early work it is possible to detect the influence of Charles Voysey.

Designs by Lindsay P. Butterfield

BELOW 'Hydrangeas', c.1896,. This was used both as a textile and as a wallpaper.

OPPOSITE, CLOCKWISE FROM TOP LEFT 'Malaga', a wallpaper design printed by Essex & Co.; 'Pomegranate', a tapestry design; 'Tudor', a tapestry design for David Barbour & Co.; 'Berry', a wallpaper design printed by Essex & Co.

ABOVE LEFT A Moorcroft 'Flamminian Ware' vase, c.1910.

BELOW LEFT 'Brown Cornflower' (or 'Brown Chrysanthemum') vase, c.1913.

We are fortunate that in later life Butterfield gave many of the original drawings for his work to the Victoria and Albert Museum. He also published two books, *Floral Forms in Historic Design*, which had notes and a preface by W.G. Paulson Townsend, and *Roses and Other Flower Designs*. He was a keen gardener and these books show his love of the flowers familiar in English gardens – roses, poppies, sweet peas, lilies, etc. Perhaps because of his botanical knowledge, he tended to depict foliage in more detail than most other designers, the foliage often vying for attention with the flowers. He was clever in his ability to arrange his subject matter, and his designs were always natural, his effects never forced or overly contrived. From what little is known he seems to have been a freelance designer and apart from Morton's sold designs to Warner & Sons, Thomas Wardle, Turnbull & Stockdale, Smith & Neuman, and G.P. and J. Baker Ltd – the leading manufacturers of the period.

Just as the name of Archibald Knox seems to dominate silver and pewter design in the early years of the twentieth century, so William Moorcroft dominates ceramic design. Liberty's stocked ceramics from various manufacturers. Apart from ceramics by Brannam (see page 84), as early as 1884 they had sold ceramics from Bretby Art Pottery, established in 1883 by Harry Tooth and William Ault. Tooth had been the manager at the Linthorpe Art Pottery in Middlesbrough, where Christopher Dresser had been the art director. 'Linthorpe Ware' had been sold at the Art Furnishers Alliance and was later sold at Liberty's. The Linthorpe Art Pottery did not exist for long – possibly ten years or so – but its products would even today be considered modern and stylish. Liberty's also sold garden pots made by the Compton Pottery in Surrey. Established by Mary Watts, wife of the painter G.F. Watts, this had originally begun as pottery classes for locals but rapidly became a commercial venture. Archibald Knox also designed ceramics for Compton's, as is clear from the *Garden Pottery* catalogue the firm published in about 1905. Another designer who did work for them was Gertrude Jekyll, who lived a couple of miles away at Busbridge. Mary Watts also designed some carpets and rugs (a rug called 'The Pelican' being one example), which were made in Donegal.

BELOW, CLOCKWISE FROM LEFT William Moorcroft in about 1930; a group of 'Florian Ware' pieces for Liberty's; a Liberty's advertisement for the 'Florian Ware' range, c.1910.

Pelican' being one example), which were made in Donegal. Whereas Knox's carpet designs were unsigned, hers were signed – a very rare concession by Liberty's. Mary Watts also ran the Yattendon metalwork classes and Liberty's would sell their copper work, which had much in common with the more familiar Newlyn and Keswick work.[18]

The Moorcroft label was originally started as a studio pottery by James Macintyre & Co. to produce 'art pottery' to complement their normal commercial work. William Moorcroft (1872–1945) was born in Burslem in Staffordshire and studied art at the local technical college and also in London and in Paris before being employed by Macintyre's in 1897 at the age of twenty-four. Within a year he was put in charge of their art pottery studio. Moorcroft contributed designs to their 'Aurelian Ware', which had transfer-printed and enamelled decoration in reds, blues

and golds – all rather high Victorian. The first range for which he was entirely responsible, 'Florian Ware', was a great success and won a gold medal at the St Louis International Exhibition in 1904. Liberty's retailed the line and it was illustrated in their *Yule-Tide Gifts* catalogue in 1901. The caption claimed that the decoration of some pieces was 'reminiscent of Pompeian models, others are adapted from Italian and contemporary schools'. Such marketing flannel was quite common, but in reality the decoration is pure Arts and Crafts infused with a touch of Art Nouveau flamboyance, probably derived from Moorcroft's studies in Paris. 'Florian Ware' was decorated with heavy slip and translucent glazes, which produced brilliant colours.

Macintyre's gained considerably from the success of the art pottery ranges, which were exhibited extensively and won many awards. However, the acclaim fell on William

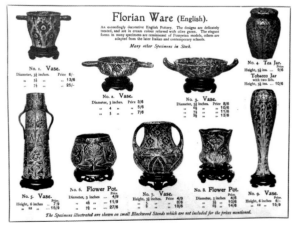

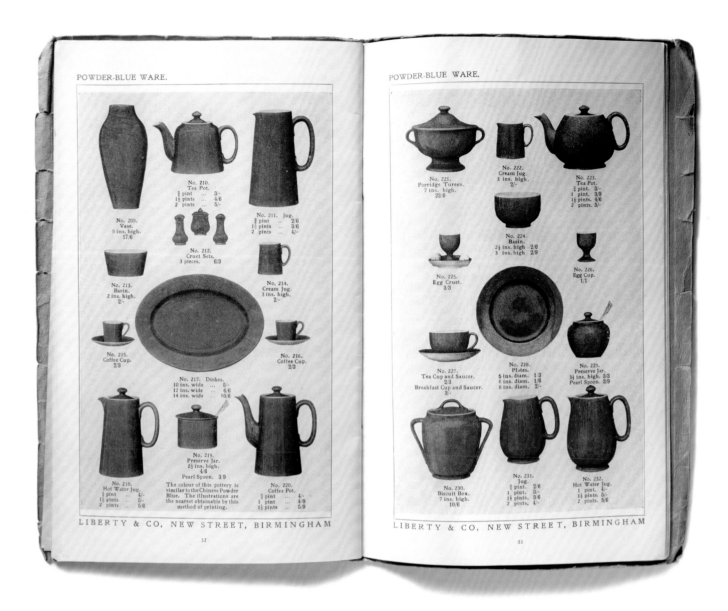

No. 209.
Vase.
9 ins. high.
17/6

No. 210.
Tea Pot.
½ pint ... 3/-
1½ pints ... 4/6
2 pints ... 5/-

No. 211. Jug.
½ pint ... 2/6
1½ pints ... 3/6
2 pints ... 4/-

No. 212.
Cruet Sets,
3 pieces. 6/3

No. 213.
Basin.
2 ins. high.
2/-

No. 214.
Cream Jug.
3 ins. high.
2/-

No. 215.
Coffee Cup.
2/3

No. 216.
Coffee Cup.
2/3

No. 217. Dishes.
10 ins. wide ... 5/-
12 ins. wide ... 6/6
14 ins. wide ... 10/6

No. 218.
Hot Water Jug.
½ pint ... 4/-
1½ pints ... 5/-
2 pints ... 5/6

No. 219.
Preserve Jar.
2½ ins. high.
4/6
Pearl Spoon. 3/9

The colour of this pottery is
similar to the Chinese Powder
Blue. The illustrations are
the nearest obtainable by this
method of printing.

No. 220.
Coffee Pot.
½ pint ... 4/-
1 pint ... 4/9
1½ pints ... 5/9

No. 221.
Porridge Tureen.
7 ins. high.
22/6

No. 222.
Cream Jug.
3 ins. high.
2/-

No. 223.
Tea Pot.
½ pint ... 3/-
1 pint ... 3/9
1½ pints ... 4/6
2 pints. 5/-

No. 224.
Basin.
2½ ins. high 2/6
3 ins. high 2/9

No. 225.
Egg Cruet.
3/3

No. 226.
Egg Cup.
1/1

No. 227.
Tea Cup and Saucer.
2/3
Breakfast Cup and Saucer.
3/-

No. 228.
Plates.
5 ins. diam. 1/3
6 ins. diam. 1/6
8 ins. diam. 2/-

No. 229.
Preserve Jar.
3½ ins. high. 3/3
Pearl Spoon. 3/9

No. 230.
Biscuit Box.
7 ins. high.
10/6

No. 231.
Jug.
½ pint ... 2/6
1 pint ... 3/-
1½ pints ... 3/6
2 pints. 4/-

No. 232.
Hot Water Jug.
1 pint ... 4/-
1½ pints ... 5/-
2 pints. 5/6

Moorcroft and eventually the success of the art pottery was felt to be overshadowing the main business. It seems that he was eventually asked to leave: they wrote to him on 21 November 1912 informing him of their decision to close the art pottery department on 30 June 1913. Arthur Liberty came to the rescue with an offer of financial help, with the result that William Moorcroft Ltd was formed, with two directors, William himself and Alwyn Lasenby, who was Arthur Liberty's cousin and close friend. After protracted negotiations with Macintyre's, Arthur Liberty was able to buy William Moorcroft's shape moulds, and it seems that the agreement also transferred many of the employees. Moorcroft opened a new purpose-built factory, the Cobridge Works in Sandbach Road, Burslem, Staffordshire, where it remains to this day. The factory was

all on one level, so there was no need to carry trays of pots up and down stairs, which allowed for an easy flow from raw clay to finished product. It was also built so that the floors could be hosed down each day to reduce dust. In its day it was the most modern factory in the Potteries.

It was probably Alwyn Lasenby (1867–1952) who realized that art pottery alone would never make the works a commercial success, or even a viable concern. More mundane products were needed to help pay the wage bill. The company developed a range of tableware known as 'Powder Blue' or 'Moorcroft Blue', which was used in Liberty's tea rooms. It was enormously successful and remained in production until 1963. The impact of 'Powder Blue' lies in its modern and distinctive shapes, which make it seem as if it were straight out of the 1950s or 1960s, though it was actually created in 1913.

"SUNRAY" WARE (MOORCROFT)

LIBERTY & CO LTD   REGENT STREET   LONDON W.1

34

OPPOSITE A page from Liberty's Birmingham 1922-23 *Yule-tide Gifts* catalogue, promoting 'Powder Blue'.

ABOVE A Liberty's London catalogue page showing 'Sunray', the sister range to 'Powder Blue'.

LEFT Mrs William Moorcroft's wedding dress, made by Liberty's in 1928.

However, changes in technology were to kill it off. 'Powder Blue' was a labour-intensive product, as each piece had to be dipped and the excess slip, or liquid clay, had to be turned off from the foot. Also it was unpredictable in firing, so assembling sets that matched was a bit like completing a giant jigsaw puzzle, and the firm ended up with a shed full of oddments. However, it could be placed in the hottest parts of the bottle kiln (around the firing holes or 'bags'), where nothing else could be positioned, and so it effectively cost nothing to fire. The Clean Air Act of 1956 meant there had to be a gradual shift to electric kilns (which have a more even temperature, with no 'hot spots'), radically changing the economics, so that 'Powder Blue' was no longer able to pay its way. It was basically an earthenware product, but to make it pay the firm needed to charge a bone china price.

Moorcroft pottery was quite distinct from the products of contemporary competitors because of the techniques involved in its manufacture, particularly the firing, traditionally called biscuit firing, which fuses the limited range of colours with the body. Moorcroft typically used very refined clay, which it was possible to fire at high temperatures – temperatures more often used to make electric insulation wares and in the pharmaceutical and chemical industries. Another characteristic of the range was the use of slip-trailing, which as a technique has a long history in the pottery towns of the British midlands. It is akin to icing a cake, but instead of having relatively easily controlled thick icing and a piping bag, you had slip, the liquid clay, and what was called an ink pot. This was small stoneware pot a couple of inches high, with a small hole towards the base on one side. A quill was fixed into the hole and this was used to direct the slip, using the thumb to restrict, increase or stop the flow. It must have been a nightmare to use this technique on a pot, especially as the ink pot had to be kept upright. William Moorcroft came up with the idea of using a bag, rather than a pot, for the slip – in essence he adapted the kitchen icing bag – which allowed much greater control of the slip, and made it possible

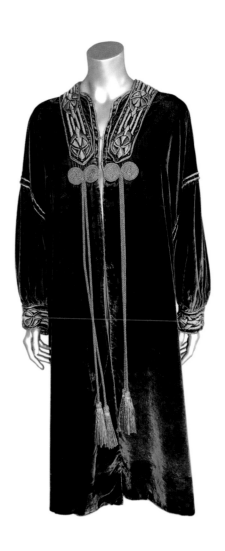

certainly does not seem to have been starved of investment. In the early 1920s Moorcroft built a new kiln at the Cobridge factory in order to try his hand at high-temperature transmutation glazes. Particularly prized was the rich red found on Chinese porcelain, a copper reduction which gained the name *rouge flambé*. Liberty's marketed a range in the 1920s and 1930s as 'Moorcroft Rouge Flambé', which is today highly sought after. Liberty's were to retain their shareholding in Moorcroft until 1962, when the Moorcroft family bought them out.

William Moorcroft became a firm friend of Arthur Liberty and his family. William's first wife, Florence Moorcroft, died in 1927 and the following year he married Hazel Lasenby, Alwyn Lasenby's sister and Sir Arthur's cousin,[19] which drew the two families even closer. In Liberty's publicity material goods were labelled 'Moorcroft', the firm being one of the few suppliers who were actually identified. Liberty's encouraged Moorcroft to exhibit and, following the First World War, he exhibited far and wide, his exhibitions being a regular feature at the British Industries Fairs: perhaps the most important was the 1924 British Empire Exhibition held at Wembley. He received a good press and from an early stage enjoyed the patronage of the Royal Family: Queen Mary, in particular, was an enthusiast for his work, and in 1928 Moorcroft received a royal warrant, becoming 'Potter to H.M. The Queen'.

Supporting and promoting artists working in the Art Nouveau style of the time and selling their creations was one more way in which Liberty's showed themselves to be at the cutting edge of style and fashion. But Liberty's did more than sell individual pieces of furniture, fabric and *objets d'art*; they also created whole rooms and whole houses.

to achieve much longer lines. This technique is usually referred to as tube-lining, the term slip-trailing being used for the older form of decoration.

This new technique enabled Moorcroft to produce designs with long, flowing lines of plant stems and leaves, which were perfect for the sort of designs then popular. The technique could ultimately be used as the main decorative feature, as can be seen in Moorcroft's famous 'Fish' vase, where the details of the fish's scales and fin are all done by tube-lining; the colouring is a secondary element, used merely to enhance the effect. Seeing how the technique could be used to portray the artistic vogue of Art Nouveau, other potters and also tile manufacturers soon took it up.

When William Moorcroft Ltd was established the loan from Liberty's was converted into two-thirds of the shares, which gave Liberty's effective control of the business. However, William Moorcroft remained in charge, free to do what he wanted artistically and commercially. The business

MAKING ROOM: INTERIOR DECORATION

I n the Victorian and Edwardian era – as in others – those who had made a fortune in business had a desire to build themselves into respectability: land and houses (especially a country house) would sanctify their new riches. The result was a building boom in the countryside, and in the towns as well. Cities such as Birmingham, Manchester and Bradford were, at least until the Second World War, at their heart Victorian. Queen Victoria herself built two new palaces, the Italianate Osborne House on the Isle of Wight and the baronial Balmoral Castle in Scotland; and in 1865 the Prince of Wales created the neo-Jacobean Sandringham House in Norfolk. These styles were widely admired and imitated. The classicism of Osborne, for instance, is reflected in the white stucco houses beloved of Londoners today (many of them by Thomas Cubitt, the builder of Osborne). Architects like Lutyens, Voysey and Baillie Scott built very little for the old gentry; they catered mainly for the aspiring middle classes – who also formed the bedrock of Liberty's customers.

The nature of society was also changing, with the establishment of hotels and restaurants. Indeed most of what we think of today as the grand London hotels – Claridge's, the Connaught, Brown's Hotel and the Savoy – date from the nineteenth century, while the Ritz opened in 1906. Ladies rarely dined in restaurants, but towards the end of the nineteenth century it became fashionable to be seen at hotels such as the Savoy. Liberty's established a contracts department quite early on, and it was kept busy with the decoration of hotels and restaurants, supplying furniture and all manner of soft furnishings. From the 1880s it was also in great demand for transforming dreary public buildings for charity functions, which were regular features of Victorian society. Such events obviously brought Liberty's to the attention of a wider public.

As the world changed, Liberty's worked increasingly for private clients, not only people who were building new houses but also the owners of older country houses seeking to make their homes more comfortable and inviting. The rapid expansion of the railway allowed places that had once been impossibly remote to be easily accessible, making the weekend house party and a house full of guests a more frequent occurrence.

Adept at marketing, Liberty's quickly caught on to the idea of using catalogues as a promotional tool. The first was *Eastern Art Manufacturers and Decorative Objects*, published in 1881, and it was the precursor of hundreds of similar publications. They also, quite early on, began to display and market goods within themed room sets, so that objects for sale had a context to which people could relate; the first of these was 'Indian Furniture and Decoration', created in 1883 and designed by Leonard Wyburd (see page 52). One of the most influential of Liberty's catalogues was the *Handbook of Sketches*, published in 1889 (it went into several impressions, all of which are undated) and republished in a slightly augmented version in about 1900 as *A Book of Sketches*. It seems to have been intended that customers would borrow the handbook, so that they could peruse the contents at leisure in their own homes. Promoting the company's interior design service, this gave customers the idea that one could, if so inclined, have a 'Jacobean style' hall and staircase or an 'Adam style' drawing room. (Alas, many clients chose to pick and mix.)

Rooms designed by Liberty's were also frequently shown in *The Studio*, almost from the magazine's inception in April 1893 – sometimes with black and white photographs, but occasionally in charming watercolours. Interiors by the company were also featured in H.C. Davison's *The Book of the Home: A Practical Guide to Household Management*, published in 1901. This extensive guide to running a house ((eight volumes) also drew on examples from other companies, such as Heal's, but the first volume contained four rooms by Liberty's and further rooms were illustrated in the next volume. It was, of course, all good publicity for Liberty's.

Though Liberty's contract department worked in a variety of different styles, they were particularly famous for their take on the fashionable Arts and Crafts style, and renowned for their panelling, particularly linenfold. Ideal for halls and corridors, libraries, billiard rooms and the like, the style might be characterized as 'Abbotsford Baronial', similar to 'Balmoral Baronial' but lighter and without the acres of tartan. Because no records have survived, it is almost impossible to deduce where Liberty's worked and for whom, except at a very few places. We know they worked at Wadhurst Park in Sussex, for Julius Drew (for whom Sir Edwin Lutyens was to build Castle Drogo in Devon), and at the Piccadilly Hotel in London. Later they did a great deal of work at Buckhurst Park near Ascot (now the home of the Dowager Queen of Jordan) for the oil magnate Sir Henri Deterding; various rooms were illustrated in the firm's staff magazine, *Liberty Lamp*, in 1927, being noted as recent works. They also seem to have done some work for George Bernard Shaw, at his London flat in Adelphi Terrace, which was demolished in 1935.[1]

Almost invariably the work was designed by Guy Bentley, who had an encyclopaedic knowledge of interior decoration. It was Bentley who prepared all the papers Sir Arthur gave at various august institutions on such topics as English pewter and the history of English furniture.

LEFT A watercolour sketch of a drawing room, from *The Studio Yearbook* of 1906.

ABOVE LEFT An Elizabethan-style hall, a typical Liberty's design.

BELOW LEFT An inglenook in the billiard room at Wadhurst Park, designed for Julius Drew.

BELOW Two morning room fireplaces, as shown in *The Studio Yearbook* of 1906.

Bentley was, by all accounts, a very elegant man. He always carried a furled umbrella, which doubled as his tape measure – assistants heard measurements described as 'Height four umbrellas; width two umbrellas plus two ferrules'.[2] He retired in April 1931 after 'acting as outdoor representative for the Soft Furnishings Department for nearly 40 years'.[3]

Liberty's style was popular not only in Britain but also across Europe and further afield. They were in the middle of a large order for the Archduke Franz Ferdinand of Austria when he was murdered in Sarajevo, the act that precipitated the outbreak of the First World War. Another order was in progress for Tsar Nicholas II for one of his residences – either the Alexander Palace at Tsarskoye Selo near St Petersburg or, more likely, the Livadia Palace near Yalta – but the war prevented its completion. Today little of their work survives – or, more correctly, it may well survive, but we know nothing about it. However, one glorious example is to be found in – of all places – southern Sweden.

Tjolöholm Slott (*slott* is Swedish for castle) is a fascinating example of Liberty's work, particularly so because a large collection of correspondence survives in the castle archive. The estate has a long history. It is first recorded in 1231, when it belonged to King Valdemar, the conqueror of Denmark. It passed through various hands until 1774, when it was bought by Anders Swalin, a merchant in Gothenburg. It changed hands again in 1841 when Richard Dann, an Englishman, bought it, only for his heirs to sell it in 1863 to Werner Santesson, who built a mansion in the then popular Italian Renaissance style (although, on the evidence of the surviving photographs, with some Russian touches). The Santesson family sold the house to Mr and Mrs James Dickson in 1892. Despite their British name, the Dicksons were Swedish, though of British descent; they were merchants in Gothenburg and said to be the richest family in Sweden.

The Italianate house the Dicksons bought was found to be in poor condition and, upon closer inspection, basically beyond repair: many of the timbers were rotting and chunks of the exterior render fell off each year. One problem seems to have been the quality of the mortar: a

proportion of sea sand had been used in the mortar mix, with
disastrous consequences. There seemed to be no option but
to demolish the house and rebuild. The Dicksons initially
engaged the architect Ferdinand Boberg (1860–1946), who
was the brother-in-law of the painter Julius Kronberg, of
whom they were patrons. Boberg had apparently studied
'the comfort that is said to be general indoors' in England,
which seemed to suit the Dicksons' tastes. Mr Dickson
wrote that he 'envisaged that a building in the style of a very
diminutive Windsor Castle would suit both place and the
building material'.[4] Despite his use of the word 'diminutive'
what was contemplated was a very substantial house indeed.
In the event Boberg's mini Windsor did not find favour and
he was dismissed. They then decided to hold a competition
to find an architect. As bait they offered a large prize of
2,000 kronor (at the time about £110) to the winner, with
a 1,000-kronor prize for each to the second- and third-
placed entries.[5] They specified that the building should be
in the 'Elizabethan style'; room should be made for Julius
Kronberg's huge picture *The Queen of Sheba*; the drawing
room should be on the first floor; and the bedroom should
face to the east (presumably for the morning sun and light),
the kitchen to the west. There were fifteen entries. The result
was published on 12 June 1897: the competition was won by
Erik Josephson (1864–1929), with Lars Wahlman (1870–
1952) coming second.

When the Dicksons studied the proposed designs in
more detail they found they much preferred Wahlman's,
so he was awarded the commission. Wahlman was much
influenced by the English Arts and Crafts Movement, and by
Baillie Scott in particular. He seems to have known Voysey
(they certainly met) and, although we have no firm evidence
that he knew Baillie Scott, he may well have done. He was
certainly aware of his work, which was published in *The
Studio*. Wahlman was to produce a substantial house with a
faint whiff of the Tudor style, reminiscent of some mansions
built about the same time and subsequently – in the interwar
years – in various parts of the United States. Tenders were
invited in November 1897 from building contractors and
a contract was awarded in February 1898. Wahlman would
supply measurements and architectural drawings for the

BELOW An aerial
photograph of Tjolöholm
Slott, showing its
magnificent position.

rooms, and the designs, which would be done by Liberty's, would be created from these. Liberty's men – Mr Butters and Mr Whittington – were to spend two years working on the house.

Unfortunately, on 14 March 1898 James Dickson died. He had attended a dinner for the Field Riding Club, where he gave a speech, which, according to a not entirely dependable contemporary report, entailed standing with his left foot on his chair and his right foot on the table. Having had a great deal to drink, he fell over and cut his hand on some broken glass. One finger was very badly cut, so it was bandaged to stop the bleeding, using a cigarette paper and the foil from a champagne bottle – not a sensible choice. Unsurprisingly, this led to septicaemia; he died a few weeks later.

His widow, Blanche Dickson (1856–1906), decided to carry on with the rebuilding of Tjolöholm, and after a two-week halt for mourning work began in earnest. Liberty's involvement commenced in mid- to late 1898; the first letter that survives is dated 3 January 1899, acknowledging receipt of plans Mrs Dickson had sent for the dining room and Great Hall. The correspondence with Liberty's, though by no means complete, draws a fascinating picture of the creation of the castle. Besides the letters there are also accounts and estimates for the works to be undertaken, but although there are a number of references to plans and coloured sketches or designs throughout the correspondence, it seems that none of these have survived. Although the correspondence is one-sided (the letters are, with a single exception, all from

BELOW The doorbell

BELOW The garden front.

Liberty's), Blanche Dickson comes across as a demanding and at times rather difficult client. However, she does not always seem to have been particularly well served by her architect: a letter from Mr Palmer at Liberty's drily noted, 'I am pleased to hear you have had a visit from your architect at last.'[6] Mrs Dickson was at the time (1902) pressing for more progress, convinced that the old mansion would probably not survive another winter. She also appears to have done quite a bit of the project management herself. A letter from Liberty's in January 1903 reveals her concern about spiralling costs, but equally shows Liberty's desire to maintain control of their designs to ensure that they were installed and finished correctly.[7]

Liberty's influence at the castle is all-pervasive and immediately apparent: the front doorbell plate is in the form of a duck (or it could be a curlew) ringing a bell, the bell button being the bird's eye.[8] It is charming and witty. You enter a vaulted lobby, decorated with wall paintings depicting *The Dreamer and Sorrow*: two women sitting beneath an old oak tree with its foliage spreading across the walls. The small red floor tiles were supplied by Liberty's, as were the Art Nouveau tiles in the adjoining cloakroom, which feature stylized mushrooms. These tiles caused not a little trouble, for Mrs Dickson was dissatisfied with the texture and the way they had been laid. It was pointed out that they would be irregular because they were made by hand, rather than machine-made, which would have ensured they were perfectly regular in shape and texture. However, more tiles had to be ordered to get a slightly more consistent effect; this married happily with the mosaic floor Liberty's also supplied. Who made the tiles is unknown – the only manufacturer mentioned is Edward's of Ruabons – but we know they cost £25 10*s*. (the extra tiles that were needed cost £1 12*s*. ½*d*.) and the mosaic floor £10 17*s*. 6*d*.[9]

At the heart of the house is the Great Hall, with a very baronial inglenook fireplace that is some 26 feet (8 metres) tall. It is emblazoned with the family arms; their motto was *Coelum versus*, 'Towards heaven', to which the soaring edifice might also refer. The fireplace competes for attention with a huge painting, *The Queen of Sheba* by Julius Kronberg (1850–1921), set into the panelling, all of which

BELOW, CLOCKWISE FROM
TOP LEFT The Great Hall;
the stylized mushroom
tiles in the cloakroom; the
Moorish smoking room,
probably designed by
Wahlman but certainly
inspired by Liberty's work.

was designed by Walhman and carved by either Thor Nerpin
or Oskar Nilsson of Stockholm. The hall and the dining room
were the first rooms Mrs Dickson consulted Liberty's about,
but she did not like the plans they submitted. They produced
a 'Chippendale style' dining room to be done in mahogany,
a rather strange choice for this type of house; possibly this was
in response to the original instruction received. Ultimately
their involvement in these two rooms seems to have been
mostly restricted to the fireplaces, although they also supplied
some furniture for the hall and decorative items such as a
collection of old swords.

Opposite the dining room a door opened into a small
lobby with a door to the garden, and this area effectively
formed a gentleman's suite: to the left was the smoking room
and beyond the billiard room. Liberty's supplied a design for
the smoking room which was rejected, but the Moorish style
of the room, in which all the windows have lattice screens,
must surely be based upon their initial proposal, as redrawn
by Wahlman, for in their *Handbook of Sketches*, published
around 1890, there is an example of such a room in what they
called 'Saracen-style' (see page 52), and, as mentioned earlier,

the company did much work of this type (it was jokingly said that Leonard Wyburd could draw Moorish lattice with his eyes closed). We know that Liberty's supplied the fireplace tiles, for these are listed on a surviving account as costing £12 12s. Off the lobby to the right was what had been intended as Mr Dickson's study. His wife wanted the room just as it had been planned and this is pure Liberty's. She wrote to her architect: 'I am ordering that room from England and feel you will fall in love with the chimneypiece there as I have done, it is just after your heart I feel sure but it would be very difficult to get made here.'[10] What Mrs Dickson had fallen in love with was a deep fireplace complete with cupboards above the hearth.

Everything required for this room was prepared in the Liberty's factory and shipped over, unassembled and unfinished (to avoid import duties), and then assembled *in situ*. The room was decorated around a theme of red, with a plain red carpet and red fabric hung above the tall oak panelling. A Knole sofa in red velvet was shipped and curtains were made in (probably) brown 'Utrecht Velvet' at 37½d. a yard. Liberty's also supplied the conical wall lights (which look a bit like witches' hats), copper light switches, sockets and bell pushes.

The broad staircase, laid with plain red 'Turkey carpet' held in place by Liberty's wrought-iron stair rods, led up to a gallery landing overlooking the Great Hall. Ahead lay the large first-floor drawing room. Again this was basically a

Liberty's room. It was slightly more classical in feeling, with a panelled dado and the wall papered above in 'Lustrelle'. The Wilton carpet was a grassy green, as were the curtains made of 'Thorian Velvet' costing 22½d. a yard, made up with merino lining and interlined; they cost over £25 to make. Of course the idea of the green carpet and curtains was to echo the huge grass lawn outside, which stretched towards the fjord at the garden's edge. The slightly oriental-looking overmantel was probably not Liberty's work, but they did supply the lustre tiles (like those in the smoking room downstairs), the fireback, firedogs and irons. Much of the furniture also appears to have been supplied by the company, or at least was closely modelled on patterns popular in England at the time.

The drawing room opened into the large oak-panelled library, also designed by Liberty's. The plaster strapwork ceiling was done by local craftsmen, as was the detailing around the inglenook fireplace, but it was Butters and Whittington who did most of the panelling. In one corner is a built-in sofa, complete with draught curtain in brown velvet with a decorative border formed from a gold braid, echoing the curtains for the main window.

Walhman's design for the castle was complicated, with numerous changes in level, which can seem confusing. Had he been older and more experienced when he designed it, perhaps he would have simplified the plan somewhat and created a house that flowed better.

OPPOSITE Mr Dickson's study: the fireplace and a lantern, both supplied by Liberty's.

BELOW The drawing room. The wallpaper is a modern replacement.

BOTTOM A sofa and chairs from a contemporary Liberty's catalogue.

No. 76. Chesterfield Sofa, upholstered in cretonne, with buttoned back and front. Plain seat. Length, 6 ft.

No. 84. Small Easy chair, in calico.
No. 84a. Loose cover of cretonne.

No. 85. Easy Chair, upholstered in calico.
No. 85a. Loose cover of cretonne.

The library, which opens off the drawing room. **CLOCKWISE FROM TOP LEFT** Towards the window, with original curtains supplied by Liberty's; a view of the corner sofa complete with the original draught curtain; towards the fireplace.

BELOW The White Passage. On the right is a detail of the wallpaper, supplied by Liberty's, The design, 'Haddon', appeared in *The Studio Yearbook* of 1915.

RIGHT Blanche Dickson's bathroom. The amazing shower was bought in London and Liberty's supplied the 'Dolphin' tiles.

Before reaching the Great Hall gallery there is one of these numerous changes in level: a small landing affording access to the guest corridor, known as the White Passage. The three simple rooms here, all done by Liberty's, are now used as offices, the furniture long ago dispersed, save for the final room with a pink-tiled fireplace and inglenook, which was once the Italian Guest Suite; its Italian walnut furniture is now in the principal guest room on the top floor.

Blanche Dickson's suite opened off a mezzanine above the Great Hall gallery. The bedroom was quite spacious, but Mrs Dickson was never really satisfied with it. The ceilings are all low, because it is above the dining room; it is rather dark, too, about which she complained, but, as Walhman pointed out, she would not allow alterations to the façades for larger windows. The room is panelled in oak with a deep frieze in gold on a red ground that imitated Spanish leather, the red being picked up from the bed curtains and velvet upholstery. There were even red tiles for the fireplace and washstand, upon which stood a pewter toilet set manufactured by Haseler's, who were in partnership with Liberty's; as it was a special commission the pewter is unmarked. The dressing room, which opens off the bedroom, was done in green. It is lighter than the bedroom and a corner seat was built to take advantage of this. Beyond this was Mrs Dickson's bathroom, complete with tiles supplied by Liberty's. There is a large freestanding shower fitment, bought in London, and an enormous built-in tile bath, which looks like a plunge pool. The tiles, in a washed pink, have a border of 'Dolphin' tiles. The dolphin theme is continued in the light fittings specially made for the room. These tiles, in various colours, were used in all the bathrooms in the castle.

Tjolöholm is a house full of quirks. Blanche Dickson's sitting room, for instance, was above the lobby and had a window looking into the Great Hall. The decoration was based around Shakespeare's *A Midsummer Night's Dream*, with caryatids in the form of characters such as Titania, Oberon and Hippolyta, while Puck sits on top of a bookcase. Blanche's desk stood in the turret, lit by large windows. A tiny staircase leads down to a walnut-panelled room known as the Pharmacy Room, but perhaps intended as either a jewellery cabinet or, more likely, a muniment room. The architect had neatly inserted this tiny room above the cloakroom.

Mrs Dickson's bedroom.
CLOCKWISE FROM OPPOSITE The dressing table especially made for the room; the four-poster bed made by Liberty's, incorporating an old piece of embroidery she had acquired; a frieze paper made to imitate Spanish leatherwork.

Off the landing opens a barrel-vaulted passage known as the Rose Passage, so called because it is painted with branches of pink roses. Beyond an oak door the passage changes character. Now it has a flat ceiling and the walls are papered, for this was the nursery. Both rooms here – presumably night and day nursery – have white-painted panelling. The last room in the series is the Peasant Room (also known as the Scanian Room or Halland Room), which has the lowest of all the ceilings and simple tongue-and-groove boarding. These rooms were served by another bathroom with 'Dolphin' tiles (blue, in this instance).

Mrs Dickson may have been disappointed with her own suite, but she seems to have been very pleased with the room known as the King's Room, on the third floor.

The Dicksons were on friendly terms with the Swedish royal family, and the room was created as a 'state bedroom'. Although the King of Sweden dined at the castle, no king has ever stayed here (though the Duke of Edinburgh did on one occasion). The large oak bed, specially made by Liberty's, was a copy (albeit rather smaller in scale) of the Great Bed of Ware, famous for being mentioned in Shakespeare's *Twelfth Night* and now in the Victoria and Albert Museum in London. The ceiling has moulded ribs in oak and there is a 'Tynecastle Frieze' (Liberty's imitation of Spanish leatherwork), similar though not identical to the frieze in Mrs Dickson's own bedroom. Liberty's also built the large wardrobe with a washstand, its glass mosaic depicting three lions drawn from the Swedish royal arms.

The bathroom serving the King's Room (and other rooms on this floor).

CLOCKWISE FROM TOP LEFT The 'Dolphin' tiles used in all the bathrooms; a dolphin cupboard latch;

dolphins decorating the radiator grilles; the large shower and bath bought in London.

OPPOSITE Blanche
Dickson and her sister
Caline, in Ceylon in 1906.
She died on the way
back, so she never saw
her home again.

Originally this room was to be served by a dressing room and a drawing room, but when built the plan was slightly modified and what had been intended as the King's Drawing Room became the principal guest bedroom. Designed by Liberty's, this is very Art Nouveau in style, with white-painted panelling inlaid with stylized roses and tendrils picked out in yellow. Alas, the bedroom furniture has gone, replaced by the Italian Renaissance-style furniture formerly in the Italian Guest Suite on the floor below (see page 122). On the upper landing are two smaller guest rooms, again panelled and furnished by Liberty's.

To modern eyes the castle appears to be very short of bathrooms. This was indicative of the times: Sir Edwin Lutyens always bemoaned the fact that he could only rarely persuade his clients to allow for a bathroom with every bedroom – most considered such generous provision to be wanton extravagance. Although there are five bedrooms on this floor, they are served by just one bathroom – but what a splendid creation it is! The room is done in white-painted panelling and green 'Dolphin' tiles. The built-in corner washstand even has decorative grilles with stylized dolphins, which concealed the heating system, while the latch of the tall cupboard is formed by a dolphin.

Having the builders in is always stressful. Nothing ever seems to go according to plan, and the building of Tjolöholm was no exception. That Mrs Dickson was pleased with the chimneypieces supplied for her own bedroom and for the King's Room was a relief to Mr Palmer, for, he related, 'they had a narrow escape this end; a steam crane frightened the 2 horses attached to our van at the docks, the driver was thrown from his seat and somewhat badly hurt and the van was stopped by an iron post when the horses were within a few feet of the Thames.'[11] In April 1904, when the furniture for the study and Mrs Dickson's bedroom was shipped over, it was discovered that some pieces did not fit 'their respective positions'. A further letter reveals that alterations were necessary; these were carried out by the local joinery contractor for a cost of £7 10s. but, Mr Palmer noted, 'We much regret that there should be any necessity for these alterations, as the greatest care was taken in making seats in study exactly to the sizes supplied by your Architect,

on whom the responsibility rests for the measurements not being strictly accurate.'[12]

But when the building work is completed, all the petty irritations and arguments are soon forgotten, and you begin to enjoy what was so laboriously created. Sadly, though, after Blanche Dickson moved into Tjolöholm in 1904, her enjoyment of the house and estate was to be all too fleeting. In March 1906 she accompanied her sister Caline on a five-week visit to their brothers Oscar and Axel, who owned tea plantations in Ceylon. She never returned to Tjolöholm.

On the return voyage she contracted dysentery. She died a few days later and was buried at sea. The Tjolöholm estate was inherited by her daughter, Countess Blanche Bonde, who used it as her summer residence for the next forty years. Then in the 1950s the Countess began to use a smaller country house at Sörö for the summer, abandoning Tjolöholm, and in 1959 tenders were invited for its demolition – it was considered far too large and expensive to run. However, the Countess died in 1960 and the house was inherited by her eldest son, who decided to sell the estate. The oil company British Petroleum (now BP) took an option on the estate as a suitable site for an oil refinery. However after a long battle the estate was ultimately purchased by the City of Gothenburg, with most of the contents but not all, some having been sold at auction and some retained by the family.

Gothenburg City Council undertook a major programme of restoration and repair, while respecting the character of the castle. Of course it has to pay its way (or try to), which inevitably means there have had to be some compromises; nevertheless Tjolöholm Slott, as an example of an Arts and Crafts country house largely decorated by Liberty's, is a rare survivor. We are fortunate that it has been preserved.

Liberty's interior decoration business carried on until the beginning of the Second World War. It does not seem, from surviving records, to have been revived after the war, which is a pity, but understandable given the restrictions on building works which remained in force until the beginning of the 1950s. And of course times and tastes had changed. The world moved on and so, once again, did Liberty's.

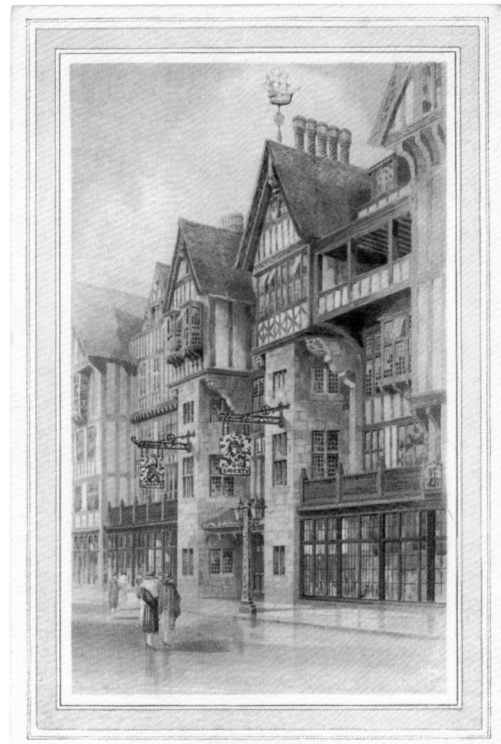

LIBERTY'S
REGENT STREET
"ONE OF THE SIGHTS OF LONDON"

TUDOR
RENAISSANCE

Despite the privations caused by the First World War, when he died in 1917 Sir Arthur left a business in fine form: the profit declared in the following year was in excess of £61,000. Liberty's had always been run on a conservative basis, so it had solid foundations. Part of this conservative philosophy was property investment. Harold Blackmore, another of Sir Arthur's nephews, who had been a director since 1900, had gradually, over the preceding twenty years, bought up the surrounding properties. Liberty's could never own East India House on Regent Street, as the whole street belongs to the Crown Estate. But they eventually owned an entire island site formed by Great Marlborough Street (what was then Argyll Place), Foubert's Place, Little Marlborough Street and Kingly Street, directly at the back of East India House.

Rebuilding Regent Street had been mooted at the end of the nineteenth century. Shopping had changed beyond all recognition since the days of Nash, and this was the prime motivation behind the Crown Estate's decision to redevelop the street. The Office of Works had asked the architect Norman Shaw to produce designs. These proved unsatisfactory. Shaw had taken his inspiration from Florence – specifically fifteenth-century Florence, where the glorious Renaissance palaces of the Medici and others were as much fortresses as palaces. Not surprisingly, the plans were hardly amenable to nineteenth-century Regent Street. But before Shaw could revise them he died (in 1912). The war prevented further plans. After the war Sir Reginald Blomfield, president of the Royal Institute of British Architects, was asked to look at the matter and revise Shaw's designs. He produced a revised plan and a set of basic principles to which, it was stipulated, all Regent Street buildings should adhere. The 'new' East India House, designed by Edwin Thomas Hall and his son Edwin Stanley Hall, followed Shaw's and Blomfield's principles. The new general pattern, as revised by Blomfield, was more French classic than Florentine fortress, but either way Liberty's hated it. The lofty pillared marble halls were not Liberty's way, but if they wished to retain their Regent Street presence they had no choice but to comply.

A new building on Liberty's freehold site was, however, a different matter. It is tempting to speculate that the firm looked back across the dark years of the war to the golden age of the long reign of Elizabeth I, when English merchants sailed across the high seas and brought back silks, spices and other goods from all corners of the globe. After all, Liberty's founder, Sir Arthur, was

BELOW HMS *Britannia*
and HMS *Hindustan* (left)
and HMS *Impregnable*
(right) on the River Dart,
where they served as
training ships, The timbers
from *Hindustan* and
Impregnable were used in
Liberty's Tudor building.

himself a latter-day merchant adventurer. However, it seems more likely that inspiration for the new building came from a less romantic source. John Llewellyn, Sir Arthur's close colleague and confidant, had, since Sir Arthur's death, held sway over all artistic matters and it seems it was his 'emphatic advice' that the new building should be in the Tudor style.[1] Llewellyn lived at Ashwell Court near Great Missenden, which was a good example of 'Stockbroker Tudor' (though it should be noted that its panelling came from a monastic building at Blois in France).

In any event, it was decided that the building should be designed in the Tudor style, and that (probably under the inspiration of the Rows in Chester) it should appear to be a series of buildings rather than the unified whole that it actually was. The building was planned around three enormous light wells (or rather, small internal courtyards), and it is composed of a series of 'rooms' rather than the immense floors that were and are usual with department stores. This was following one of Sir Arthur's principles.

He believed that goods should be displayed in small rooms, more closely resembling those found in customers' houses; this would allow a customer to imagine something in the shop in their own home.

For eighteen months a team of twenty carpenters laboured over the timbers for the new building. These were recycled from two Royal Navy warships: HMS *Impregnable* and HMS *Hindustan*.[2] Over three thousand oak trees are said to have been felled to build *Impregnable* (which was very similar to HMS *Victory*, though slightly longer), and a similar number had probably gone into *Hindustan*. It is said that the shop's frontage on Great Marlborough Street is the same length as *Impregnable*'s gun deck (197 feet/60 metres), and the height of the building, from pavement to eaves, is equal to that of the ship from the water line to the tip of the main mast. *Impregnable*'s old figurehead of Admiral Howe (the ship was originally christened HMS *Howe*) ended up guarding the gates of Pipers, Arthur Liberty's nephew's house at The Lee.

BELOW Another postcard from the 'Sights of London' series, showing the bridge linking the Tudor shop with East India House on Regent Street.

The stonework was all of Portland stone; there were Tudor brick chimneys (entirely false, of course) and handmade roof tiles, and the whole glorious confection was topped by a gilded weather vane in the form of the *Mayflower*. For those who didn't quite get the point, the main doors were detailed with the coats of arms of each of Henry VIII's six wives, while the gable facing Regent Street (actually on the corner of Great Marlborough and Kingly Streets) was emblazoned with the arms of his daughter, Elizabeth I. It was a very shrewd piece of publicity. Such was the public interest in the building that Liberty's produced a modest booklet about it, published in the late 1920s. The only major mistake the architects made was in positioning the main doors. Although they neatly terminated the vista formed by Argyll Street, their positioning meant that customers coming from Regent Street had to walk halfway down Great Marlborough Street before they could enter the shop. The gable facing Regent Street was all window. There was a linking 'bridge' between East India House and the Tudor building, but the achitects had evidently not properly considered the all-important flow of foot traffic. The gable was soon altered and made into doors to give easier access from Regent Street.

The new building was completed quite quickly, and it was opened by William Judd, who had helped to open the very first shop fifty years before, on 24 October 1925. Exceptions to the general acclaim included most of the architectural establishment. Pevsner was particularly scornful: 'The timbers are the real article; they come from genuine men-of-war; they are not just stuck on. The roofing tiles are hand-made, the windows leaded. So technically there is nothing wrong – but functionally and intellectually everything. The scale is wrong, the symmetry is wrong, the proximity to a classical façade put up by the same firm at the same time is wrong, and the goings-on of a store behind such a façade (and below those twisted Tudor chimneys) are wrongest of all.'[3] The public didn't agree: they loved it and still do. They liked the Tudor pastiche, the illusion that the building had come down from the days of 'Good Queen Bess'; and they loved the intimacy of the store, the small rooms, the elegant 'Tudoresque' plasterwork, and the general impression that you were in a huge Tudor mansion.

LIBERTY'S
RECENT STREET.
"ONE OF THE SIGHTS
OF LONDON."

Wills's Cigarettes

Liberty's "East India House", Regent Street

Work soon began on rebuilding the Regent Street buildings. Higgs & Hill were the contractors. Liberty's were anxious to maintain a presence while the rebuilding was being done, so kept a series of display cases in Regent Street. Not that this was necessary, for the rebuilding was achieved at impressive speed. It was complete by 1926. The new East India House is a very graceful addition to Regent Street, the elegant curve of the upper storeys reflecting the sweeping curve of Nash's street. The beautiful Portland stone creation was topped by a graceful half-size frieze, some 115 feet (35 metres) long and sculpted by Charles L.J. Donian and Thomas J. Chapperton, depicting the goods of faraway lands being borne by camels, elephants and it seems any means possible to the United Kingdom, which is represented by the towering figure of Britannia. Today it appears hopelessly jingoistic and politically incorrect, but it captures the spirit of the times in which it was created. The 'new' Regent Street was officially opened by George V on 24 June 1927 (the centenary

of the street), when he and Queen Mary drove in state down the street to the acclaim of cheering crowds.

In many ways the early 1920s were not especially happy years for Liberty's, but perhaps that was to be expected. When a business is very much one man's creation, it is likely to lose its sense of direction and purpose when that man is no longer in control. Liberty's had always been a leader of fashion and of taste, as had been Arthur Liberty's aim from the beginning. With the death of Sir Arthur the firm lost not only its revered founder, and an all-powerful benign autocrat, but also the visionary who had enabled it to be that leader. The shop became a follower of fashion, no longer avant-garde but merely safe and dependable.

From the perspective of design history what is most striking about the interwar period is the lack of big design names producing goods for Liberty's. Who was there to compare with the designers who had dominated Liberty's from its foundation in 1875 up until the First World War?

It wasn't that no one was producing innovative and well-designed products: the interwar years were a period of great creativity. It was more the case that no one at Liberty's was searching out new designers – and this shows a degree of stagnation and complacency.

Of course the problem was compounded by the First World War. The terrible tragedy of the war had shaken the foundations of society in the United Kingdom and even more so in Continental Europe. Many of the young men at Liberty's who would have succeeded to managerial positions went to war, never to return. As their world fell apart around them the older staff who had been left in post became ever more conservative, more anxious about change, more wary of innovation. These department heads were autocrats with their own little fiefdoms, which they defended tenaciously. They chose the merchandise that was sold; they chose the staff who sold it. The board of directors was remote and failed to offer sufficient leadership and direction. Hilary Blackmore (Harold Blackmore's son and Sir Arthur's great-nephew), who joined the printworks at Merton Abbey in 1926, recorded his dismay at finding that 'not even the colourways of designs had been changed between 1920 and 1924, let alone any new designs introduced.' Further, he castigated the board for 'the self-satisfaction and atmosphere of laissez-faire', and bemoaned the 'lack of young people in the shop'.[4] Liberty's could still trade on its reputation, and the new rich – those who had done quite well out of the war from a financial point of view – flocked to Liberty's because of that reputation. However, their old customers had not fared quite so well. They still came, but spent less with every passing year.

Most, though, could afford to buy one of the famous Liberty scarves. In the late 1930s a hand-printed scarf (52 by 18 inches/132 by 46 centimetres) produced at Merton on silk crêpe cost 9s. 6d. In former times Liberty's used to do a brisk trade in souvenir handkerchiefs to commemorate the winner of the Derby. As soon as the winner was known, a messenger would ride like the wind from Epsom to the works at Merton, 'where printers would stamp the winner's name on to the already printed handkerchiefs. These would be on sale in the neighbouring streets and taverns almost as soon as the first race-goers were returning through Merton to London.'[5] Scarves were popular fashion accessories and Liberty's were justly famous for them. When you walked through the main doors in Great Marlborough Street you immediately entered what might be termed the gift department (known to staff as K department), which sold scarves, handkerchiefs and other small items including leather goods and even lampshades.[6] Some of the designs used for scarves were adaptations of earlier fabric designs by people such as Voysey and Butterfield, and their paisley designs were, then as now, good steady sellers. Liberty's also continued to design commemorative scarves like those produced for the coronations of George VI in 1937 and Elizabeth II in 1953.

It is hardly surprising that the precarious interwar period was marked by nostalgia. There was, of course, a building boom – and the designs of 'homes fit for heroes' drew heavily on the architecture of the Arts and Crafts Movement and on what can best be characterized as 'Mock Tudor' or 'Stockbroker Tudor' (of which the new Liberty shop was a premier example). Inevitably those who bought such houses would buy safe period furniture to fill them, and this is amply demonstrated by Liberty's literature of the period. Chippendale, Hepplewhite and Sheraton revival pieces, popular since the 1880s, now became all the rage.

BELOW A page from a catalogue of the early 1930s, depicting scarves and shawls.

BOTTOM A booklet produced by Liberty's to promote their scarves and show customers ways to wear them. Produced in the 1930, revised in the 1960s.

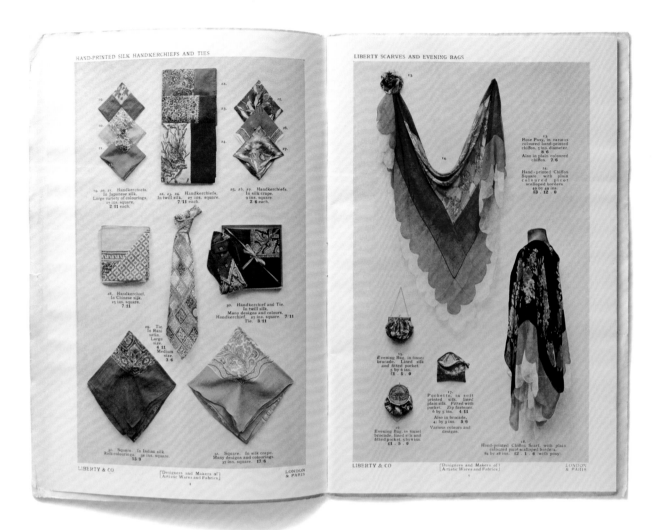

Duckpond

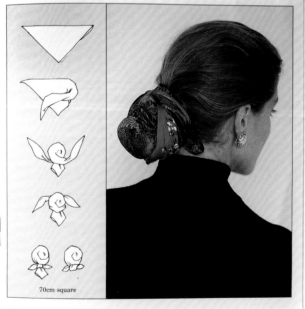

70cm square

Specially
printed for
Jane Kingsley
1939

These silk squares are printed by British Craftsmen on heavy British Silk Twill.   You may have any name
specially printed in the centre medallion.

Each square is 28 ins. wide.   Any of these combinations of colours.   Price 10/6.   When ordering state No. of colour.

LIBERTY & CO LTD   10   REGENT STREET LONDON W1

ABOVE A page from a
Liberty's gift catalogue
of 1939, showing their
commemorative scarves.

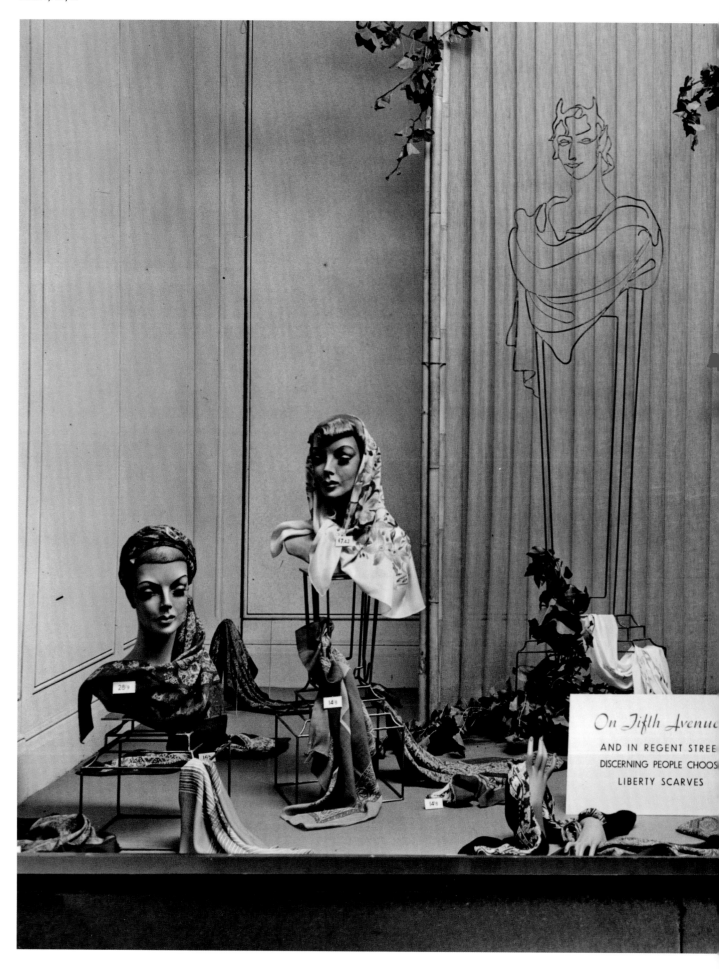

'On Fifth Avenue and in Regent Street, discerning people choose Liberty scarves.' A 1950s window display arranged by Eric Lucking.

During the 1920s Liberty's greatly expanded their range of dress and furnishing fabrics, catering for different shoppers. The luxury end of the market was served by the hand-blocked fabrics produced in relatively small runs at the Merton Abbey works. Liberty's used the works as a marketing tool, producing a small booklet on *The Renaissance of Merton Abbey* in the 1930s and even opening them to the public by appointment on Wednesdays. Hand-block printing is a slow and expensive process, so fabrics produced this way were more than double the cost of machine-printed fabrics. A single block might take a week to make, and a complex pattern could have thirty or more blocks. With a complex pattern it might be possible to produce 30 yards in a day, in contrast to the 180 yards that could be produced by silkscreen printing, or the 300 yards an hour that might be produced by machine roller printing.

The furnishing fabrics produced at the time tended to be traditionally based floral patterns (what are often erroneously termed 'chintzes'), in quite muted colours; dark backgrounds were popular in the 1920s. Bold Art Deco patterns with abstract patterns in strong colours, which were popular on the Continent, found little favour and were not really popular with the British public. And they didn't appeal to Liberty's. A request to the Silver Studio for a few 'modernistic patterns' was met with incredulity, and was considered so unusual and out of character that it was noted in the day diary – 'Mr Cram [of Liberty's] actually suggested that we should send him one or two modernists.'[7] Liberty's did sell a few abstract patterns during the 1930s, most notably one designed by Frank Ormrod, which comprised stylized birds set within geometric shapes, all based upon a Caucasian rug.

One of the themes of the later 1920s and early 1930s was the taste for chinoiserie. The renowned decorator John Fowler (of Colefax & Fowler) actually started his career painting Chinese wallpapers in the studio of Thornton Smith, a Soho decorating firm. Such wallpapers were immensely popular. There was also a taste for chinoiserie furniture, usually lacquered in black, or red or green. This taste influenced fabric design: many fabrics of the period had dark backgrounds, which worked well with the black lacquer furniture. The taste for the oriental was clearly shown in two cretonnes that were produced in the 1920s: 'Peacock and Peony' and 'Pheasant', both of

BELOW The 'Phoenix' portrait of Elizabeth I by Nicholas Hilliard, used as the cover for a Liberty's gift catalogue of the 1930s.

which were bestsellers, breaking all previous records, not only at Liberty's but also in the trade in general. As the 1920s slipped into the 1930s, the fashion for dark, heavy backgrounds declined and there was a desire for lighter fabrics in brighter colours on paler backgrounds. This trend was heightened in the years after the Second World War, when manufacturers had to adjust their colours to work with brighter lighting and changing tastes (encouraged by the advent of mass travel, usually to destinations in the Mediterranean). Today it would be impossible to sell the muted colours that were once so popular.

That the 1920s and 1930s was in Britain an age of nostalgia, looking back to perceived better, richer times, is underlined by Liberty's promotional material, which frequently alluded to the past, mentioning, for instance, how their patterns were drawn from 'old examples' or that 'Whether it be Tudor, Jacobean, Adam or some other bygone period Liberty's will gladly wait upon you'. The British are on the whole a conservative people, wary of newfangled ideas and concepts, preferring the safety of tradition and continuity. They also tend to have no strong feeling for design, and to prefer illusion to precision – another reasons why modernism had so little appeal. It would have been pointless for Liberty's to stock – for example – the avant-garde furniture that Metz & Co, their distributor in the Netherlands, carried. It would not have sold.

Dress fabrics of the period were often small-scale floral designs, usually produced in clear pastel colours and actually very similar to what had been produced before the war. These fabrics suited the fashions of the period and continued to be popular until the Second World War. The range of fashion fabrics Liberty's produced was vast and many of them were exclusive to the company. They had their own cotton lawn fabric, known as 'Tana' lawn, and their own crêpe range, known as 'Runis'.[8] These were made from natural fibres, but in the 1920s they introduced a range of viscose rayon fabrics under the brand 'Woodray', and later a blend of rayon and silk or wool known as 'Sungleam', a range that became immensely popular – so much so that it had its own mini department in the shop.

GAINSBOROUGH

OLIVIA. Tea Gown in Liberty silk-crape, with filmy gauze tucker and ruffle

9½ guineas

LIBERTY & CO. LONDON & PARIS

LIBERTY & CO. LONDON & PARIS

PART II. NOVELTIES
FOR THE SEASON
LIBERTY & CO
LONDON & PARIS

PART II. NOVELTIES
FOR THE SEASON
LIBERTY & CO
LONDON & PARIS

Peire. Evening Gown, in Accolotol silk and shaded ninon. Applique embroidery: 12½ guineas

Toinette. Dance gown, in lola satin and filmy lace, finish in contrasting shades: From 11 guineas

Pages from a Liberty's
dress catalogue.

LEFT AND RIGHT 'Gowns
Never Out of Fashion'.

BELOW LEFT 'Gowns of the
New Season'.

In the 1920s and 1930s there was a great demand for dress fabrics because many women made their own clothes rather than buying ready-to-wear. Liberty's manufactured clothes, but they also catered to the home sewing market, even offering a pattern-cutting service so that customers could make up the latest Paris fashions found in *Vogue*.[9]

The costume department issued regular catalogues, as it had before the war. The first catalogue of dresses issued after the war, in 1919, followed the old pre-war formula and was in two parts, the first being 'Gowns Never Out of Fashion' and the second 'Gowns of the New Season'. The first section featured Ancient Greek-style gowns or 'Empire' gowns, which were already deeply unfashionable, although they may have appealed to some older customers. The second section was more contemporary, but not exactly cutting edge, more a continuation of the Belle Epoque of the old pre-war world: it was not until the late 1920s that there was a clearer contemporary feel to the designs offered.

Liberty's had maintained a Paris presence since opening a shop there in 1890, but the Great Depression brought this to an end. The Wall Street crash of 1929 and the subsequent recession hit the Parisian fashion scene badly. Many firms went bankrupt, including the House of Poiret, owned by Paul Poiret.[10] Sterling abandoned the gold standard in 1931, but the imposition of tariffs, as well as the depreciation of sterling against the French franc, made Maison Liberty uneconomic and it closed in 1932. Paul St George Perrott, who had run the branch, returned to London. At his suggestion, in May 1932 Liberty's set up a model gown department (within the costume department), which, according to the literature sent out to customers, would be 'under the direct supervision of a Paris dress designer', and in which all the gowns would be at attractive prices and made from Liberty fabrics.

Paul Poiret had founded his own house in 1903 and made his name with the kimono. His fame grew rapidly and in 1909, to the consternation of the entire British garment trade, Margot Asquith, wife of the Prime Minister – who was never renowned for tact or diplomacy – invited him to show his latest collection at 10 Downing Street. He had a gift for marketing, and was the first couturier to expand his activities to include furniture, décor and fragrances.

After the First World War, during which he was in the military, he returned to his fashion house, but he had rather lost touch. Designers like Coco Chanel were producing garments that were not only simpler and more elegant in design but also beautifully made (it might seem surprising but Poiret's creations were not noted for their meticulous workmanship).

Poiret was known to Liberty's, for he had used their fabrics in the pre-war days. He also opened a London store at 10 Albemarle Street, with the restaurateur Marcel Boulestin as manager, dividing the premises between his couture business and his decorating business, l'Atelier Martine.[11] The furniture was designed by Pierre Fauconnet and was mostly painted. It did not find favour with everyone; the Duchesse de Gramont described it as 'a night of bad dreams after eating potted hare'.[12] Needless to say, painted pieces of this kind were not something Liberty's were really interested in, preferring the (relative) honesty and simplicity of polished wood.

As supervisor of Liberty's model gown department, Poiret seems to have designed only four collections for Liberty's, starting in autumn 1932, so one is left to assume that his creations did not sell particularly well, or else the relationship would surely have continued. Liberty's probably realized that fashion, that destructive dame, had moved on and Poiret had not. He certainly designed a collection for 1933 (an invitation to a 'Dress Parade' held on 3, 4 and 5 October 1933 survives) but it seems there was no autumn 1934 collection. A few of his creations survive, clearly labelled 'Liberty by Poiret' – naming the designer being an unusual departure for Liberty's, although in this case it was probably an essential aid to marketing – but they seem to be from another age.

The photographer Cecil Beaton relays a story told by Poiret's nephew, Jean Bongard, about a time (probably in 1931 or early 1932) when his uncle was living in the top two floors of the Salle Pleyel in Paris, without the means to pay the rent. Two men from Liberty's came to see him and advanced him the large sum of 10,000 francs, on the strength of which Poiret invited his young nephew to a celebratory lunch. He arrived to find that Poiret had

BELOW 'Poiret for Liberty': left, a velvet house robe, the belt threaded through gold lace; right, a rose pink satin cape with berry-embroidered borders and tassels.

OPPOSITE, CLOCKWISE FROM TOP A woven silk and velvet shawl made for Liberty's in the mid-1920s; a printed velvet coat from the early 1930s; a purple velvet and damask satin reversible evening cape from the early 1920s; a wool cape with green silk embroiderery.

spent the entire sum on a telescope, with which to view the heavens, and a refrigerator, with which to chill the champagne necessary for such an occupation.[13] Bongard got no lunch. However, Poiret honoured his contract with Liberty's. A senior member of staff clearly remembered him walking through the London store, cutting a rather striking figure, 'a small man with a jaunty beard clad in a velvet jacket and peach coloured trousers with a stripe down the leg'.[14]

Liberty's costume department (known in the company as 'H' department) was quite an extensive affair, with a large workroom that would have been equal, if not superior, to what Poiret had enjoyed in his heyday. The dressmaking workshop had a 'French room', a 'pleating room', an 'embroidery room', a 'model room', etc. Liberty's buyers would go to Paris to view the collections, and they would order *toiles* – fabric prototypes of designs – or paper patterns and occasionally buy models, and then copy the designs in the workroom, using Liberty's fabrics. Their embroidery room was renowned for the quality of its work, and this gained them extensive patronage; their customers included the Queens of Spain and Romania, the Princess of Monaco

and the Duchess of York, later Queen Elizabeth The Queen Mother. Equally, although Liberty's had no wholesale department until 1939, they had from the earliest days sold fabrics to others at wholesale prices. The salesmen in the 'trade room' would call at all the great couture houses, such as Worth and Chanel in Paris and Hartnell and Hardy Amies in London, to sell silks and other fabrics. But the fabrics were only ever sold to the couture houses and never to the developing ready-to-wear manufacturers.

In those pre-war days it would be quite common to see Great Marlborough Street filled with chauffeured Daimlers and Rolls-Royces, sometimes even with an attendant footman. The atmosphere on the shop floor was perfectly captured by the 1970s television sitcom *Are you Being Served?*, which, although not based on Liberty's, epitomized department stores of the times. There were always two commissionaires at each door, in top hats and liveried coats, and shop-walkers (or floor-walkers), veritable 'Captain Peacock' figures, who were known as cicerones. One such, A.W. Foster, who was a cicerone for over thirty years, cut a dashing figure in a light grey frock

RIGHT A page from a Liberty's gift catalogue of the late 1930s, showing Chinese-inspired jackets and robes.

coat and cravat; another was a tall, elegant figure with a little pointed beard and so aristocratic a bearing and manner that he could have passed for a duke. Assistants served in order of seniority, which was probably very hard on the most junior members of staff. A customer might simply say in conclusion, 'Please put it on my account' and 'Kindly have it sent' – no lady would be seen carrying shopping – and the hapless assistant would have to know whom he or she was serving.

Taking a break from all the shopping, you could pop downstairs to the new tea rooms. These were a clever blend of pseudo-Gothic architecture, dominated by a huge cowled fireplace, small oak tables and Riemerschmid-style chairs, which Liberty's had sold from the turn of the century. Iron-banded lanterns and a large Eastern Buddha completed the exotic scene. The tea rooms continued to use Moorcroft's 'Powder Blue' table ware (see page 104), which probably contributed to the popularity of the brand.

Tastes in china and glass, and metalwork too, continued after the First World War much as they had before. Liberty's continued to produce Archibald Knox pewter designs, but in 1927 the partnership with Haseler's – Liberty & Co. (Cymric) Ltd – was dissolved. Production of the Tudric range was to continue for a few years but finally came to an end in 1939 when Haseler's surrendered all

but four of the iron moulds to the government for the war effort. Knox produced no new designs after 1912. During the 1920s very few new designs were introduced and those that were are basically revivalist in nature.

Liberty's continued to offer Moorcroft wares just as before, but they no longer seemed to stock what had been known as 'Austrian' glass – not actually Austrian but produced by manufacturers such as Loetz. Instead they sold 'Monart' glass, made in Perth by John Moncrieff Ltd, who employed craftsmen from Catalonia in Spain. Prior to 1922, Moncrieff's had been specialist producers, mainly manufacturing for the chemical and engineering industries. In 1922 they employed Salvador Ysart and his son Paul Ysart, who had previously worked for Cochran's in Glasgow and before that for Charles and Ernest Schneider, who had a small glass factory at Epinay-sur-Seine near Paris. Mrs Isabel Moncrieff seems to have been the driving force behind the development of this art glass, even supplying designs. The 'Paisley Shawl' pattern was popular and a masterpiece of the glassmaker's art, but even more technically accomplished was the 'Cloisonné' pattern, which required the piece to be reheated and plunged in cold water. Monart found a contrast in the range of modern French glass Liberty's also sold, which was manufactured by Gabriel Argy-Rousseau, although in the various catalogues of the period this product range appears only briefly.

LEFT The new tea rooms in the basement, with its huge cowled fireplace and Riemerschmid furniture.

RIGHT Another watercolour of the Tudor building, used for a *Yule-Tide Gifts* catalogue.

ABOVE One of Liberty's
costume workshops in 1900.

BELOW Evening gowns
from a 1930s gift catalogue.

Left.—CYNTHIA

Semi-Evening Gown in Liberty Gulmar velvet, with slim-fitting waistline becoming to all figures. Colours : bottle green, cherry, dark blue, reseda, old rose, mulberry and black. Hip sizes : 36, 38, 40, 42, 44.

8 guineas.

Right.—HONEYBUNCH

The charm of this Evening Gown in Liberty taffeta is the tight-fitting bodice and attractive bows. In glorious ' shot ' colourings of turquoise/gold, green/ amber, blue/rose, blue/green, navy/ sapphire, wine/blue. Hip sizes : 36, 38, 40, 42, 44.

7 guineas.

The above are examples taken from Liberty's collection of Smart Frocks to be seen in the Inexpensive Dress Department, First Floor, Regent Street.

BEAUTIFUL EXAMPLES OF BRITISH GLASS AND LAMPS

331. Vase.
7¾ ins. high.
£1 . 1 . 0

332. Vase.
8½ ins. high.
£1 . 5 . 0

335. Lamp and Shade.
£4 . 7 . 6
(With flex, plug and fittings.)

334. Vase.
9½ ins. high.
£1 . 1 . 0

336. Vase.
9½ ins. high.
£1 . 1 . 0

333. Vase.
3¼ ins. high.
8/6

337. Vase.
3½ ins. high.
8/6

339. Vase.
12¾ ins. high.
£1 . 12 . 6

338. Vase.
5 ins. high.
8/6

340. Vase.
4¼ ins. high.
8/6

341. Vase.
12¼ ins. high.
£1 . 7 . 6

342. Vase.
11½ ins. high.
£1 . 7 . 6

343. Bowl.
10 ins. diameter.
£1 . 1 . 0

344. Lamp and Shade.
£3 . 7 . 6
(With flex, plug and fittings.)

345. Bowl.
8¾ ins. diameter.
£1 . 7 . 6

346. Bowl.
12½ ins. diameter. £1 . 19 . 6
10½ ins. diameter. £1 . 12 . 6

347. Bowl.
6 ins. diameter.
9/6

348. Bowl.
10½ ins. diameter.
£1 . 7 . 6

349. Bowl.
4½ ins. diameter.
6/6

350. Bowl.
14¼ ins. diameter. £2 . 5 . 0
12 ins. diameter. £1 . 12 . 6

LIBERTY & CO LTD   REGENT STREET   LONDON W.1
33

Rather surprisingly, Liberty's do not seem to have been great promoters of Clarice Cliff's iconic pottery. They stocked her wares, but none appear in any of the many catalogues Liberty's issued. She produced a pattern in the 'Bizarre' range (it also, although less frequently, appears in the 'Fantasque' range) known as 'Liberty Band', which Liberty's retailed, although it does not seem to have been exclusive to them. This was merely simple bands of colour in various thicknesses and a variety of colours, and it was created from the remains of that day's paint mixings – hence the random colours used. It was untypical of Cliff's work, and is not particularly prized today. However, Liberty's do seem to have sought to capitalize on Cliff's success by stocking a range of Japanese pottery that bore a striking resemblance to her work.

Liberty's continued to sell Japanese and oriental goods, as can be seen in many of the catalogues of the period, but these were no longer the core of the business. Perhaps from a desire to revive this side of things, in 1923 they invested heavily in a jade mining syndicate: the Burchin Syndicate, which had a concession at Tawmaw in the Kachin Hills in Burma.[15] Liberty's had always been noted for jade and in 1919 had produced a small booklet on jade amulets, beads and carvings, which explained the significance of jade in Chinese society. However, investing in the mine was a daft idea. Did the board fall for the sales patter of the mining engineer who appeared at the door bearing a lump of jade the size of a football, or were the company profits burning a hole in their pockets? Either way, one suspects that had Sir Arthur been alive the whole enterprise would have been given very short shrift. Leaving aside the jade (which in the end, in an effort to sell it at a reasonable price, they had to ship to Shanghai), the jewellery department was one of the few to reflect contemporary fashion. The settings they sold were often Art Deco in style and some reflected Native American art, upon which Art Deco drew heavily.

Liberty's were hard hit by the economic slump and found it necessary to make one person redundant from every department – an unheard-of event. As staff tended to stay for ever, this was a sad and upsetting time for all concerned. Gradually, though, the American economy stabilized and American visitors came once more. As things picked up on the Continent too, there was an upsurge in foreign shoppers. Liberty's buyers embraced those improved times with enthusiasm and stock levels increased. But across the Channel the dark clouds of war were gathering.

OPPOSITE 'Monart' glass, made by John Moncrieff Ltd, as shown in a 1930s gift catalogue.

ABOVE 'Monart' glass from a Liberty's Birmingham catalogue.

FOLLOWING PAGES Pearl, diamond and jade jewellery offered by Liberty's in the 1930s.

JADE SET WITH DIAMONDS IN PLATINUM AND 18ct. WHITE GOLD

43.
Jade and Diamond Brooch.
£95 . 0 . 0

42.
Jade and Diamond
Earrings.
£27 . 10 . 0

45.
Jade and Diamond
Ring.
£10 . 10 . 0

46.
Jade and Diamond
Ring.
£37 . 10 . 0

47.
Jade and Diamond Bar Brooch.
£14 . 14 . 0

48.
Jade and White Gold
Ring.
£5 . 5 . 0

51. Jade and Diamond
Earrings.
£45 . 0 . 0

49. Jade Necklace.
16 ins. **£12 . 12 . 0**
30 ins. **£22 . 10 . 0**

50. Jade and Diamond
Pendant.
£25 . 0 . 0

52.
Jade and White Gold Brooch.
£6 . 6 . 0

53. Jade and White Gold Bracelet.
£25 . 0 . 0

LIBERTY & CO LTD   REGENT STREET   LONDON W.1
6

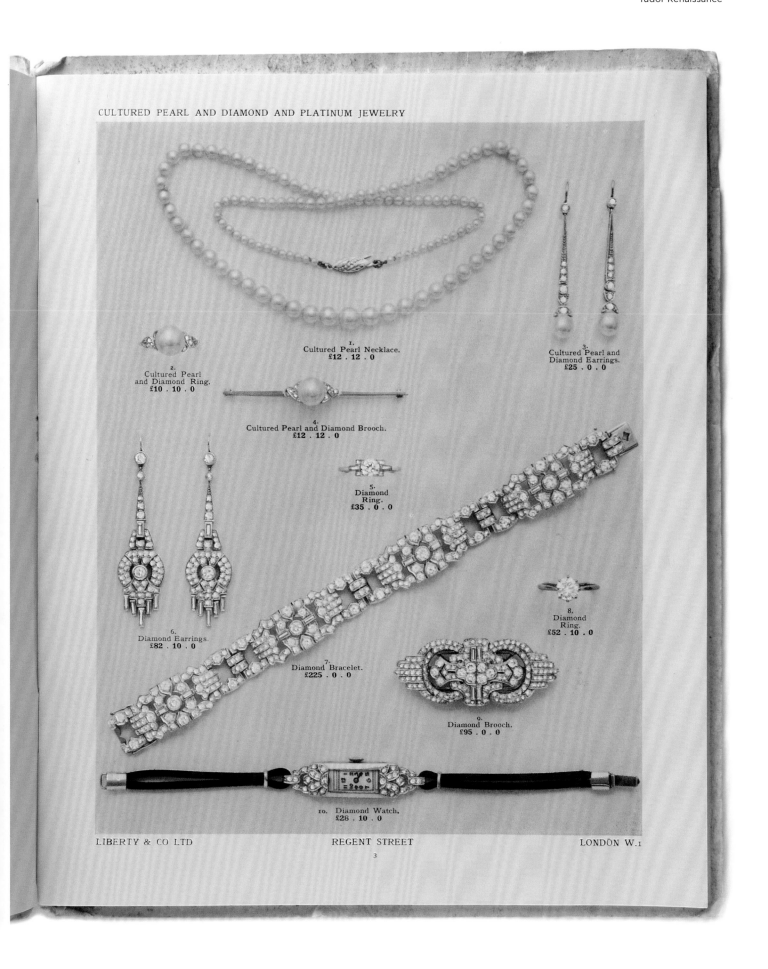

CULTURED PEARL AND DIAMOND AND PLATINUM JEWELRY

1.
Cultured Pearl Necklace.
£12 . 12 . 0

2.
Cultured Pearl
and Diamond Ring.
£10 . 10 . 0

3.
Cultured Pearl and
Diamond Earrings.
£25 . 0 . 0

4.
Cultured Pearl and Diamond Brooch.
£12 . 12 . 0

5.
Diamond
Ring.
£35 . 0 . 0

6.
Diamond Earrings.
£82 . 10 . 0

7.
Diamond Bracelet.
£225 . 0 . 0

8.
Diamond
Ring.
£52 . 10 . 0

9.
Diamond Brooch.
£95 . 0 . 0

10. Diamond Watch.
£28 . 10 . 0

LIBERTY & CO LTD   REGENT STREET   LONDON W.1
3

A BRAVE NEW WORLD

An Eric Lucking window
display, c.1950.

In September 1939 Britain found itself once more at war with Germany. At the outbreak of war Liberty's was seriously overstocked: the demand for luxury goods had declined as the European crisis grew. Overstocking often proves to be disastrous for businesses, but in this case it proved to be Liberty's salvation. They had, for example, bought a huge consignment of leather handbags, and throughout the Second World War Liberty's was about the only place in London where such an item might be purchased, as the use of leather for making handbags had been very quickly prohibited.

Gradually more and more raw materials and goods were rationed. Rationing was to have a profound effect on many areas of life and many of the restrictions were to remain until the Queen's Coronation in 1953. Clothes rationing was introduced in June 1941 and the regulations were tightened the following year. There were limits on the number of pleats there could be, if any at all. The width of sleeves was regulated, as were the number of button and the size and depth of collars, and so on. Everything possible was done to save labour in manufacturing and to save fabric. The Board of Trade set up committees to regulate designs, which produced detailed specifications about the amount of material and labour that could be used, giving rise to the term 'Utility clothing'. A number of leading figures were to produce Utility designs: for example, Norman Hartnell, couturier to the Queen, and Hardy Amies (who served in the Special Operations Executive) both designed ranges for mass manufacture (both were considered a great success).

Soon, in August 1942, domestic pottery was restricted to a narrow range of very plain items – cups were produced with no handles, even, in the effort to save materials. Two months later the manufacture of all furniture was restricted to twenty-two items, each with a specific timber content, being produced in two qualities. There were usually three designs for each permitted item. The committee responsible for Utility furniture was composed of a number of design luminaries, and the design panel was eventually chaired by the Cotswold furniture-maker Gordon Russell (1892–1980).[1] Because of Russell's background, much Utility furniture was based upon Arts and Crafts designs, which would have been familiar to Liberty's customers. More specifically, because of Russell the committee drew heavily on the work of Ernest Gimson and the Cotswold School. The Utility designs were inevitably simplified and, of course, devoid of most of the decoration. Nevertheless, Russell set out with the objective of providing people with 'something better than they might have expected'; he also sought to make the Utility specification a benchmark for quality after the war, and basically he achieved this. In clothing, too, many of the Utility patterns continued to be produced well after the war, and certainly informed and influenced post-war fashions.

Liberty's, like other businesses, struggled to cope. As the situation grew ever bleaker, more and more staff were called up to do essential war work. The tea rooms in the 'crypt' were turned into a canteen for Air Raid Wardens (the ARP) and even the chairman, Harold Blackmore, was on fire watch duty, doing two nights on and two nights off. The London Blitz brought terrible destruction to large parts of the capital, but here the gods seem to have favoured Liberty's. A bomb in Conduit Street shattered all the windows in East India House, and a direct hit on the premises of the International Dental Companies in Great Marlborough Street shattered the windows in the accounts office (apparently the following morning the sold ledger office was strewn with false teeth, causing the finance director to observe drily that it was the first time there had been any teeth in Liberty's debt collecting.)[2] But Liberty's and their iconic building both survived the war, perhaps a little battered, but relatively unscathed.

Peace did not immediately bring plenty; indeed, many wartime restrictions actually became harsher. Britain was victorious, but bankrupt and exhausted. As the 1940s drew to a close, however, restrictions began to ease. At Liberty's too things were changing. Harold Blackmore retired from his position as chairman in 1950. He was succeeded by Ivor Stewart-Liberty, who, however, died suddenly in 1952 and was in turn succeeded by his son, Arthur Stewart-Liberty.[3] The brave new world that was dawning did not sit happily with the traditional ethos of Liberty's, epitomized in the Tudor building; indeed to many people Liberty's was indelibly characterized by the Tudor building, which suggested that all that was to be found inside it were traditional designs and beautiful workmanship. If it were to have any hope of survival, Liberty's needed to reinvent itself and dispel its old-fashioned image, appealing to a new, younger generation.

In 1949 the board decided to open a department aimed at the young, selling the sort of merchandise that would appeal to them. 'Young Liberty' was allocated

space in the Tudor building and Hulme Chadwick, who was noted for designing aircraft interiors, was engaged to design the space. He installed a false ceiling to cover the beams and turned the windows into lit display cases. Everything was done in primrose, grey and green, and rather than use oak he used sapele mahogany and the rare South African wood avodiré.

Arthur Stewart-Liberty (1916–90) and his cousin and fellow director Hilary Blackmore (1904–83), who ran the wholesale company, were the driving force behind many of the changes Liberty's underwent in the late 1940s and the 1950s. Both had great enthusiasm and determination, and both were interested in contemporary styles. They kept a close eye on prevailing trends and fashions, and this led to the establishment of the advisory design committee. This was a clever idea, as it immediately overthrew the tyranny of the departmental heads. It enabled Liberty's to instil a much-needed design focus and it also provided a forum in which new ideas could be aired and discussed. A balance needed to be struck between the avant-garde and the traditional. Liberty's was, after all, a well-established business with a well-established customer base, which you alienated at your peril. Even acknowledging this, however, the committee realized that they could make a huge difference in two areas in particular: window displays and textiles.

When Arthur Stewart-Liberty returned from active service, he was aware that he knew nothing about retailing, but he was determined to learn. He took a course on window display at the Reiman School in Horseferry Road. A window is the picture a business presents to the world, and imaginative, arresting window displays can have a huge impact. Stewart-Liberty was introduced to Eric Lucking and persuaded the board to appoint Lucking to a new position of display manager. This was in 1946. It was quite a challenge to create imaginative windows, especially as Liberty's windows had a backdrop of walnut panelling. Lucking went hunting and found a quantity of timber battens and some blackout fabric. He made a series of screens, spraying the blackout white, and made figures out of wire, wire netting, straw – anything, in fact, that would serve his purpose.

RIGHT Harold Blackmore, chairman until 1950.

FAR RIGHT Ivor Stewart-Liberty, who briefly succeeded as chairman but died in 1952.

BELOW A meeting of the advisory design committee in the early 1950s: clockwise from the top: Hilary Blackmore (at the head of the table), Colleen Farr (standing), William Dorrell, Arthur Stewart-Liberty (standing), Carole Thomas, Rosemary Boland, Mr Browning.

'Young Liberty' and
Christofle silver: one of
Eric Lucking's memorable
window displays from the
late 1940s.

RIGHT A 'white' window of children's dresses, 1950.

FOLLOWING PAGES A silver promotion, probably from the late 1940s.

One famous window featured a giraffe with a series of Liberty's scarves tied around its neck to keep out the cold. (It probably needed them: the winter of 1947 was among the coldest on record.) For one Christmas display Lucking made long tendrils that each terminated in a hand offering a gift. His displays were always imaginative and often had a touch of the surreal – shades of Salvador Dalí and lobster telephones – and they were immensely popular with the public.

The textile business had always been at the heart of Liberty's and the firm held a huge archive, even if management had at times not properly appreciated this. Hilary Blackmore, who had, of course, been the manager at Merton Abbey before the war, quickly realized that the old fabric designs for which Liberty's were famous could be transformed simply by recolouring or rescaling. In many ways the 1950s are characterized not just by the shock of the new, of the avant-garde, but also by revivalism. Older customers who were repairing the ravages of war wanted the familiar and the nostalgic, so there was a healthy trade in older patterns – florals of one sort or another – in traditional colourways. Liberty's still owned the Merton Abbey printworks, but hand-block printing was gradually becoming more and more uneconomic. It was fine for silks used in the dress department or for scarves or for men's ties, which are basically luxury products, but useless for the vast majority of furnishing fabrics, which are more price-sensitive. A complex paisley pattern might have as many as thirty blocks, so production proceeded at a snail's pace, one block at a time. The board decided to modernize Merton Abbey, and in 1966 a press release announced the purchase of a Meccanotessile screen-printing machine, which could handle fabrics 60 inches (152 centimetres) wide and run eighteen colours.[4] It was a brave try at holding back the tide, but eventually the works were sold and they now no longer exist.

While they could draw on the design archive, Liberty's still needed fresh work. Perhaps the most significant designer to work for them in the 1950s was Colleen Farr. Arthur Stewart-Liberty spotted her work at the Royal College of Art diploma show and asked her to contact him. She initially worked for Roosen Silks, but after a year or so she did get in touch with Liberty's and was immediately engaged.

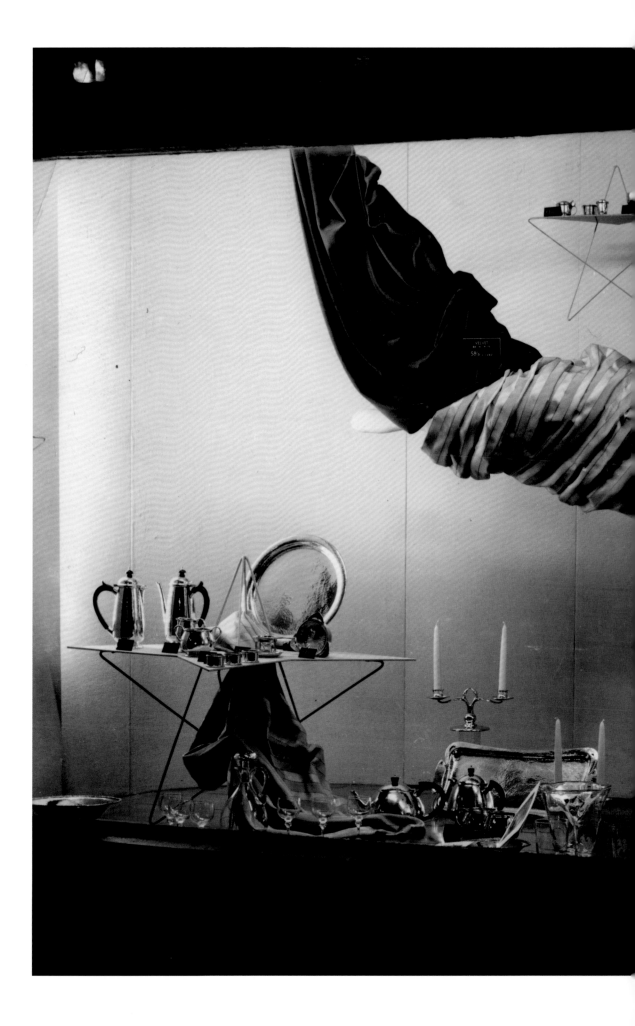

'Liberty's Lunch Room', a
window display of furnishing
fabrics, c.1950.

A menswear window
display by Eric Lucking,
summer 1951.

An arrangement of Chinese
and Japanese goods,
recalling Liberty's roots.
By Eric Lucking, c.1949.

Jean Muir dresses made
for the actress Joanna
Lumley.

LEFT TO RIGHT A printed
silk 'peasant' dress and
shawl in striped paisley
fabric and a printed silk
dress in bold primary
colours, both 1960s; a
printed silk dress with
a high waistline and
buttoned bodice and a
moss-crêpe evening dress
with a stand-up collar
and deep cuffs, 1970s.

Farr started working with Hilary Blackmore, who ran
the wholesale division, and soon suggested they establish
a design studio, which they did. When you walked out
on to Kingly Street in those days, the fashion trade was
all around you, so it was comparatively easy to keep up
with current trends and developments. In those days,
within a short walking distance of Liberty's, you could
find workrooms making garments, buttons, *passementerie*
and almost anything else you might need. There was an
upholstery workshop within a stone's throw of Portland
Place. One of Farr's patterns, 'Blackberry', won a gold
medal at the Sacramento International Fair in 1955. It
was subsequently used by the fashion designer Jean Muir,
as was another Farr design, 'Mexicana', which had been
inspired by a trip to Mexico. In 1962 Farr left Liberty's to
begin a teaching career at the Central School of Art and
Design. However, for a number of years she continued
to supply the company with designs on a freelance basis.
And, naturally, many of her students went on to design for
the company.

It was not unusual for the impetus for change in the
business to come from staff. In 1958 William Poole, who
was assistant to Gustav Weiner of Merton Abbey, went to
Paris and by chance saw a small exhibition devoted to Art
Nouveau. It transpired that another exhibition was planned
in Amsterdam for the following year and a much larger
one in June 1960 at the Museum of Modern Art in New
York. Hilary Blackmore immediately saw the potential and
a search at Merton produced many old pattern books with
Art Nouveau designs. Probably a dozen furnishing fabrics
were selected and William Poole redrew them for silk-screen
printing, recolouring some of them. They were sold as dress
fabrics printed on silk, wool chiffon and organza under
the 'Lotus' collection brand. This was a huge hit with the
fashion houses in Paris and particularly in Rome, where the
Fontana sisters produced an entire sub-collection around
the fabrics, which was shown to great acclaim.[5] The fourteen
designs in the Lotus range formed the basis for Liberty's
1960 spring collection. The timing was perfect and the
range sold very strongly, particularly in the United States.

ABOVE RIGHT A Jean
Muir Art Nouveau print
satin evening dress, 1970s.

BELOW RIGHT A detail of
the fabric 'Burnham'.

OPPOSITE The 'Lotus'
collection, photographed
here in the Crush Bar of
the Royal Opera House,
c.1960.

The following year they had yet another major success
with a follow-up collection by the designer and decorator
Martin Battersby. He studied the designs by Léon Bakst
for Diaghilev's Ballets Russes, and also drew on the work
of Paul Poiret, who had briefly designed costumes for
Liberty's in the 1930s (see pages 145–9), and on the
fashion plates of George Barbier and Georges Lepape.
From these sources Battersby produced six designs for the
Bakst/Poiret range.

In 1960 Cecil Beaton came to them when he was doing
My Fair Lady, wanting to have printed some of the fabrics
used in the first production of *Patience* in 1881. The blocks
were found, but not the necessary number of printers, the
Merton Abbey staff having been reduced to eighteen or
even fewer. Beaton got his fabrics, though, as they were
able to create screens from the original blocks. The Liberty
archive was an almost inexhaustible well, and very wisely
they had decided to record all the designs drawn from
the old printing blocks. In 1962 they began to dispose of
the original blocks, working on the assumption that most
would never be used again.

William Poole left Liberty's in 1962 for the United
States and was replaced by Bernard Nevill as design
consultant. Nevill already had his own design studio, but
Arthur Stewart-Liberty persuaded him to join Liberty's.
Though they were to enjoy a rather spiky relationship,
it was a shrewd appointment. Nevill brought a fresh
approach, creating new modernist patterns and updating
the old. His training was as a fashion designer, so his eye
was attuned to fashion rather than fabrics. He explained:
'I worked backwards from the dress to the textile because
I've had very good antennae for picking up vibes and trends
before they happen, that's a very important thing to have
as a designer.' Whether he had a 'feeling for maxi, for long
skirts, or short skirts or loose clothes or tight clothes it
would affect my designs for textiles'. Of course having a
vision does not necessarily mean that others will share that
vision or that confidence. Nevill also remarked: 'It was sheer
perseverance to convince them [Liberty's] that my feelings,
my antennae for where the wind was blowing, were worth
following commercially.'[6]

Building on the work of Martin Battersby, and what might be termed the Art Deco revival, Nevill produced a number of Art-Deco-inspired fabrics. One, the 'Landscape' range, which was produced in 1968, could have derived from a 1930s Art Deco travel poster or a Batsford book cover, only it was done in more muted shades. Islamic art provided the inspiration for a collection in 1965, while an earlier group of fabrics with large, bold abstract flowers was based on the work of Henri Matisse. His antennae ever twitching, when in 1969 there was an exhibition at the Tate of Elizabethan portraiture, Nevill created a collection of winter wool fabrics inspired by sixteenth-century damasks. This caught the eye of Yves Saint Laurent, who ordered thirteen designs in thirty-four colourways. When Nevill left Liberty's in 1972 his place was taken by Susan Collier, who continued where he left off, developing more modern designs and colourings.

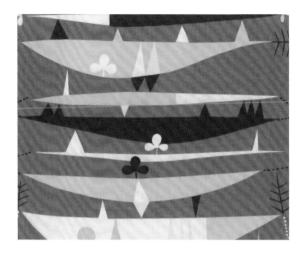

In the early 1950s there was a great hunger for consumer goods, a pent-up demand that had been suppressed since 1940. You could, as Sir Terence Conran remarked, 'sell almost anything'.[7] Although best known for his furniture designs and the Habitat brand, Conran originally trained as a textile designer and, having sold some textile designs to Horrockses Fashions Ltd, he was able to sell more to Liberty's.[8] Conran was one of the bright young things who were revolutionizing fashion and design in general at the time. In the world of fashion three names, especially, are prominent. Mary Quant opened her boutique, Bazaar, in the King's Road in 1955. Although she did not invent the style, Mary Quant is famous for her promotion of the mini-skirt. She was queen of the avant-garde, and her clientele were usually reasonably well off, with money to spare and to spend. Barbara Hulanicki was another significant fashion icon: her shop, Biba in Kensington, which opened in 1964, was a sensation. Biba was, if anything, more cutting edge than Bazaar, catering for a different market, the bedsit kids who would buy something to soon discard it and move on. The third name is Laura Ashley, who opened her first shop in South Kensington in 1968, peddling a romantic and nostalgic vision which had huge appeal at the end of the 1960s.

Three sketches by Yves
Saint Laurent: a midi skirt
using 'Macedonia', c.1966;
a coat in one of Liberty's
new prints, c.1966; a
Mexican-inspired full-
sleeved dress with deep
printed border, 1973.

Liberty children's
dresses, all made in
'Tana' lawn or 'Varuna'
wool in the late 1970s.

Dramatic window
displays for the 'Lotus'
collection promotion.

LEFT A recycled aluminium 'BA' chair, designed by Ernest Race in 1945.

Liberty's was never going to be a Bazaar or a Biba. Like Laura Ashley, in fashion terms the company traded more on nostalgia. Liberty's buyers would go to shows in Paris, as they had done before the war, and also to shows in Rome and Madrid. As before, they would buy some models and *toiles*, so that a customer could have the latest Paris fashions produced in Liberty's own fabrics in their own workrooms. Because of the continuation of wartime restrictions Liberty's customers had missed out on Dior's 'New Look', with its extravagant use of fabric, but later you could buy a 'Dior' coat, or a suit designed by Givenchy, or a dress from a design by Visconti or Rodriguez. The range was diverse and extensive.

Just as they opened 'Young Liberty' in 1949 as an outlet for more youthful fashions, so in July 1950 they opened a contemporary furniture department to promote new British and European design. The project, which seems to have been a long time in the planning, was put in the hands of Frank Martin. He was faced with the problem of how to show strikingly contemporary furniture and *objets d'art* in the traditional setting of the Tudor building. By using a variety of different treatments for the walls, and subtle subdivisions, Martin was able to create a series of spaces in which the contemporary furniture looked appealing. Liberty's then found there was a demand for similar accessories, such as lamps, ceramics and glass. The interest was huge, particularly following the Festival of Britain in 1951, which promoted contemporary British design, and after the Utility regulations ended in 1953.

The sort of contemporary furniture Liberty's stocked had its origins in the modern movement and the pre-war world. It was characterized by flowing curves and sleek shapes – a style we tend to think of as Scandinavian design. Liberty's were understandably nervous about it (although they had, of course, sold some contemporary furniture before the war, stocking works by Alvar Aalto, for example) and decided to mix the modern with antique country pieces, which always appealed to a large section of the British public. This was probably not a good idea, as it gave a rather muddled message in design terms. Designers who were well known in their own right – Arne Jacobsen, Stig Lindberg, Paolo Venini and Piero Fornasetti, for example – were of course credited with their work. And occasionally designers would be given one-man shows, such as that held in 1957 for Gio Ponti. However, following their long-standing tradition, Liberty's would often refer to the country of origin – rather than the name – of the designer: objects were Danish, Swedish, Finnish, Italian or French.

Among British manufacturers who produced contemporary furniture, Race Furniture was outstanding. Ernest Race was an architect who was also a trained tool-and-die maker, and he founded his company in 1945 to create furniture that utilized modern engineering principles. His famous 'BA' chair, which he designed in 1945, with the intention that it would be made from scrap aluminium recycled from wartime aircraft, has become a design classic. Liberty's were stockists of Race furniture and the products of many other contemporary manufacturers. They also commissioned exclusive pieces. Probably the most famous of these was the 'Boomerang' table, which was designed for them by A.M. Lewis. It was intended to fit around a chair or a sofa, and came in a variety of different woods and finishes.

The trade in ceramics in the post-war years was probably more extensive than that in furniture. Liberty's retailed the wares of many manufacturers, including Spode, Royal Doulton and Wedgwood. Of more interest are the studio potters Liberty's supported, some of whom are famous names today. Bernard Leach was extensively promoted, his work featuring in their published catalogues, but also being given one-man exhibitions. Leach was already an established name in the 1950s (as of course was Lucy Rie, also sold at Liberty's) but the company was also very good at fostering new talent.

One such was Geoffrey Curran, who owned the Fen Pottery in Godmanchester, Huntingdonshire. Before the war Curran had run a printing company in Cornwall, and then, briefly, worked in advertising in London. He joined the RAF on the first day of the war, hoping to be a pilot, but a minor eye defect put paid to that. He ended up in Aden (modern-day Yemen), commanding an armoured car unit with instructions – shades of *Lawrence of Arabia* – to cause the Japanese as much trouble as possible should they invade.[9] Fortunately, they didn't. It must have been a most extraordinary decision, just after the war, for a former RAF officer to decide to go to Leicester College of Art and Technology to study pottery, but that is what Curran did. His pottery was opened in in 1947 (by the Emperor Haile Selassie, whose acquaintance Curran had somehow made during a brief wartime stint in Ethiopia). In his early days Geoffrey Curran was influenced by Bernard Leach and produced straightforward utilitarian objects, which derived great beauty from their simplicity. Liberty's was an early customer, and probably his most important. A small art pottery employing probably no more than about twenty people, Fen Pottery was just the sort of business Sir Arthur Liberty would have encouraged.[10]

In 1973 Liberty's acquired their Continental distributor, Metz & Co. in the Netherlands. This old-established company (founded by Moses Samuels in 1740), based in Amsterdam and with a branch in The Hague, had been their distributor since 1898. Such was the relationship that they would issue joint catalogues. The business had been owned by Joseph de Leeuw (1872–1944), who was a man of great taste. He admired Liberty's and became a friend of Sir Arthur. In all probability some Continental manufacturers and artists gained an introduction to Liberty's through him. After the First World War he went into furniture production, commissioning designs from Paul Bromberg and then the interior decorator Willem Penaat. De Leeuw's taste was decidedly more avant-garde than the prevailing ethos at Liberty's, and he was to commission furniture from the architect and designer Gerrit Rietveld, a leading member of the Dutch artistic movement De Stijl. Tragically, during the Second World War Joseph de Leeuw

perished in the Theresienstadt concentration camp. However, his son Hendrik de Leeuw (1908–78) survived and carried on the business.[11] Hendrik de Leeuw had his father's artistic eye: he spotted Terence Conran and engaged him to open a kitchen and tableware department in the basement of Metz & Co. in 1952 which was a sort of pre-Habitat. By the early 1970s Hendrik de Leeuw wanted to retire, but his son, the pianist and conductor Reinbert de Leeuw, was developing his musical career, which he understandably did not wish to relinquish, so it was decided (in consultation with the staff) to offer the business to Liberty's.

Liberty's celebrated its centenary in 1975, the anniversary being marked by a large exhibition at the Victoria and Albert Museum and smaller exhibitions in the Regent Street and Tudor shops. These events reminded the public, and design world, of the pivotal role Liberty's had played in fostering good design, for the exhibitions were rich in famous designers who had worked for Liberty's. The attendant publicity markedly increased visitor numbers to the store. So in 1979 the company began a major renovation and restoration of its famous Tudor building, the work being supervised by the Derek Forsyth Partnership. They soon discovered that under all the accumulated detritus lay the original linenfold panelling and this was restored, giving the building a uniformity that had hitherto been lacking.

RIGHT A 'Supperleggera' chair, designed by Gio Ponti in 1957. Inspired by Italian country furniture, it was made of ash with a woven cane seat.

ABOVE 'Liberty's Living Rooms', a display featured in *The Studio Yearbook* of 1951.

LEFT A 'Liberty's Living Rooms' display which appeared in *The Studio Yearbook* in 1955. The curtain to the left is 'Macrihanish' by Robert Stewart.

BELOW A window display promoting an exhibition of the work of the designer Gio Ponti, held in April 1957.

RIGHT The Homeware department in the early 1960s.

BELOW LEFT The Metz & Co. building in Amsterdam.

BELOW RIGHT A Liberty's advertisement from the early 1950s. Note the 'Boomerang' table in the centre.

Liberty

Liberty's live up to their reputation for matchless quality and design with their contemporary collection of price-controlled English, Scottish and Scandinavian furniture . . . Swedish glass . . . modern light fittings . . . and their own Liberty-designed occasional pieces and hand-printed furnishing fabrics.

of Regent Street

Arthur Stewart-Liberty died in 1990, and his death marked the beginning of the end of Sir Arthur Liberty's family's involvement with the business. Like Sir Arthur Liberty before him, Arthur Stewart-Liberty had been a charismatic man with vision and taste. After his death, once more the company began to drift and to flounder. A succession of chairmen and managing directors came, saw, did little and left as quickly as they had arrived. Under Arthur Stewart-Liberty the company had been very profitable, but now there was a slow, inexorable decline in profits, exacerbated by poor leadership and lack of vision. One by one the branches outside London, such as the long-established outlets in Birmingham and Manchester, and the more recent branches (opened in the 1950s) in Croydon and Kingston upon Thames, were closed or sold off, the business retreating to its London base. Arthur Stewart-

Liberty's two sons, Richard and Oliver, both resigned from the board in 1995, leaving Anthony Blackmore (Hilary Blackmore's son) the only family member on the board. A series of bitter battles ensued, culminating in the family marshalling enough support to oust the chairman. This, however, proved to be a pyrrhic victory. In 2000 Marylebone Warwick Balfour Group bought out the family members, thus severing all connections with the family that had created the business. There began a process of retrenchment and in 2006 the lease on East India House was sold to an investment group, which brought to an end Liberty's connection with Regent Street, where it had all begun 131 years earlier. In June 2010 BlueGem Capital Partners LLP acquired the business. They bought the famous Tudor building with its 70,000 square feet (21,336 square metres) of space arrayed over six floors; they also

The Christmas-themed
windows on Great
Marlborough Street,
November 2007.

acquired the Liberty Art Fabrics business, which was based
in London and Tokyo and distributed Liberty's printed
fabrics to the fashion industry, drawing on Liberty's unique
archive of over 43,000 designs. This almost inexhaustible
well continues to provide designs that remain enormously
popular with the publc.

Those designs lie at the heart of Liberty's long history.
When Sir Arthur Liberty opened his shop on 17 May
1875 he had the ambition 'not to follow existing fashion
but to create new ones' and remarkably, as we have seen,
he managed to do exactly that. The business grew at an
astonishing pace because Sir Arthur had such assured taste.
It still flourishes more than a century later. There is probably
no other department store in the world that has employed
the services of so many famous designers. And that was
really the secret of Liberty's success: an eye for great design.

NOTES

A MAN WITH A VISION

1 Arthur Liberty, *De Libertat: A Historical and Genealogical Review, Comprising an Account of the Submission of the City of Marseilles*, T. Pettitt & Co. of London, 1888.

2 James Laver, *The Liberty Story*, Liberty & Co, 1959, p. 3. This booklet states: 'They emigrated to England after the French Revolution and it was then that they Anglicized their name.' This is totally incorrect, although a romantic idea.

3 Liberty is an Anglo-Saxon name, thought to derive from the Old English words *lead* and *beatere*, meaning 'he who beats lead'.

4 Arthur Liberty's great-great- grandfather was Daniel Liberty, who died on 9 December 1785, and whose wife was Mary, who died on 22 February 1791. Liberty's great-grandfather was also Daniel Liberty, who was born in 1731 at Kensworth and died on 29 August 1815 at Dunstable. He married Elizabeth Herbert on 5 January 1756. The Liberty family seems to have been long established in the Kensworth area and a christening record exists for a William Liberty there on 17 February 1632.

5 Thomas Liberty (1772/3–1820) married Margaret Edwards on 3 June 1802. Their children were: John Edwards, christened 17 May 1803, died December 1877; Thomas Deamer, christened 24 March 1805; George, christened 28 September 1806, died June 1891; Margaret, christened 28 February 1808, married Robert Vernon; Maria, christened 15 October 1809, married Meshack 'Michael' Godwin 4 September 1843; Alfred, christened 13 January 1811, died 5 May 1841; Arthur, christened 25 October 1813, died 7 November 1813; and Arthur, christened 25 December 1814, who was Arthur Lasenby Liberty's father.

6 Arthur Liberty (1814–1901); Rebecca Liberty (née Lasenby) (1815–1905).

7 George Liberty (1806–91). Arthur Liberty's sister Kate was born in 1852 while the family was still living in Buckinghamshire. His sister Ada was born in November 1853 in Nottingham. She married Donald Stewart on 25 July 1883. Their son, Ivor, became Sir Arthur Liberty's heir.

8 Alison Adburgham, *Liberty's: A Biography of a Shop*, George Allen & Unwin Ltd, London 1975, p. 9

9 Ibid., p. 11. The letter is dated 6 May 1859.

10 *Business Directory of London*, 1884.

11 Anon., 'The Maker of the House Beautiful', *Fortunes Made in Business or Life Struggles of Successful People*, Amalgamated Press Ltd, London 1901, p. 212.

12 Alison Adburgham, *Liberty's: A Biography of a Shop*, op. cit., p. 11.

13 Martha Cottam (or Cotham) gave as her father William Cottam, who was described as a 'gentleman'. On her marriage certificate to Arthur Liberty his address is merely given as 'St Pancras', while her address is given as 'St. Mark, City Road', which was actually a hospital. The marriage may actually have been void, possibly a sham (it might have been bigamous), but in the event it was dissolved by divorce. Subsequently a Martha Cotham was married at St Pancras Church in April 1874. Her father was a William Cotham and was described as a mercantile clerk. The signature is remarkably similar to Martha Cottam's a few years before. Cottam did not marry Augustus Glover (she seems to disappear from public records, although that may simply be a consequence of ambiguities in spelling) and Arthur Liberty subsequently married Emma Blackmore in church. Blackmore Family Notes, courtesy of Anthony Blackmore.

14 Letter from Muriel Collie to Mary Cummins, 5 July 1953, Westminster Archives, 788/163(c).

15 Ibid.

16 Anon., 'The Maker of the House Beautiful', *Fortunes Made in Business*, op. cit., p. 214.

17 Alison Adburgham, *Liberty's: A Biography of a Shop*, op. cit., pp. 18–19, and Blackmore Family Notes, op. cit.

18 James Laver, *The Liberty Story*, op. cit., p. 9. The amount of money required might be explained by the location: 'His shop was small – it was really only half a shop – but even for this he had to pay a premium of £1800, a large sum in those days, and a high rent.'

19 'Old Friends: Mr Elsom', *Liberty Lamp*, November 1925, p. 8.

20 'The Liberty Art Movement', *British Warehouseman*, 1895, page unknown

21 Anon., 'The Maker of the House Beautiful', *Fortunes Made in Business*, op. cit., p. 213.

22 William Judd, interview, *Liberty Lamp*, March 1925, pp. 4–5.

23 *Business Directory of London*, 1884.

24 'Old Friends: Mr Elsom', *Liberty Lamp*, November 1925, p. 8.

25 Anon., 'The Maker of the House Beautiful', *Fortunes Made in Business*, p. 214.

26 The property, along with No. 14, is now occupied by the Daiwa Anglo-Japanese Foundation. No. 13 was Arthur Liberty's home from 1885 until 1893.

27 Alison Adburgham, *Liberty's: A Biography of a Shop*, op. cit., pp. 45–6.

28 A list from 1890 gives the following locations: Aberdeen, Bournemouth, Dover, Dublin, Edinburgh, Glasgow, Leeds, Liverpool, Manchester, Scarborough, Taunton and Torquay. Overseas agents included New York, Boston, Chicago, Toronto and Tasmania. There also seems to have been an agent in Yokohama, Japan. Alison Adburgham, *Liberty's: A Biography of a Shop*, op. cit., p. 65.

29 The partnership deed was dated 18 June 1887. It was dissolved on 13 November 1888 and notice of such appeared in the *London Gazette* on 16 November 1888.

30 Alison Adburgham, *Liberty's: A Biography of a Shop*, op. cit., pp. 71 and 72.

31 For the year to 31 January /1/1894 the gross profit at Liberty's was £67,805, which gave a net profit of £6,072. Westminster Archives, 1932/37; 38.

32 The Lee had originally belonged to the Russells, Earls of Bedford. In 1635 the 4th Earl, Francis Russell, leased and then later sold lands at The Lee to William Plaistowe. It is known that Thomas Plaistowe (1628?–1715) was the first of the family to own The Lee outright. In 1785 another Thomas Plaistowe passed the estate to his daughter, Elizabeth, who married Henry Deering. The estate passed back into the Plaistowe family and John Plaistowe sold it to Arthur Liberty's cousin.

33 A letter survives from H.C. Blackmore, Arthur Liberty's nephew, dated 20 December 1899, regarding an extension of the lease from twenty-one to thirty-five years for a payment of £1,000.

34 There exists a copy of a drawing of a panelled room at the Manor House, which was probably added by Sir Arthur. However, there is no indication of who drew it or where it was published, if indeed it was. Westminster Archives, 788/174(5).

35 Notes on the Blackmore Family History, courtesy of Anthony Blackmore.

36 Letter from Miss Kate Morris (later Mrs K. Ayland) to her sister, c.1938, Buckinghamshire Record Office D/X823/4.

37 Archibald Knox Society website. The cigar box is now in the Victoria and Albert Museum.

38 Westminster Archives holds copies of all their published books, together with part of a diary recording the round-the-world trip taken between 13 December 1888 and July 1889. There is also an extract from Emma Liberty's diary, 'The Levant and Back within 28 Days', Westminster Archives, 788/179 and 788/184.

39 Alison Adburgham, *Liberty's: A Biography of a Shop*, op. cit., p. 94.

40 The Libertys' published travel writings are as follows: *Springtime in the Basque Mountains*, Grant Richards, 1901; *Japan: A Pictorial Record by Mrs Lasenby Liberty*, Adam & Charles Black, 1910; *A Day in Tangier*, Adam & Charles Black, 1913; *The Treasure Hunt: The Conspirators in Constantinople*, Liberty & Co., 1915.

41 Anon., 'The Maker of the House Beautiful', *Fortunes Made in Business*, op. cit., p. 213.

42 Ivor Stewart was the son of Ada Liberty (1853–1933), who married Donald Stewart in 1883. Alison Adburgham, *Liberty's: A Biography of a Shop*, op. cit., p. 99.

FROM A FARAWAY COUNTRY TO REGENT STREET

1 Neville Chamberlain, speech broadcast on 27 September 1938. The Prime Minister was referring to the Czechoslovakia crisis. The speech was reported in *The Times* on 28 September 1938, p. 10.

2 E.W. Godwin (1833–86) was born in Bristol, the son of a prosperous leather-worker. He was educated at Exton School in Highbury and subsequently articled to William Armstrong, a civil architect and civil engineer. Godwin set up his own practice in 1854 and was fortunate enough to win a competition to design Northampton Town Hall in 1861. After his wife's death in 1865 he began an affair with Ellen Terry. This affair produced two children, but it fizzled out after five or so years, and he married Beatriz Birnie Philip (1857–96), who bore him a son. After his death she married the painter James Whistler, for whom Godwin had built a house (known as the White House) in Tite Street, Chelsea; sadly, this house was demolished in the 1960s.

3 E.W. Godwin, *The Architect*, 23 December 1876, p. 363.

4 Ibid.

5 Sir Frances Cowley Burnand (1836–1917) was editor of *Punch* from 1880 to 1906. He was a comic writer and dramatist, creating over 200 works. *The Colonel* mercilessly satirized the Aesthetic Movement. The farce was wildly successful and it made the actor-manager Edgar Bruce so much money that he built the Prince of Wales Theatre from the proceeds.

6 Anon., 'The Maker of the House Beautiful', *Fortunes Made in Business*, op. cit., p. 216.

7 E.W. Godwin, *The Architect*, 23 December 1876, p. 363.

8 Letter from Edward Burne-Jones to Liberty's, 17 December 1897, Westminster Archives, 788/164/6a.

9 The Aesthetic Movement was a rather short-lived and hard-to-define phase in decorative taste. It is generally accepted that the catalyst for its popularity was the Philadelphia Centennial Exposition held in 1876. However, the movement's roots lie in the industrialization of the United Kingdom in the nineteenth century, and it drew on historical and exotic sources, particularly Japanese influences. People like E.W. Godwin and, most notably, Christopher Dresser studied Japanese design, carefully analysing objects and their intended function. This analysis they used in their own design work, and in so doing laid the foundations of twentieth-century modernism.

10 Sir Arthur Liberty, interview in *The Daily Chronicle*, 21 February 1913, p. 7.

11 'The Liberty Art Movement', *British Warehouseman*, 1895, page unknown. Quoted in Alison Adburgham, *Liberty's: A Biography of a Shop*, op. cit., p. 73.

12 The cashmere fabrics initially imported by Liberty's did not wear very well. The yarn used in their Umritzur cashmere had a little more twist in it than the earlier cashmere and the fabric was slightly more tightly woven.

13 In weaving the warp threads pass through a sort of closed 'comb' known as a reed. After the weft thread from the shuttle passes through the open warp, it is pushed up or 'beaten' up by the reed. How close the weft thread gets to the previous thread depends in handloom weaving on the force the weaver uses. In a machine-made fabric that force is always consistent, resulting in a uniform regularity.

14 Tussar silk is a form of wild silk obtained from worms (*Antheraea mylitta* and *A. proylei*) that feed on the leaves of sal (*Shorea robusta*) and the genus *Terminalia*. *Bombyx mori*, the domesticated silk moth, prefers to feed on the leaves of the white mulberry (*Morus alba*) and does not seem to like the black mulberry (*M. nigra*), which is the species that was planted by James I.

15 Registering a design (at the Patent Office) was a form of copyright protection. The six designs registered by Wardle on behalf of Liberty's were 'Rangoon Poppy', 'Moultan May Blossom' (or 'Moultan Ray Flower'), 'Allahabad Marigold', 'Indian Diaper', 'Tanjore Lotus' and one unnamed design.

16 'The Influence of Aesthetics on English Society', *Sylvia's Home Journal*, Ward, Lock & Co., 1879, pp. 420–21.

17 Arthur Liberty, interview in the *Daily Chronicle*, 21 February 1913, p. 7.

18 Alison Adburgham, *Liberty's: A Biography of a Shop*, op. cit., p. 33.

19 From Annie Wakeman, *British and Mercantile Gazette*, quoted in Alison Adburgham, *Liberty's: A Biography of a Shop*, op. cit., pp. 56–7.

20 Arthur Liberty, interview in *The Daily Chronicle*, 21 February 1913, p. 7.

21 Merton Abbey mill is believed to have been established in about 1724 by Huguenots. It was used for open-air bleaching, and the flat water meadows, which had once belonged to the Abbey, were ideal for the purpose. Edmund Littler, who came from a family long established in the calico business, took over the mill in 1832. He began printing for Liberty's in 1876 or 1877, shortly after the shop was established, and it is said that by the 1890s his entire print production was for Liberty's. In 1904 Liberty's acquired his business and began a programme of investment, building new sheds, etc.

22 Morris had been using the services of Thomas Wardle, but he wrote to Jane, his wife, on 23 February 1881 complaining that 'Tom Wardle is a heap of trouble to us; nothing will he do right and he does write the longest winded letters containing lies of various kinds.' Morris's dissatisfaction with Wardle's dyeing techniques was one of the reasons he decided to go into manufacturing on his own account. Morris decided to move to Merton because he found the water of the River Wandle ideal for dyeing. Many of his fabrics used the indigo discharge method. The fabric was first dyed to a shade of blue using indigo; then the fabric was printed with a bleaching agent to remove the blue as the pattern required. Mordants (fixing agents) were then printed on the white parts and the fabric dyed a second time with madder, and again with yellow. The three superimposed colours gave green, purple or orange. The excess dye was washed away and then the colours were set by passing the fabrics through soapy water at nearly boiling point and drying them.

23 Alison Adburgham, *Liberty's: A Biography of a Shop*, op. cit., p. 40.

24 Monsieur Ursin Fortier is recorded as trading out of workshops in Lisle Street, Soho, in 1876 and was described as a basket maker. He moved to Carnaby Street, where he was described as a cane worker, and later to 55 Dean Street. In 1885 he is recorded at 65 Charlotte Street, Fitzroy Square. The 1901 census records an Ursin Fortier, who was born in Normandy in 1818, as a resident in a nursing home or hospital.

25 Aubrey Beardsley (1872–98) was greatly influenced by Japanese woodcuts and, following a visit to Paris, by the poster art of Henri de Toulouse-Lautrec. Beardsley was a controversial artist who was noted for his perverse images and grotesque erotica, inspired by Japanese shunga work. When his health rapidly declined (he had tuberculosis), he moved to the French Riviera. He died at Menton in March 1898.

26 Charles Holme (1848–1923) was born in Derby, where his father, George Holme, was a silk manufacturer. In 1871 he moved to Bradford and founded a woollen business. He was greatly influenced by a lecture on east Turkestan given by Robert Barkley Shaw (1839–79) to the Bradford Chamber of Commerce. In 1879 he set up Dresser & Holme at Farringdon Road in London, with a branch office in Kobe, Japan. In 1889 he bought William Morris's old home, the Red House, in Bexleyheath, Kent, for £2,900; he lived there until 1903. He retired from business in 1892 and founded *The Studio* magazine the following year with Gleeson White. In 1903 he went to live at Upton Grey, near Basingstoke in Hampshire, in a house designed by Ernest Newton with a garden designed by Gertrude Jekyll. (Restored in the 1990s, this is one of the few Jekyll gardens still in existence.)

27 Toni Huberman, Sonia Ashmore and Yasuko Suga (eds), *The Diary of Charles Holme's 1889 Visit to Japan and North America with Mrs Lasenby Liberty's Photographic Record*, Global Oriental, Folkestone 2008. Emma Liberty took something like a thousand photographs during the visit, which are now an invaluable record of Japan in the late 1880s.

28 Christopher Morley, *Dresser's Decorative Design*, Salisbury 2010, p. 21.

29 The Art Furnishers Alliance is often referred to as 'Dresser's Art Furnishers Alliance', but this is erroneous because Dresser owned only one share; he was probably contracted to work for the Alliance for a period of about three years. The Art Furnishers Alliance took a 21-year lease on premises in Bond Street on 14 June 1880. The company was incorporated on 12 April 1881 and opened for business in May 1881. The directors were George Hayton Chubb (of the safe makers), John Harrison (of the Linthorpe Art Pottery), Edward Cope (a lace manufacturer) and Sir Edward Lee (managing director of the Alexander Palace Co.). The company had a nominal capital of £50,000, divided as 10,000 shares of £5. Only 383 shares were issued, totalling £1,910. Shareholders included James Dixon, William Cooke (a wallpaper manufacturer who had £300 in shares) and Arthur Liberty. Although the rent on the Bond Street premises was £1,500 a year and the first year's turnover was £11,000, nevertheless the company went bankrupt. The stock was sold at auction on 24 August 1883 by Thurgood & Martin of Chancery Lane.

30 Dresser designed ceramics for the Linthorpe Art Pottery. This closed in 1889 and the moulds were acquired by Ault Pottery of Derbyshire. In 1893 they contracted Dresser to supply new designs and it was stipulated that these pieces were to be signed. He

designed glass for James Couper of Glasgow, who produced the 'Clutha' range sold by Liberty's. He also designed silver and plate for Hukin & Heath of Birmingham and for James Dixon & Sons of Sheffield in the late 1870s; brass and copper for Benham & Froud; and japanned metal for Richard Perry of Wolverhampton.

31 Adrian J. Tilbrook, *The Designs of Archibald Knox for Liberty & Co.*, Ornament Press, London 1976, p. 55.

32 The design is in the collection of the Nordiska Museum, Stockholm, Sweden.

33 Unlike Christopher Dresser, William Morris never designed domestic glass. He shared John Ruskin's view that 'all cut glass is barbarous'. This view probably arose from a misunderstanding about, and an ignorance of, the differences between English and Venetian glass, the latter being much admired by Ruskin. Venetian glass gains nothing from being cut, whereas English lead crystal does not fully reveal its prismatic glory until and unless it is cut.

34 A Liberty's catalogue of 1896, quoted in Stephen Calloway (ed.), *The House of Liberty: Masters of Style and Decoration*, Thames and Hudson, London 1992, p. 113.

35 Given that both types of 'Thebes' stools are based on examples held in the British Museum, it is surprising that the Patent Office granted a patent for them. However, one type of 'Thebes' stool, Patent No. 16673, had turning on the four lower legs with a leather seat attached by thonging. A design for a similar stool was produced by J.G. Grace, dated 1853 (the drawing is now in the collection of the RIBA), and Christopher Dresser and E.W. Godwin also produced designs for Egyptian-inspired furniture. The other Thebes stool had three legs and was also patented, No. 16674.

36 *Liberty Lamp*, quoted in Alison Adburgham, *Liberty's: A Biography of a Shop*, op. cit., p. 47.

37 Daryl Bennett, *Liberty's Furniture 1875–1915: The Birth of Modern Interior Design*, Antique Collectors' Club, Woodbridge 2012, page 101.

38 Alison Adburgham, *Liberty's: A Biography of a Shop*, op. cit., p. 47.

39 *The Citizen*, 10 December 1898.

THE ARCHITECTS AND THE DESIGNERS

1 Thomas James Cobden-Sanderson (1840–1922) was an artist and a bookbinder. He was born in Alnwick and attended many schools before going to Owen's College (now Manchester University) and then to Trinity College, Cambridge, where he studied law. He left without taking his degree and entered Lincoln's Inn to train as a barrister. He was a friend of William Morris and it was Morris's

wife, Jane, who persuaded him to take up bookbinding. He opened a workshop in 1884 and in 1900 he founded the Doves Press with Emery Walker.

2 The Luddites derive their name from Ned Ludd, a (probably mythical) Nottinghamshire youth who is said to have smashed two stocking frames in 1779, and the name has become synonymous with machine destroyers. The movement started in Nottinghamshire and spread to Yorkshire and Lancashire. Eventually Parliament made 'machine breaking' a capital offence. In the early years of the nineteenth century the government felt compelled to deploy the army and it is said that there were more troops fighting Luddites than Napoleon had in Spain and Portugal. Following the murder of the mill owner William Horsfall at Marsden, near Huddersfield, the authorities acted swiftly and with vigour. Horsfall's murderers were tried at York Assizes in 1813 and hanged. A number of subsequent trials were held, with harsh sentences being handed down, and these events effectively crushed the movement. The Pentrich Rising in Derbyshire in 1817 was its last gasp. The ringleaders were convicted of high treason and hanged in front of Derby Gaol.

3 Bedford Park, begun in 1876, was the first garden suburb, designed as a utopia for aspiring aesthetes. E.W. Godwin designed the first eighteen houses, but his designs were not well received, so he and the developer, Jonathan Carr, who had bought the 24 acres (9.7. hectares) in 1875, parted company. Norman Shaw completed the project and although his houses vary slightly they are basically solid examples of the Queen Anne Revival, a style in which he excelled.

4 William Morris was from a wealthy family. When he came of age in 1855 he came into an annual income of £700. The basis of the family fortune was stockbroking; his father was a partner in Sanderson & Co. In 1844, when Morris was ten, his father and uncle bought 304 £1 shares (out of a total of only 1,024 shares issued) in the new Devonshire Great Consolidated Copper Mining Co. The mine was soon found to have far richer deposits than first thought and within six months the shares Morris Snr owned were worth over £230,000, a huge fortune then. Morris Snr died in September 1847 and left an estate in excess of £60,000. In 1855 Morris inherited thirteen Devon Great Consolidated shares, which paid a dividend of £57 a share, giving Morris an income that year of £741. In 1866 the shares paid a dividend of £43 a share. Thereafter the company rapidly declined, paying no dividend in 1872 or ever again after that, and losing value until it was effectively worthless.

5 Walter Crane, *Ideals in Art: Papers Theoretical, Practical, Critical*, George Bell & Sons, London 1905, p. 22.

6 The Art Workers Guild was established in January 1884 at the Charing Cross Hotel by a group of five architects who were associated with the Arts and Crafts Movement: W.R. Lethaby, Edward Prior, Ernest Newton, Mervyn McCartney and Gerald C. Horsley, all of whom worked in the office of the architect Norman Shaw.

7 Cretonnes were originally a strong, white fabric with a hempen warp and a linen weft, but the term is comonly applied to any printed cotton (or linen) of a heavier weight than chintz, and unglazed. The word is said to derive from the village of Creton or Courtonne in Normandy. The fabric may also be named after the seventeenth-century French weaver Paul Creton (who is also said to have invented chintz).

8 William Judd, 'A Few Early Recollections', *Liberty Lamp*, March 1925, pp. 4–5.

9 *The Studio*, April 1893, pp. 232–3.

10 Ibid., p. 233.

11 The history of the company was chronicled in Jocelyn Morton, *Three Generations in a Family Textile Firm*, Routledge & Kegan Paul Ltd, London 1971.

12 Woven fabrics are produced on tappet, dobbie or jacquard looms. These terms refer to the machinery used to lift the warp threads. A tappet loom uses cams and is restricted to relatively uncomplicated patterns – simple twills and plain weaves. A dobbie loom is more versatile and can produce more elaborate patterns, but large complex patterns can only be produced by jacquard looms, which employ a system for lifting warp threads. The details of this system depend on how the machinery is set up. A double cloth is a compound fabric in which two component cloths are held together in one of a number of different ways. Sometimes it can be by centre-stitching, where a series of special threads lie between the two cloths and interlace alternately, binding them together. Another method is self-stitching, where threads from each cloth interchange with each face (back warp threads over a face weft thread). Yet another method is interchanging, where the two cloths are woven to interchange with each other; sometimes they are completely interchangeable, but in others it might be only warp or only weft threads.

13 Roderick Gradidge, *Dream Homes: The Edwardian Ideal*, Constable, London 1980, p. 180. An early version of the Blackwell plan was published in *The Studio* in January 1895, which might have influenced Voysey. Gradidge points out that comparing the 'two halls shows that they are only similar in the most superficial way, and Baillie Scott's is the more interesting in his use of space'. However, overall Gradidge found Broadleys the better house.

14 Adrian J. Tilbrook, *The Designs of Archibald Knox for Liberty & Co.*, op. cit., p. 37.

15 M. H. Baillie Scott, 'The Ideal Suburban House', *The Studio*, January 1895.

16 James D. Kornwolf, *M.H. Baillie Scott and the Arts and Crafts Movement*, Johns Hopkins Press, Baltimore and London 1972, p. 163.

17 John Parish White (1855–1917) was apprenticed to a builder in Biggleswade, Bedfordshire. He set up his own company at Dunmow in Essex, but by the mid-1880s he had acquired the Bedford firm of John Hull. In 1896 he established the Pyghtle Works (*pyghtle* being an Anglo-Saxon word meaning 'a small parcel of land, or small enclosure, or a croft'). How he met Baillie Scott is unknown. A number of catalogues were issued, all of which are now rare. The most important is probably *Furniture Made at the Pyghtle Works Bedford by John P. White Designed by M. H. Baillie Scott*, published in 1901, about 40 pages.

18 Lionel Lambourne, *Utopian Craftsmen: The Arts and Crafts Movement from the Cotswolds to Chicago*, Astragal Books, London 1980, p. 40.

19 Ibid, p. 47.

20 The exhibition was held 7–13 March 1903. Liberty's produced a catalogue, *Founding a National Industry: Irish Carpets*. The descriptions given in this catalogue, together with a number of contemporary photographs make it possible to identify some, but not all, of the carpets displayed.

21 *The Citizen*, 10 December 1898.

STILE LIBERTY: THE ART NOUVEAU MOVEMENT

1 Siegfried Bing was born in Hamburg in February 1838. He went to live in Paris in 1854 to manage a ceramics business belonging to part of the family. He lived in France for the rest of his life and became a French citizen in 1876. In 1873 he gained control of all the family's French businesses and established an import-export business, specializing in importing Japanese and Asian *objets d'art* while exporting French goods to Japan. The interiors of Maison de l'Art Nouveau were designed by Henry van de Velde and had stained glass from Tiffany's in New York. The gallery sold fabrics by William Morris, glass from Tiffany's and some goods from Liberty's. The fashion for Art Nouveau was short and Bing closed the gallery in 1904. He died the following year. He is often confusingly called 'Samuel' Bing, but Samuel Bing was actually his younger brother, Samuel Otto Bing (1850–1905). Siegfried's son, Marcel Bing (1875–1920), was a famous Art Nouveau jewellery designer.

2 The glass entrances for the stations at Porte Dauphine and Abbesses are the only original structures left. The rest are modern copies.

3 The term is drawn from a description of *Cyclamen*, a wall hanging produced by Hermann Obrist in 1894. It was described in *Pan* magazine as having 'sudden violent curves generated by the cracking of a whip': hence the term whiplash. Alastair Duncan, *Art Nouveau: World of Art*, Thames & Hudson, New York, 1994, pp. 27–8.

4 Charles Rennie Mackintosh (1868–1928) was not, it seems, one of Liberty's designers. Born in Glasgow, he became a partner in Honeyman and Keppie in 1907, but he resigned in 1913 and opened his own practice. This, however, proved to be unsuccessful. He moved to London, but the onset of war restricted building work and made life very difficult. He and his wife, Margaret MacDonald, lived briefly in the Suffolk village of Walberswick, where they painted (both were accomplished watercolour artists) and began designing textiles. With his Glaswegian accent and limp Mackintosh must have cut a rather peculiar figure and he was arrested as a suspected German spy after trying to repair a lamp at his coastal cottage. Letters from Hermann Muthesius and Joseph Olbrich (of the German Arts and Crafts Movement) seemed to be conclusive proof and he was brought before Southwold magistrates. After a discreet intervention by a figure in Whitehall he was instructed by the bench 'never to darken our coastline again'. The Mackintoshes were friends of Claud Lovat Fraser, who designed work for Liberty's, and it was almost certainly Fraser who introduced them to William Foxton, who in 1903 established the textile house of W. Fraser Ltd, regarded as one of the most innovative textile houses. Unfortunately all their papers were lost in an air raid in 1942. Fraser certainly printed some designs by the Mackintoshes, but whether or not these were retailed by Liberty's is unknown.

5 Insular art is a term (derived from the *insula*, the Latin for island) used to define art produced in the post-Roman period in the British Isles, also sometimes known as Hiberno-Saxon art. Britain and Ireland shared a largely common style that differed from that found in the rest of Europe during the period.

6 Adrian J. Tilbrook, *The Designs of Archibald Knox for Liberty & Co.*, op cit, p. 23.

7 *Jade Amulets: Historic Notes With Coloured Illustrations and Interpretations of the most Characteristic Forms*, Liberty & Co, London 1925, 33 pages.

8 Most associated with Matthew Boulton, Sheffield plate is basically a copper core sandwiched between two plates of silver (although it can be one plate of silver backed by copper), which are fused together with heat and thus the resulting product behaves as one. Because of this its surface is identical to that of solid silver, but gradually over time the silver surface wears away, allowing the copper core to show through.

9 The composition of English pewter was protected by the Worshipful Company of Pewterers. High-grade pewter was required to contain 94 per cent tin, the balance being made up of other metals, including lead. The finest grade, known as 'fine metal', which was used for tableware, was basically tin with about 1 per cent copper. The second grade, known as 'trifling metal' or 'trifle', used for hollow ware, contained copper and up to 4 per cent lead. Inferior pewter, known as 'lay metal' or 'ley metal' and used only for things which did not come into contact with food, could contain as much as 15 per cent lead.

10 Arthur L. Liberty, 'Pewter and the Revival of its Use', *Journal of the Society of Arts* 10 June 1904, pp. 626–44. The paper was read to the society on 17 May 1904.

11 Toynbee Hall was founded in 1883 and named in memory of the Oxford historian Arnold Toynbee. It provided a base where Oxford and Cambridge students lived as residential volunteers. Others known to have been associated with Toynbee include the Labour Prime Minister Clement Attlee; William Beveridge, the social reformer widely regarded as the author of the welfare state; and John Profumo, who devoted much of his time to the Hall after his resignation from the House of Commons.

12 Lionel Lambourne, *Utopian Craftsmen: The Arts and Crafts Movement from the Cotswolds to Chicago*, op. cit, p.126.

13 Ibid., p. 130.

14 C.R. Ashbee, *Should We Stop Teaching Art*, Batsford 1911.

15 Christopher Morley, *Dresser's Decorative Design*, op. cit, p. 62.

16 *The Studio*, volume 3, page 117.

17 Mario Amaya, *Art Nouveau*, Studio Vista, 1966.

18 The Keswick School of Industrial Art and the Newlyn Art Metal Industry were repoussé metalwork classes, established in 1884 and 1890. The Yattendon school was established in about 1890 by Mrs Waterhouse, wife of the architect Alfred Price Waterhouse. The school was active until 1914. Their products were featured in *The Studio* between 1895 and 1902. The Newlyn School lasted for about thirty years and the Keswick School finally closed in 1984.

19 Stephen Calloway (ed.), *The House of Liberty: Masters of Style and Decoration*, op. cit., p. 156.

MAKING ROOM: INTERIOR DECORATION

1 Alice McEwan, letter to the author 21 August 2013. Liberty's undertook the redecoration of the flat for Shaw in 1922. The work was just painting and maybe making some curtains, and was probably for Charlotte Shaw rather than Shaw himself. It has been suggested that Liberty's also worked at Shaw's Corner, but there is no evidence of this.

2 Alison Adburgham, *Liberty's: A Biography of a Shop*, op. cit., p. 97.

3 *Liberty Lamp*, April 1931, p. 25.

4 Quoted in Anne Sumner, *Tjolöholm: A Woman's Achievement*, Tjolöholm Foundation, Fjärås, Sweden 2001, p. 42.

5 The Swedish kronor formed part of the Scandinavian Monetary Union in 1873 with Norway and Denmark.

6 Liberty's to Mrs Blanche Dickson, 29 July 1902, Tjolöholm Foundation Archive.

7 Liberty's to Mrs Blanche Dickson, 5 January 1903, Tjolöholm Foundation Archive.

8 The design of the doorbell plate is mentioned in the correspondence (1 March 1904, with a quote of £7 10s.), but does not seem to appear in the surviving bills. It may be the work of W. Karlsson of Huddinge near Stockholm, who produced some of the decorative metalwork. Most of the fingerplates, light switches and power sockets were made by Liberty's and can be traced to the accounts that survive.

9 Liberty's to Mrs Blanche Dickson, 6 July 1901. This letter mentions Edward's, together with costings for various sizes of tiles. Whether these costings refer to bathroom tiles or to tiles used for the fireplaces is unclear. Liberty's Account, 30 May 1904, Tjolöholm Foundation Archive and Göteborgs Stad Fastighetskontoret.

10 Anne Sumner, *Tjolöholm*, op, cit., p. 89.

11 Liberty's to Mrs Blanche Dickson, 2 December 1902, Tjolöholm Foundation Archive.

12 Liberty's to Mrs Blanche Dickson, 3 May 1904 and 8 August 1904, Tjolöholm Foundation Archive.

TUDOR RENAISSANCE

1 John Llewellyn was a director of the company from 1898 until 1935.

2 HMS *Hindustan* was ordered in September 1819, had her keel laid in 1828 and was finally launched in 1841. She was an eighty-gun second-rate ship of the line, but became a training ship in 1868. She was renamed HMS *Fisgard III* in 1905 but became *Hindostan* again in 1920 before being sold in 1921. HMS *Impregnable* was launched in 1860 at Pembroke Dockyard as HMS *Howe*, named after Admiral Richard Howe. She was

renamed HMS *Bulwark* in 1885, and then HMS *Impregnable* in 1886, when she became a training ship. She was sold and broken up in 1921.

3 Nikolaus Pevsner and Bridget Cherry, *The Buildings of England, London Volume One: The Cities of London and Westminster*, Penguin Books, Harmondsworth 1973, p. 579.

4 Alison Adburgham, *Liberty's: A Biography of a Shop*, op. cit., p. 107.

5 Anon., *The Renaissance of Merton Abbey*, Liberty & Co, London n.d., p. 11.

6 By 1880 the business had been 'departmentalized'. The original departments were as follows: A, Carpets; B, Curios; C, Embroideries; D, Furniture; E, Miscellaneous; F, Porcelain; G, Silks. Later departments were: H, Costume; J, Silver and Jewellery; K, which seems to have just grown of its own accord.

7 Stephen Calloway (ed.), *The House of Liberty: Masters of Style and Decoration*, op. cit., p. 140. The request was made in October 1933.

8 The name of 'Tana' lawn is derived from Tana Lake in Ethiopia. The fabric was made from Ethiopian cotton and was originally devised by William Hayes Dorell, who was then the head cotton buyer.

9 Stephen Calloway (ed.), *The House of Liberty: Masters of Style and Decoration*, op. cit., p. 145.

10 Paul Poiret (1879–1944), the son of a cloth merchant, was born in Les Halles, then a poor neighbourhood of Paris, . His parents apprenticed him to an umbrella maker, but while still a teenager he took a collection of sketches to Madeleine Chéruit (died 1935), who promptly bought some of them. He sold sketches to many major couture houses and in 1896 was employed by Jacques Doucet (1853–1929); then he moved to the House of Worth, the grandest of all the Parisian fashion houses, before establishing his own house in 1903. In 1911 the magazine *Art et Décoration* published a set of photographs of Poiret's clothes by Edward Steichen, which are regarded as the first fashion photography shoot. Poiret enjoyed considerable success before the First World War, but afterwards he seemed to lose his way and his house went bankrupt. The arrangement with Liberty's was not a success and he became very poor, selling drawings to customers of Paris cafés. During the Second World War he drifted to the Riviera, cutting a sad figure wearing a suit he had fashioned from a beach peignoir and relying on any charitable soul to buy him lunch. He died in Paris in 1944 and would have had a pauper's funeral had it not been for the generosity of his friend Elsa Schiaparelli.

11 Martin Battersby, *The Decorative Twenties*, Studio Vista, London, 1969, p. 113. Poiret's fashion house went bankrupt in 1929, although *Harper's Bazaar* carried a report of his autumn collection and in 1930 mentioned the decorating business.

12 Alison Adburgham, *Liberty's: A Biography of a Shop*, op. cit., p. 95.

13 Cecil Beaton, *The Glass of Fashion*, Weidenfeld & Nicolson, London, 1954, p. 118.

14 Alison Adburgham, *Liberty's: A Biography of a Shop*, op. cit., p. 119.

15 Ibid., p. 102.

A BRAVE NEW WORLD

1 The Utility Furniture Advisory Committee was set up in 1942 by the President of the Board of Trade, Hugh Dalton, and drew heavily on advice from Sir Gordon Russell, Ernest Clench, Herman Lebus and John Gloag. The committee produced the *Utility Furniture Catalogue* in 1943.

2 Alison Adburgham, *Liberty's: A Biography of a Shop*, op. cit., p. 123.

3 Harold Blackmore was chairman from 1936 to 1950 and had been a director since 1900. Ivor Stewart-Liberty was appointed a director in 1916 and was chairman from 1950 to 1952. He was succeeded by his son, Arthur Stewart-Liberty, who remained chairman until his own death in 1990. Arthur Stewart-Liberty had started to work for the company just before the Second World War, and returned to the company after active service. He started to learn about retailing by doing a window-dressing course. He was just thirty-six when he succeeded his father.

4 Press release, March 1966, Westminster Archives, Ref 788/96(21).

5 The Fontana sisters – Giovanna (1915–2004), Micol (b. 1913) and Zoe (1911–79) – founded their fashion house in Rome in 1943 with capital of just 500 lire.

6 Professor Bernard Nevill, interview with staff, Victoria and Albert Museum, April 2006.

7 Sir Terence Conran, interview with the author, 4 August 2008. Conran originally trained as a textile designer at the Central School of Art and Design. He worked in the Festival of Britain in 1951 and for Dennis Lennon's architectural company. He started his own design company in 1956 with the Summa furniture range and designed a shop for Mary Quant. In 1964 he opened Habitat in Chelsea, which was merged with British Home Stores in 1986 to form Storehouse plc.

8 Anna Buruma, *Liberty and Co. in the Fifties and Sixties: A Taste for Design*, Antique Collectors' Club, Woodbridge 2009, page 56.

9 James Curran, letter to the author, 29 July 2013. Geoffrey Curran (1911–68) was born in Devon. He started a printing company in Cornwall and then worked in advertising in London before the Second World War. After the war he established Fen Pottery, which he ran for a number of years before selling the company to a Mr de Grey, who promptly died. His son continued to run the pottery, although not very successfully and it eventually closed.

10 Tricia Jameson, interview with the author, 12 July 2013. Mrs Jameson is Geoffrey Curran's daughter. She remembers that her father would employ potters from Stoke-on-Trent and although he could pot himself his role gradually became more marketing and design.

11 Hendrik de Leeuw was in Paris when the Germans invaded The Netherlands and was unable to return home. He fled from France (via England and Portugal) and became a refugee in the United States.

APPENDIX

DESIGNERS, MANUFACTURERS AND SUPPLIERS KNOWN TO HAVE SUPPLIED LIBERTY'S

This catalogue is compiled from a wide variety of sources and is by no means exhaustive. Any attempt to create such a catalogue is fraught with difficulties. Liberty's would, particularly in the earlier years, commission or buy designs from designers, and then have them manufactured: these were exclusive designs. They would also buy in products from various manufacturers, many of whom employed noted designers, whose work was thus sold by Liberty's; this was particularly common after the Second World War.

Many of the designers and manufacturers listed here are well known, and well known for their work for Liberty's, but many are not. Where the designer or manufacturer is less well known, a reference to the source has been given.

The following abbreviations are used (for full details, see Bibliography):

Buruma: Anna Buruma, *Liberty and Co.
    in the Fifties and Sixties*
Calloway: Stephen Calloway (ed.),
    The House of Liberty
LD: Barbara Morris, *Liberty Design*
LS: Mervyn Levy, *Liberty Style:
    The Classic Years 1898–1910*
V&A: Victoria and Albert Museum,
    Liberty's 1875–1975
WA: Westminster City Archives Centre

Aalto, Alvar (1898–1976)
Finnish architect and designer much influenced by classicism and amongst the first to design in the style termed Nordic Classicism, which gradually evolved into a form of modernism. He designed furniture, some of which was sold by Liberty's.
Ref. Calloway

Albeck, Pat (1930–)
Trained at the College of Arts and Crafts in Hull and at the Royal College of Arts. Designed fabrics in the 1950s.
Ref. V&A G7

Aldin, Cecil Charles Windsor (1870–1935)
An artist and illustrator who is best known for his sketches and paintings of rural life, sports and animals. His first published works appeared in *The Building News* in 1890. He designed nursery wallpapers for Liberty's in 1898. 'Mother Duck' and 'Dog and Cock' were his designs.
Ref. LD

Aller Vale Pottery
Formed in 1865 on the edge of the village of Kingskerswell, near Newton Abbot, Devon, although a pottery is thought to have existed on the site in medieval times. In 1868 it was taken over by John Phillips (1835–97), a clay merchant from Newton Abbot. It was later owned by Hexter, Humpherson & Co. Liberty's were a stockist between 1887 and 1901.
Ref. LS

Arabia Pottery
Founded in 1873 by the Swedish company Rörstrand near Helsinki, Finland. The company passed into Finnish hands during the First World War and by 1939 was the largest porcelain producer in Europe. In the 1950s Arabia were famous for their Scandinavian-designed wares by designers such as Kaj Franck and Anja Juwrikkola. Liberty's stocked their wares in the 1950s.
Ref. V&A G28

Ault & Co.
Of Midland Road, Swadlincote, Derbyshire. Founded in 1887 by William Ault, who created his own style of pottery, which bore the mark 'Ault Faience'. He opened a London showroom and exhibited widely. His designs, often with artwork by his daughters Clarissa and Gertrude, were derived from designs developed by the Linthorpe Art Pottery in Yorkshire.

R.B. Ayers Upholstery Ltd
Upholstery company, which went into liquidation in 1971. Supplied upholstered furniture in the 1960s.
Ref. WA 1166/235

Baillie-Scott, M.H. (1865–1945)
One of the major figures of the Arts and Crafts Movement. An architect by training, he was a prolific designer of all manner of items, most notably textiles, wallpapers and furniture. He designed furniture for J.P. White of Bedford.

G.P. and J. Baker Ltd
Founded in 1884 by George Percival and James Baker, who were the sons of George Baker (1822–??), who had been a gardener at the British Embassy in Therapia near Constantinople. He began exporting Turkish goods, establishing a London warehouse. He sent his two sons to England, where they set up their own company and bought the Swaisland Fabric Printing Company, acquiring their extensive archive, dating back to the eighteenth century. Baker's produced many fabrics for Liberty's as well as supplying Liberty's with their own-label designs by many celebrated names of the period.
Ref. V&A, D30, 32, 35, 261

Baker, Oliver (1856–1939)
Born in Birmingham, Baker was the son of the artist Samuel Henry Baker (1824–1909),

noted for his landscapes. He became an artist and trained in his father's studio, and was also an etcher, designer and silversmith. He is best remembered for his contribution to the 'Cymric' silverware range.
Ref. V&A

Bankart, George Percy (1866–1929)
Bankart was articled to the Midlands Arts and Crafts architect Isaac Barradale, and later worked for various architects in London. He had met Ernest Gimson (1864–1919). His name frequently occurs in relation to plasterwork and he became one of the leading exponents of the art, his work appearing frequently in *The Studio Yearbook of Decorative Art*. He was also noted for his decorative leadwork. He published a number of books on plasterwork.

David Barbour & Co.
Textile manufacturers. Supplied Liberty's c.1900.
Ref. V&A, D260

Battersby, Martin (1914–82)
George Martin Battersby was a theatrical set decorator and *trompe l'oeil* artist. An expert on Art Nouveau, he wrote extensively on the topic. Originally trained as a draughtsman, he later worked at Liberty's before studying acting at RADA, but he was more interested in set design than treading the boards. He designed dress fabrics in the 1960s.

Bechert, E.
Textile designs in the 1950s.
Ref. Buruma

Benson, William Arthur Smith (1854–1924)
An English architect and designer who founded a workshop in order to manufacture metalwork in 1880 and later, in 1887, opened a shop in Bond Street, London. He was a founding member of the Art Workers Guild. From 1896 he directed the furniture department at Morris and Co. He also created designs intended for mass production. Liberty's seem to have retailed some of his metalwork.

Berge, T.
Designed glass for Almeric Walter of Nancy, France, in around 1905.
Ref. V&A, D253

H.J. Berry & Sons Ltd
Famous furniture manufacturer at Kirk Mills, Chipping, Preston, Lancashire, established in 1840. They supplied the Bowland range of chairs and tables to Liberty's in 1953.
Ref. WA 1166/231

William Birch Ltd
A noted furniture designer and manufacturer, based in High Wycombe. According to family tradition the Birch

family began chair-making in the 1840s, although the company first appeared in trade directories in 1853. William Birch is thought to have begun manufacturing in the mid-1890s and was a major supplier of Liberty's. In 1901 he moved to larger premises and was joined by a number of well-known designers, including George Whitehead and Edward G. Punnett (q.v.). In the 1950s the company made a range called Birchcraft. The factory was taken over by E. Gomme Ltd in 1954 (founded by Ebenezer Gomme, 1858–1931) and is best remembered today as the manufacturers of G-Plan furniture.

Bojesen, Kay (1886–1958)
Danish silversmith and designer. He worked for Georg Jensen before starting in business on his own. His early work was clearly Art Nouveau in style, while his later work is simpler and more functional. In 1922 he began designing wooden toys, which were very popular. His cutlery design, exhibited at the Milan Triennale in 1951, won the Grand Prix – hence its name.
Ref. Calloway

Bradley, Martin (1931–)
Designed textiles in the 1950s.
Ref. Buruma

C.H. Brannam Ltd
Thomas Backway Brannam (1815–97) acquired the lease to a pottery in North Walk, Barnstaple in Devon, in 1848, which had formerly belonged to John Rendell, who also owned a second pottery in Litchdon Street. In 1853 Brannam (or 'Brannan') also acquired those premises. Brannam was very successful at producing sgraffito pottery (the term is derived from the Italian *graffiare*, meaning 'to scratch'). In 1881 his son, Charles Hubert Brannam (1855–1937), took over the pottery and developed the business, receiving an order from the Queen in 1885. The following year he registered Royal Barum Ware, which was extremely successful. Although he was a skilled potter, C.H. Brannam employed two talented designers, John Dewdney and William Baron, and pots were often marked with their initials. Liberty's became the pottery's sole agents in 1882 and remained so until 1914; they continued to stock Brannam's pottery until the late 1930s.

Bretby Art Pottery
Founded by Henry Tooth and William Ault in 1882, the pottery – in Woodville, Derbyshire – registered the famous 'Sunburst' mark in 1884. The partnership was of short duration and was dissolved in 1887. The company was renamed Tooth and Co. and then used a new mark of 'Bretby'. Liberty's *Yule-Tide Gifts* catalogue of 1888 contained a number of Bretby designs. Tooth's new partner, John Downing Wragg, resigned in 1912, and a new company was formed, H. Tooth & Co. Ltd.

Henry's son, William, sold the business in 1932 and the company continued until the 1990s.

Peter Brunn Workshop
Supplied furniture to Liberty's in the 1950s.
Ref. Calloway

Buckley, E.J.
Manufacturer of printed textiles in Manchester. Supplied Liberty's in the 1890s.
Ref. V&A, D13

Butterfield, Lindsay P. (1869–1948)
Noted textile designer who worked freelance and supplied Liberty's with many designs. He also supplied designs to the Silver Studio.

Campbell, Sarah
Together with her sister, Susan Collier, she founded Collier Campbell in 1979. Designed furnishing fabrics for Liberty's in the 1970s.

Giuseppe Cantagalli & Sons
The family pottery in Florence, taken over by the sons of Giuseppe Cantagalli – Ulisse and Romeo – in 1878, was noted for their majolica ware. Liberty's sold their glazed earthenware with decoration in bronze lustres and blues. They were probably introduced to Liberty's by William de Morgan (1839–1917), who spent the winters in Florence.

Carter, Stabler & Adams Ltd
Originally founded as Carter's Industrial Tile Manufactory. Jesse Carter, together with the designers Harold Stabler and Phoebie Stabler, was joined by the potters John Adams and Truda Adams (Truda Carter) to form the company in the 1920s. They produced Art Deco pottery, and the company produced much of the ceramic tiling used on London Underground stations built in the 1930s. It became Poole Pottery and produced lines such as 'Twintone'. Liberty's were a stockist.
Ref. V&A, F27

Cassina
The Amedeo Cassina company was founded by Cesare and Umberto Cassina in 1927 at Meda, Brianza, in northern Italy. They specialize in producing high-quality furniture. In 1964 they acquired the rights to Le Corbusier designs and they have subsequently acquired rights to Bauhaus, Gerrit Rietveld, Lloyd Wright and Mackintosh.
Ref. V&A, G1

Casson, Michael (1925–2003)
Potter and contributor to the Liberty's Centenary Exhibition in 1975.
Ref. V&A

Clarke, Nigel
Painted silks. Contributor to the Liberty's Centenary Exhibition in 1975.
Ref. V&A

Cliff, Clarice (1899–1972)
One of the most recognizable names in twentieth-century ceramics and particularly famous for her Art Deco designs. At seventeen she joined A.J. Wilkinson's Royal Staffordshire Pottery as a lithographer. She studied at evening classes at the Burslem School of Art and at the Royal College of Art in 1927. She returned to Wilkinson's and set up a small studio in the Newport Pottery, which they owned. In 1930 she became art director. The Newport Pottery produced 'Liberty Band' pattern, which was produced in the early 1930s, as part of the 'Bizarre' range.

Collier, Susan (1938–2011)
Both she and her sister, Sarah Campbell (q.v.), worked in the Liberty design studio. Susan Collier became design consultant in 1971. In 1979 she and her sister founded Collier Campbell

Collis, Charles
Worked as a designer and decorator at the Della Robbia Pottery.
Ref. V&A, C29

Compton Pottery
Founded in 1899 by Mary Fraser-Tytler (Mrs G.F. Watts), wife of the painter George Frederic Watts, at Compton in Surrey and known as the Compton Potters' Arts Guild. The pottery's output was extensive, but it is famous for innovative terracotta garden ornaments, which it began to produce at the suggestion of Gertrude Jekyll, who contributed some designs. Mostly the designs were Arts and Crafts and latterly Art Nouveau in style, many with Celtic-inspired decoration and some designed by Archibald Knox. The pottery continued to produce until 1954

Messrs Connell & Co.
Of Cheapside, London. Connell's acquired most of Archibald Knox's pewter designs from Liberty's in about 1909/10 and attempted to compete with their Tudric range.

Conran, Terence (b. 1931)
Designer of furniture and fabrics who is perhaps better known as the founder of Habitat. He opened the first Habitat shop in Chelsea in 1964.
Ref. Buruma

Cooper, Billy McCarty
See McCarty.

Corrieri, Gina
Supplied textile designs in the 1950s.
Ref. Buruma

Couldridge, Alan
Noted milliner and contributor to the Liberty's Centenary Exhibition in 1975.
Ref. V&A

James Couper & Sons
Founded by James Couper in 1950 as the City Flint Glassworks in Kyle Street, Glasgow. The factory produced a wide

variety of decorative glassware and industrial glass. They are most famous for their production of Christopher Dresser's 'Clutha' glass. The factory closed in 1922.

Crane, Walter (1845–1915)
Born in Liverpool, Crane was the second son of the portrait painter Thomas Crane. He was apprenticed to the wood-engraver W.J. Linton and subsequently did engravings of works by Rossetti and Millais. A close associate of William Morris, he was greatly influenced by his politics. Crane designed fabrics for Liberty's in the 1890s.

Craythorn, H.C. (1881–1949)
A brilliant silversmith and designer who worked for W.H. Haseler Ltd (q.v.) for more than forty years. It was Craythorn who worked most of Knox's silver designs.

Curran, Geoffrey P. (1911–68)
Former Royal Air Force officer, who after service during the Second World War studied pottery at Leicester College of Art, and then established the Fen Pottery at Godmanchester, in Huntingdonshire, in about 1947. Liberty's were enormously helpful and encouraging and sold his pottery, as did Heal's.

Cuzner, Bernard (1877–1956)
Born in Alcester in Warwickshire, Cuzner initially trained as a watchmaker, but following an interest in silversmithing he took evening classes in Redditch and then at the Victoria Street School of Jewellery and Silversmithing in Birmingham. He subsequently began to teach at the school and started designing for W.H. Haseler (q.v.) and Liberty's. From 1910 until 1942 he was head of metalwork at the Birmingham School of Art.

Day, Désirée Lucienne (1917–2010)
Born in Coulsdon in Surrey (née Conradi), she became a student at the Croydon School of Art, where she discovered a love for textiles, particularly printed textiles. She went on to study at the Royal College of Art. She became a very successful industrial designer, producing not only fabrics but also carpets. She collaborated with Heal's for more than twenty years. In 1942 she married the furniture designer Robin Day.

Della Robbia Pottery
The factory in Birkenhead, Merseyside, had a brief life, from 1894 to 1906. It was founded by Harold Steward Rathbone (1858–1929) and Conrad Gustave d'Huc Dressler (1856–1940). Rathbone had been a pupil of the artist Ford Madox Brown and was the son of a wealthy local businessman. Dressler, by contrast, was a sculptor and potter. He also invented the continuous firing tunnel kiln, which revolutionised the kiln firing process. Dressler left in 1897 to establish his own pottery, the Medmenham Pottery in Buckinghamshire. In early 1894 Giovanni

Carlo Valentino Manzoni (1855–1910) joined, but he left a year later to establish his own pottery, the Minerva Art Ware Manufacturers in Hanley, Staffordshire. He returned in June 1898 and remained until the pottery closed.

Lizzie Derriey Design Studio
The Lizzie Derriey Design Studio in Paris was a textile and wallpaper design house, active from 1928 until 1994. The studio produced designs for some of the best couture houses and supplied Liberty's with many designs in the 1950s. The studio was located on rue du Faubourg, the heart of the Parisian fashion world. At any one time twenty-five designers worked at the studio, which appears to have been a design co-operative. Little is known about Lizzie Derriey and details of the design studio are sketchy.

Dickson of Ipswich
Furniture manufacturer. Supplied c.1963.
Ref. WA 1166/225

Dinzl, Contessa Friedlinde di Colbertaldo
Well-known and established freelance designer based in Rome. Designed for companies like Edinburgh Weavers, Sanderson's and Warner's.

Dresser, Christopher (1834–1904)
Probably the finest industrial designer of the Victorian period and a direct contemporary of William Morris. He was a close friend of Sir Arthur Liberty. The shop stocked Dresser's Clutha glass and other items of his design.

Duresta Upholstery Ltd
Well-known manufacturer of upholstered furniture. Supplier to Liberty's in the 1980s.
Ref. WA 1166/238

Durkin, Hilda
Prolific designer of textiles during the 1950s.

J.C. Edwards (Ruabon) Ltd,
Tile and brick manufacturers of Ruabon, Denbighshire, Wales. Mentioned in correspondence 1901. Supplier of tiles.
Ref. Tjolöholm Archive

Farnham Potteries
Farnham in Surrey had been a major pottery centre from Roman times and in Tudor times provided a substantial part of the pottery needs of London. In 1872 the Farnham Pottery was owned by Absalom Harris and was making utility items such as tiles and drainpipes. In the early 1880s Harris was asked to copy a French vase and after some trial and error he produced one, using a lead glaze to which he added copper oxide. This gave a wonderful green colour and the resulting range was known as 'Green Ware'. Liberty's were a major stockist. Later the artist William Herbert Allen (1863–1943) designed for Farnham Potteries until his death.

Farr, Colleen
Arthur Stewart-Liberty saw Farr's work at the Royal College of Art diploma show and invited her to contact him. She worked for a year for Roosen Silks and then for a brief period as a freelance textile designer, but in the early 1950s (1952 or 1953) she set up a design studio at Liberty's. She remained its head until 1962. Farr was admired for her skill as a designer and her sharp eye for commercial designs. Her fabrics were used extensively by the fashion designer Jean Muir. Farr left Liberty's in 1962 and started teaching at the Central School of Art and Design, eventually becoming head of the textile department.

Farr, Gillian
Colleen Farr's sister, who trained at the Harrow School of Art. She worked in the Liberty's design studio with Colleen and went on to supply designs to Conran Fabrics.

Fen Pottery
See Curran, Geoffrey.

Few, Alice Dorothy
An American student of Lindsay Butterfield. Liberty's bought two of her designs ('Bird & Wisteria' and 'Chinese Panel') in 1926.
Ref. LD

Finmar Ltd
A major importer of Scandinavian furniture from 1934 until 1965. Before the Second World War Finmar imported plywood furniture by Alvar Aalto. However, after the war the company was sold to Paul Stemann, who was Danish. The company expanded under his direction, importing Danish factory-made versions of Windsor chairs that complied with the Utility regulations. They sold furniture not only to Liberty's but also to other stores, including Heal's.

Fletcher, Mr
Designed 'Damasque Wallpaper' for Liberty's wallpaper department in 1887. This was supposed to resemble silken brocades.
Ref. LD.

Foley Pottery
See Wileman & Co.
Ref. V&A

Fornasetti, Piero (1913–88)
Italian painter, sculptor, interior decorator and engraver, who lived most of his life in Milan, where he attended the Brera Art Academy in the 1930s. Liberty's retailed some of his furniture in the late 1950s and 1960s.

Forsyth, Gordon M. (1879–1952)
Studied at the Royal College of Art before becoming art director at Minton Hollins in Stoke-on-Trent, Staffordshire. Subsequently he took the same position at Pilkington Tile and Pottery (Pilkington's Royal Lancastrian Pottery) near Manchester. From 1921 he did freelance designing for A.E. Gray & Co. Ltd. Forsyth is famous for his sumptuous lustre work at Pilkington's, where he used medieval

motifs, sailing boats, lions and other heraldic symbols. The ceramic designer Susie Cooper also worked at Gray's Pottery, leaving in 1929.
Ref. V&A, D229

Fortescue-Brickdale, Eleanor (1871–1945)
Artist who trained at the Crystal Palace School of Art. She exhibited regularly at the Royal Academy and became a teacher at John Byam Shaw's art school, which he founded in 1911. She was a designer and enamel painter for Liberty's, specialising in the depiction of figures in landscapes.
Ref. LS

Fortier, Ursin (1818–1902?)
Responsible for making much of Liberty's bamboo furniture in the 1880s.

Franck, Kaj (1911–89)
A leading Finnish designer. He was artistic director of the Wärtsilä Group (now the Littala Group), but he is better known as a teacher of several generations of professional designers. He is noted for his glass designs.
Ref. Calloway

Fraser, Claud Lovat (1890–1921)
Studied at the Westminster School of Art, where one of his tutors was Walter Sickert. After the First World War he produced the designs for a production of Shakespeare's *As You Like It* in Stratford-upon-Avon and later for a production of John Gay's *The Beggar's Opera*. He became friendly with the artist Paul Nash and died while on holiday with the Nash family. Liberty's produced a dress fabric in 1973 based on one of Lovat's designs.

The Furniture Industries Ltd
Founded in the late 1950s in Princes Risborough, Buckinghamshire. Now part of Ercol Furniture Ltd.
Ref. Calloway

Gariboldi, Giovanni (1908–71)
Designed tableware for Richard-Ginori (q.v.). He also designed furniture.
Ref. V&A, G26

Gaskin, Arthur (1862–1928) and Georgie (1868–1934)
Arthur Gaskin was an illustrator, painter, teacher and most notably designer of jewellery and enamelwork. He and his wife, Georgie (also a jewellery designer), were both members of the Birmingham School).
Refs. LD; LS; V&A, D156

Gibbings, Terence Harold Robsjohn (1905–76)
Having studied architecture at London University, he worked for the Widdicomb Furniture Company in Grand Rapids, Michigan, from 1943 to 1956. In 1960 he met Susan and Eleftherios Sardis, Greek cabinetmakers, and together they created the Klismos range of furniture. Liberty's

retailed their furniture, all of which was inspired by that of Ancient Greece, in 1961-3. Gibbings later worked as designer to the ship owner Aristotle Onassis.
Ref. V&A

Ginori
See Richard-Ginori.

Godwin, E.W. (1833–86)
Architect, theatre critic and a leading member of the Aesthetic Movement. Appointed dress consultant to Liberty's in 1884.

Gouda
Gouda in Arnhem, The Netherlands, was famous for pottery. Its Breda Ware was produced exclusively for Liberty's and was manufactured by Plateelbakkerij Zuid-Holland, or PZH for short, which had been established in 1898.

Groag, Jacqueline (1903–86)
Born in Czechoslovakia, she studied textile design under Josef Hofmann in Vienna during the 1920s. Subsequently she designed textiles for the Wiener Werkstatte in Vienna and designed for many Parisian fashion houses such as Chanel. She came to England in 1939 and Liberty's bought designs from her in the 1950s.

Gustavsberg
Swedish ceramic manufacturer founded in 1826, which continued until 1993. In the nineteenth century the factory was noted for its English-style creamware. In 1917 the potter and artist Wilhelm Kåge (1889–1960), who had studied under Henri Matisse, joined, later becoming artistic director. He left in 1949 and was succeeded by Stig Lindberg.
Ref. Calloway

Guyatt, Richard (1914–2007)
The youngest ever professor at the Royal College of Art when appointed in 1948. He acted as a consultant designer for Wedgwood, and Liberty's commissioned a Lemonade Set, which he designed and which was made by Wedgwood.
Ref. V&A, G25

Fritz Hansen
Furniture manufacturer in Allerod, Denmark, established in 1872, which produced works by Arne Jacobsen, Poul Kjaerholm, Hans J. Wegner and Piet Hein.
Ref. V&A, G2

Harford, Ronald
Designed furniture in conjunction with Henry Long.
Ref. Calloway P191.

A. Harris & Son
See Farnham Potteries.
Ref. V&A, C28

H. Harris (Textiles) Ltd
Fabric wholesalers who supplied tapestries, brocades and damask fabrics to Liberty's in the 1970s.
Ref. WA 1166/241

W.H. Haseler
Of 16-26 Hylton Street, Birmingham. Founded in 1870 by Willaim Hair Haseler. In 1898, the firm went into partnership with Liberty's as Liberty and Co. (Cymric) Ltd. Together they launched the 'Cymric' silver range. The partnership was dissolved in 1926.

Hassell, John (1868–1948)
Born in Walmer in Kent, Hassall is famous as an illustrator. He designed nursery wallpapers.

Havinden, Ashley (1903–73)
Art director at W.S. Crawford Ltd, one of London's top advertising agents, he designed packaging for Liberty's perfumes.

Haward, Sidney
A friend of Arthur Liberty, he established the Haward Studio in Kensington, which later moved to Twickenham.
Ref. *The Studio Yearbook of Decorative Art 1911*, p. 129, design for cretonne

Hawes & Murray (Upholstery) Ltd
Supplier of upholstered furniture, c.1955. The company, which was at 69 Shrubland Road, London E8, was liquidated in 1965.
Ref. WA 1166/239

W.W. Hawkins
Cabinetmakers in Bond Street, Ipswich. Their design for a bedside cabinet survives, dating from the early 1960s.
Ref. WA 1166/232

Heaton, Butler and Bayne
Stained glass manufacturers from 1855.

Heaton, Clement John (1861–1940)
A noted designer of stained glass and a partner in Heaton, Butler and Bayne, he left in 1885 to found his own company, Heaton's Cloisonné Mosaics Ltd, in order to manufacture cloisonné enamels. He designed and manufactured cloisonné enamel for Liberty's.

Heaton's Cloisonné Mosaics Ltd
See Heaton, Clement John.

Hexter, Humpherson & Co.
Owned Aller Vale Pottery (q.v.).

S. Hille & Co.
Founded by Salamon Hille, a Russian émigré, to renovate and to reproduce eighteenth-century furniture. Later his daughter Ray joined the business and started to produce furniture to original designs. Liberty's sold these designs in the 1950s and 1960s. S. Hille & Co. produced designs by Robin Day, which were also sold by Liberty's.

Hirokage, Tomimatsu
Designed decorated fans sold by Liberty's; there is an example in the Victoria & Albert Museum. Other artists who designed fans included Sawada Rosui, Masuda Tetsu and Kamei Tadsu.
Ref. V&A, B28

H.K. Furniture
Founded by Howard Keith (Hans Krebs, formerly of Berlin) in 1930. His work was innovative and featured in many magazines such as *Design Journal*. His products were stocked by many shops, including Liberty's and Heal's.

Home Arts and Industries Association
Founded in 1883, with Lord Brownlow as president and Walter Besant (1836–1901) as treasurer. A leading member was Mary Fraser Tytler of Compton Pottery (q.v.). The Home Art and Industries Association helped market the works of amateur craftsmen, and Liberty's were one of their markets.
Ref. LD

Jacobsen, Arne (1902–71)
Danish architect and designer who was greatly influenced by the designers Charles and Ray Eames, and also Ernesto Rogers, the Italian architect and design historian. Jacobsen is noted for his furniture, which Liberty's retailed.

Jarvis, Gwenfred
Designed a number of fabrics for Liberty's in the 1950s and 1960s.
Ref. Buruma

Jones, A.E. (1879–1954)
Silversmith and designer who trained at the Birmingham School of Art and was also a member of the Birmingham Guild of Handicraft. He founded A.E. Jones & Co. in 1902 and in 1905 acquired Jesson & Birkett, who owned the trademark 'St. Dunstan'. Subsequently he collaborated with Howson Taylor, whose father owned the Ruskin Pottery. He is best known for silver, but also produced work in bronze, copper and brass.

Juhl, Finn (1912–89)
Danish architect, interior designer and industrial designer who was one of the leading figures in the creation of the 'Danish design' movement in the late 1940s. He is most famous for his furniture designs, which were regarded as radical.
Ref. Calloway, p. 192

Juwrikkola, Anja (1923–)
Finnish sculptor and designer who created designs for the Arabia Pottery (q.v.).
Ref. V&A, G28

Kaipiainen, Birger (1915–88)
Designed for the Arabia Pottery (q.v.). Contributor to the Liberty's Centenary Exhibition in 1975.
Ref. V&A

Kaj, Franck (1911–89)
One of the leading figures in Finnish design from 1940 until his death. He was artistic director of the Wärtsilä Group, which later became Hackman plc and is now Littala Group.
Ref. V&A, G28

J.P. Kayser Sohn, Krefeld, Germany
Founded by Jean Kayser in Krefeld in 1862. His son, Engelbert Kayser, opened a design workshop in 1894 in Cologne with the designers Hugo Levin, Karl Geyer, Hermann Fauser, Karl Berghof and Johann C. Kroner. They created over 800 different designs for pewter ware (the designs were numbered from 4,000 to 4,999), which were mass-produced until around 1925.

Keith, Howard B.
See H.K. Furniture.

Kelly, G. and A.
Of 2 Grafton Mews, London, W1. Furniture designs dated 19 February 1965 survive.
Ref. WA 1166/237

Kidd, William
Designed bold printed cotton cushion covers and frieze wallpapers for use in children's nurseries. Active c.1900.
Ref. LD

Kientz, Suzanne
Artist who designed textiles in the 1950s.
Ref. Buruma

King, Jessie M. (1875–1949)
Noted illustrator of children's books. She designed jewellery and fabrics and also painted pottery. A member of the Glasgow School. Married to the furniture designer E.A. Taylor.

Kinkokan
Porcelain manufactured in Kyoto, Japan, in the early years of the twentieth century.
Ref. V&A, B30

Knight-Gregson
Supplied 'Beiderbecke' dress fabric, produced in 1966.

Knox, Archibald (1864–1933)
Probably one of the most famous designers to produce work for Liberty's. Renowned for his Celtic-inspired design, he made a major contribution to the jewellery, silver and pewter produced in the early years of the twentieth century.

Komai of Kyoto
Sword-maker and metalworker. Liberty's imported his work in the late nineteenth century.
Ref. LD

Konoike of Yokohama
Liberty's imported his silver ware.
Ref. LD

Kydd, William (1864–1936)
Worked for the wallpaper manufacturer Hayward & Son before establishing his own company in 1891. In the early years he designed most of the papers, which were retailed by many shops including Liberty's.
Ref. V&A, D262, 263

Lancastrian Pottery
See Pilkington Lancastrian Pottery.
Ref. V&A

Landberg, Nils (1927–72)
Swedish designer who produced designs for Orrefors Glass (q.v.).
Ref. V&A, G31

Larcombe, Ethel (1876–1940)
Artist who designed a series of postcards issued by Liberty's.
Ref. V&A, D268

Läuger, Max (1864–1952)
German painter, architect, sculptor and ceramist who studied painting and interior design at Karlsrühe and worked at the potteries in Kandern before establishing his own pottery in 1895. He exhibited his work in Paris and at the St Louis Exposition of 1904. He was co-founder of the Deutscher Werkbund in 1907. Liberty's were the first to import his work.

Arthur Lee & Son Ltd
Founded by Arthur H. Lee in the mid-1880s in Bolton, Lancashire, before moving to Warrington, Cheshire, in 1888 and subsequently to Birkenhead, Merseyside, in 1908. Arthur Lee developed methods of weaving figured 'tapestries' on jacquard looms, supplementing the restricted number of weft colours (constrained by the number of shuttle boxes on power looms) with printing. These processes made his products unique. The company continued as a family business until its closure in 1970. The American branch of the firm continues as the fabric house Lee Jofa.

Lethaby, W.R. (1857–1911)
Architect and designer who was a founding member of the Art Workers Guild in 1884 and Professor of Design at the Royal College of Art in 1900. He designed fabrics for Liberty's in the 1890s.

Léveillé, Ernest-Baptiste (1841–1913)
Took over the Paris studio and shop owned by François-Eugène Rousseau (q.v.) at 43 rue Coquillère and later at 74 boulevard Haussmann. He designed and sold glass, some of which was probably made by Appert Frères, Clichy.

Leven, Hugo (1874–1956)
Designer who worked for J.P. Kayser Sohn, Kerfeld, Germany. He designed from 1895 to about 1904 many models for the Kayserzinn range of pewter stocked by Liberty's. He went on to design for the silversmiths Koch & Bergfeld.
Ref. V&A, D167

Levett-Prinsep, (Thomas Francis) Anthony (1908–83)
A member of an old Staffordshire family, he gave in to family pressure and attended Sandhurst, and then studied to become a vet, but eventually between 1931 and 1935 he studied at the Central School of Art. He became an artist and illustrator, and designed textiles during the 1950s and 1960s. He later lived in Snekkersten, Denmark.

Lewis, A.M.
Furniture designer. His most famous work was probably the 'Boomerang' table, which was retailed by Liberty's through their modern furniture department. Worked with K. McAvoy.
Ref. Calloway, p. 192

Lichtinger, Ludwig
Firm of pewter manufacturers in Munich, Germany, who were active from about 1878 until 1906.

Lindberg, Stig (1916–82)
Swedish designer of ceramics, glass, textiles, furniture, etc. One of the most important post-war designers working in Sweden, he designed ceramics for Rörstrand and Gustavsberg.
Ref. Calloway

Lindstrand, Viktor (1904–83)
Designer of glass, textiles and ceramics who was a pioneer of Swedish glass art. He joined Orrefors (q.v.) in 1928 and remained with them until he joined Kosta Glasbruk (a long-established glass manufacturers) as artistic director, a post he retained until he retired.
Ref. V&A, G31

Edmund Littler & Co.
Textile printers at Merton Abbey, Surrey, which Liberty's began to use in 1877. Liberty's bought the company in 1904 and continued to print at Merton until 1972.

Johann Lötz Witwe
The glass factory in Klostermuhle, Austria, was founded in 1836 and was bought by Johann Loetz in 1840. His widow ran the business under the name of Johann Loetz Widow and upon her death it passed to her grandson, Max Ritter von Spaun, in 1879. He modernized the factory and produced glass that was comparable to Tiffany's. The glass is sometimes marked 'Loetz, Austria'; 'Lötz' or 'Lötz, Klostermühle', all with crossed arrows in a circle.

Long, Henry
Designed furniture in conjunction with Ronald Harford.
Ref. Calloway, p. 191

McAvoy, K.
Furniture designer who worked with A.M. Lewis. Their most famous creation was the 'Nimbus' coffee table.
Ref. Calloway, p. 192

MacBeth, Ann (1875–1948)
Studied at the Glasgow School of Art from 1897 to 1899 and in 1911 succeeded Jessie Newbery as head of the embroidery department. Liberty's commissioned embroideries from her, including cushion covers and decorative panels, very much in the Art Nouveau style. She wrote five books on embroidery.
Ref. LD

McCarty, Billy (Billy McCarty Cooper) (1938–91)
Born in Florida, he worked for David Hicks before establishing his own design practice. He designed the Thebes collection of furniture. Contributor to the Liberty's Centenary Exhibition in 1975.
Ref. V&A

James Macintyre & Co.
In 1854 James Macintyre joined William Saddler Kennedy, who had set up in business at Washington Works, Burslem, Staffordshire, in 1843. Macintyre carried on the business in 1860. William Moorcroft was a designer from 1898 to 1913. After he left they concentrated on industrial products.

McClintock, Annette
Designed fabrics in the 1950s and 1960s.

McNish, Althea
Born in Trinidad and Tobago, she came to London in the 1950s and began a career as a textile designer. Her fabrics were always distinctive, with bold tropical colourings. After studying at the Royal College of Art, she was commissioned by Liberty's to design a collection the day after she graduated in 1957.

Magistretti, Vico (1920–2006)
Born in Milan, he followed family tradition and became an architect. He is today better known for his furniture designs, particularly those produced for Cassina (q.v.), such as the Carimate chair and Maralunga sofa.
Ref. Calloway, p. 193

Makepeace, John (1939–)
Noted furniture designer and craftsman who supplied designs for dining furniture in the 1960s. Contributor to the Liberty's Centenary Exhibition in 1975.
Ref. V&A

Marsden, Robert (1947–)
Silversmith and metalworker. Supplied items in the 1970s. Contributor to the Liberty's Centenary Exhibition in 1975.
Ref. V&A

Matthson, Bruno (1907–88)
The son of a carpenter, he was born in Värnamo in southern Sweden. He trained as an architect but is renowned for his furniture designs, especially his chairs.
Ref. Calloway, p. 192

Mawson, Sidney G. (1849–1941)
A landscape painter and lecturer in textile design at the Slade School of Art in London. His first known design was done for Thomas Wardle & Co. in the 1880s. He later produced designs for Morton Sundour Fabrics, which were retailed through Liberty's and also for Turnbull & Stockdale. His print 'Chatsworth' was first produced in 1909 and remained in production until recent times.

Melson Bros (London) Ltd
Upholstered furniture manufacturer of Algeon Works, Queensbridge Road, London E8, and supplier to Liberty's in the 1960s.
Ref. WA 1166/236

Middleton-Stanford, Betty
Textile designer and illustrator who designed textiles for Liberty's in the 1950s.
Ref. Buruma

Miles, Frank (1852–891)
A London society portrait artist, who usually worked in pastels. He commissioned E.W. Godwin to build him a house in Tite Street, Chelsea (No. 1, later renumbered as 44). Oscar Wilde lived with him (they may have been lovers) and Miles introduced him to society. Miles designed textiles for Liberty's from the 1880s until his death.

Miller, H.T.
Designed postcards in around 1915.
Ref. V&A, D268

Milligan, Michael
Consultant jewellery designer to Liberty's.
Ref. V&A

Mines and West Ltd
Furniture manufacturer of Downley, High Wycombe, Buckinghamshire.
Ref. WA 1166/228

John Moncrieff Ltd, Perth, Scotland
Glass manufacturers, founded in 1864, who produced 'Monart' glass, which was retailed by Liberty's from around 1925 and was often described as Scotch glass. Much of it was the work of Salvador Ysart and his son Paul, who were from Catalonia. Many of the designs were by Isabel Moncrieff.

Moorcroft, William (1872–1945)
Ceramic designer for James Macintyre & Co. before he founded his own company, which was financed by Liberty's. Much of what he produced was sold by Liberty's and Tiffany's in New York.

Morgan, William de (1839–1917)
A lifelong friend of William Morris, Morgan designed tiles, stained glass and furniture for Morris & Co. between 1863 and 1872. He is best known for his pottery and tiles, often inspired by medieval designs or Persian patterns. He founded a pottery in Chelsea in 1872, which migrated to Merton Abbey and then, in 1888, to Fulham, where it remained. Morgan left the pottery in 1907, but it continued to be run by Charles and Fred Passenger. Liberty's furniture occasionally incorporated de Morgan tiles.

Morris of Glasgow
Founded by Harris Morris in 1884, the company was famous for supplying furniture for many ocean liners built on the Clyde including the RMS *Queen Mary*. Morris became famous for their Bambi chair and Clouds occasional tables. Liberty's stocked their furniture in the 1950s and 1960s.

Alexander Morton & Co.
Founded by Alexander Morton (1844–1923) in Kilmarnock, Scotland, originally selling muslins. Their range expanded to include chenilles, woollen cloths and double cloths, for which they were noted. They founded a carpet manufacturing operation in Donegal in the late 1890s. The company bought in designs from all the leading designers of the period. In 1906 they established Morton Sundour Fabrics for printed fabrics.

Mürrle Bennett & Co.
Founded by Ernst Mürrle and a Mr Bennett in 1896, this was a wholesale jeweller's in London. Mürrle was born in Pforzheim in Germany, a town well known for jewellery, while Bennett seems to have been the English partner. The firm produced jewellery in the Jugendstil or German Art Nouveau style and much of it was probably produced in Pforzheim. Their works often carried Liberty's mark and sometimes that of Haseler (q.v.). The firm became White Redgrove and Whyte during the First World War.
Refs. LS; V&A, D145, 146

Napper, Harry (1860–1930)
Joined the Silver Studio (q.v.) in 1893 and ran it after Arthur Silver died in 1896. He left in 1898 to work as a freelance designer, but continued to use the Silver Studio as an agency. Napper produced some of the finest Art Nouveau designs, both for fabrics and wallpapers, and was also a designer of furniture and metalwork, which was produced by Norman and Stacey Ltd and shown at the Officers' Ideal Quarters Exhibition held at Earl's Court, London, in 1901. All the leading manufacturers of the period bought his designs.
Ref. V&A, D32, 37, 259, G21

Nevill, Bernard (1934–)
Studied at St Martin's College of Art, and then taught there and at the Royal College of Art. In 1960 he became consultant designer for Liberty's and remained for over ten years.
Ref. V&A, H3, 12

Niczewski, Peter (1948–)
Woodworker. A wooden table with *trompe l'oeil* decoration was featured in the Liberty's Centenary Exhibition in 1975.
Ref. V&A.

O.M.K. Design
Furniture designer and manufacturer established by Rodney Kinsman (and Jurek Olejnik and Bryan Morrison) in 1965 after he left the Central School of Art. Kinsman's designs were retailed extensively by Habitat and also by Liberty's.

Ormrod, Frank (1896–1988)
Artist and designer born in Bolton, Lancashire. He was a designer of textiles for Liberty's in the late 1920s and 1930s. He also designed posters for London Transport in 1937.

Orivit
The Orivit factory in Cologne, Germany, was founded in 1894 by Ferdinand Hubert Schmitz, who purchased an existing metalworking firm. He introduced the brand name Orivit in 1898. The designers Hermann Gradl, Walter Scherf and Georges Charles Coudray are all known to have produced designs for the factory (Theo Blum, Georg Graseggar, Vicor Heinrich Seifert and Johann Christian Kroner had some association with it too). The company went bankrupt in 1905 and was taken over by the metalware manufacturer WMF, who continued to produce Orivit products until around 1930. Georg Fredrich Schmitt became design director in 1906 and he brought with him many designs from the Orion company, which he had run previously.
Ref. D169, 170

Orrefors Glass
Swedish glass manufacturers in the village of Orrefors, founded in 1898. Prior to 1913 the company produced window glass and bottles. Thereafter they began to produce domestic glassware, and they were much influenced by Art Nouveau and the work of the French artist Émile Gallé. Liberty's were a stockist after the Second World War.
Ref. V&A, G31

Osiris
See Walter Scherf & Co.

Over, Celia
Silver designer whose work featured in the Liberty's Centenary Exhibition in 1975.
Ref. V&A

Palmqvist, Sven (1906–84)
Swedish glass designer who worked for Orrefors (q.v.). He is most famous for his 'Fuga' series of bowls.
Ref. V&A, G31

Parker Knoll
Frederick Parker founded the company in London in 1869, but soon moved it to High Wycombe, Buckinghamshire, a centre of furniture manufacture. He made furniture for liners, including the *Aquitania* and even for the Royal Yacht, and later furniture for Viceroy's House in New Delhi, which was designed by Sir Edwin Lutyens. In 1931 Parker's merged with the company founded by Willi Knoll, a German who had begun selling his designs through Heal's. Liberty's sold Parker Knoll's furniture after the Second World War.

Pattison, Edgar Edwin Lawrence (1872–1950)
An artist of note, who designed textiles from the 1890s. These seem to have been produced by J.W. & C. Ward of Halifax.
Ref. LD

Peace, David (1915–2003)
By profession a town planner, but noted for his glass engraving, which was his hobby. He was much inspired by Eric Gill, about whom he wrote a book. He held his first one-man show in 1972 at Kettle's Yard in Cambridge. He contributed to the Liberty's Centenary Exhibition in 1975.
Ref. V&A

Pearce, Charles (1943–)
The Liberty's Centenary Exhibition in 1975 featured his calligraphy.
Ref. V&A

Pearce, Simon
The Liberty's Centenary Exhibition in 1975 featured his glass.
Ref. V&A

Pearson, Colin (1923–2007)
The Liberty's Centenary Exhibition in 1975 featured his pottery.
Ref. V&A

Pearson, John (1859–1930)
A founding member, together with Charles R. Ashbee, of the Guild and School of Handicraft in 1888. He was dismissed from the guild in 1892 (for maintaining his own shop) and went to Newlyn in Cornwall, where he worked in the industrial school. He remained at Newlyn for six years. Greatly influenced by William de Morgan, he may have worked in de Morgan's workshop, perhaps making metalwork. In 1901 he returned to London and opened a new workshop at Hanway Street, W1, where he decorated ceramics and produced metalwork, some of which Liberty's sold. He closed his workshop in 1929 and retired to Canvey Island in Essex, where he died.

Richard Perry & Son, Wolverhampton
A firm of tin plate workers and japanners, founded at the beginning of the nineteenth century by Richard Perry in partnership with his son George. Eventually they also incorporated the business of another son, Edward. Perry's produced some designs by Christopher Dresser.
Ref. LD

Pilkington Lancastrian Pottery
Established in 1892 at Clifton Junction, Lancashire, originally manufacturing tiles, vases, bowls, etc. In 1903 they developed an opalescent ceramic glaze that they called 'Lancastrian'. They are famous for manufacturing designs by Walter Crane, Lewis Day and Charles Voysey. The company produced a range of pottery until 1938. It survived until 2010.

Plateelbakkerij Zuid-Holland
Produced a range of pottery known as 'Breda Ware' in Gouda in The Netherlands exclusively for Liberty's in the early years of the twentieth century. The factory was established in 1898 and closed in 1965.
Ref. V&A, D216

Plunkett, William Frederick (1928–2013)
Established his company in 1963. His furniture, which is not well known, was batch-produced in limited quantities, unlike that of many of his contemporaries, who mass-produced their designs. Some of his designs, such as the 'Kingston' range and the 'Epsom' range, were successful and remained in production for a long time. His 'Coulsdon' chair and coffee table graced one of the bars on the QE2. Liberty's sold some of his furniture.
Ref. Calloway

Pogany, Vilmos A. (1882–1955)
A prolific Hungarian illustrator of children's and other books, notably *The Rubáiyát of Omar Khayyám*, published in 1909, and best known for his pen and ink drawings of myths and fables. He certainly designed two calendars for Liberty's, the 'Omar Khayyam' in 1913 and the 'Tannhauser' in 1916. Two other calendars, the 'Hindu' produced in 1914 and the 'Shakespeare' calendar in either 1914 or 1915 may also have been Pogany's work.
Ref. V&A, D269

Poiret, Paul (1879–1944)
Paris couturier who established his own fashion house in 1903 and became one of the leading couturiers of the period. After the First World War his house was almost bankrupt and it eventually closed in 1929. Liberty's engaged him to design a number of collections – they were signed 'Paul Poiret at Liberty's'; the arrangement seems to have lasted about two years.

Poncelet, Jacqueline
The Liberty's Centenary Exhibition in 1975 featured her pottery.
Ref. V&A

Ponti, Giò (1891–1979)
Italian architect and furniture designer. He designed furniture for Cassina (q.v.) that was retailed by Liberty's. He also designed ceramics for Richard Ginori (q.v.), sanitary ware for Ideal Standard, and lamps for Artemide, Fontana Arte and Venini.

Poole Pottery
See Carter, Stabler & Adams Ltd.

James Powell & Sons
Also known as Whitefriars Glass. The company is thought to have been established in 1680 in Whitefriars, London, and was purchased by James Powell in 1834. They became famous for stained glass and also for quarry glass, which was mass-produced by moulding and printing. In the late nineteenth century they were associated with many leading designers, including T.G. Jackson, Edward Burne-Jones, William de Morgan, James Doyle and Philip Webb; the last used their glass in his designs for William Morris. The company also produced domestic glass, to which Liberty's added Archibald Knox mounts.

Pride, Blair (19??–1971)
Designer who updated the 'Tana Lawn' range in the 1960s. He died suddenly in 1971.
Ref. Calloway

Punnett, Edward G. (1887–1948)
Son of a publican (at the Old Globe on the Mile End Road), Punnett joined William Birch Ltd (q.v.). Punnett's name appears in Birch's cost and design books in October 1901 when he was just fourteen.

Pye, David William (1914–1993)
The Liberty's Centenary Exhibition in 1975 featured his woodware.
Ref. V&A

Race, Ernest (1913–64)
Textile and furniture designer, born in Newcastle, who is famous for his aluminium chair, designed in 1945, and also for his 'Antelope' chair, designed for the Festival of Britain in 1951. Liberty's sold his furniture in the 1940s and 1950s. He traded under the name Ernest Race Ltd and later as Race Furniture.
Ref. Calloway

G.T. Rackstraw Ltd
Manufacturers of furniture in Droitwich, West Midlands. Supplied Liberty's in the 1960s and 1970s.
Ref. WA 1166/226; 227

Rathbone, Harold S. (1858–1929)
Owner of the Della Robbia Pottery, which he founded in 1894 with Conrad Gustave d'Huc Dressler (1856–1940). Rathbone had been a pupil of Ford Madox Brown. Della Robbia pottery was sold extensively at Liberty's. The pottery closed in 1906.
Ref. V&A, C29

Ravilious, Eric William (1903–42)
Brought up in Sussex, Ravilious is noted for his watercolours of the South Downs. In 1936 he was invited by Wedgwood to create designs for ceramics. His best-known work was the 'Garden' series of plates featuring different plants, which continued in production into the 1950s. He was a war artist and was killed while with the RAF.
Ref. V&A, G24

Reimerschmid, Richard (1868–1957)
German architect, painter and designer. He was a leading figure in the Jugendstil and co-founder of Vereinigte Wekstätte für Kunst im Handwerk (United Workshops for Art in Handcrafts). He was greatly influenced by the English Arts and Crafts Movement and went on to create furniture, carpets, fabric and wallpapers; he also designed porcelain for Meissen. At the Vereinigte Wekstätte he developed a programme of machine production of art furniture. An example was his 'music room' chair, which was exhibited at the German Art Exhibition in Dresden in 1899. This proved to be so popular that the Vereinigte Wekstätte immediately put it into production, and it was manufactured and retailed at Liberty's the following year.
Ref. D5, 6

Reuter, Edmund George (1845– after 1912)
Born in Geneva, Reuter came to London in 1870, lodging in Chelsea. He illustrated William Morris's *The Roots of the Mountains*, published in 1894, and did other work for the Kelmscott Press. He moved to Stoke-on-Trent, Staffordshire, where he was employed by Minton Tiles. In 1901 he was employed as designer by the Vine Pottery, which had been established in 1894. He is said to have designed textiles for Liberty's in the 1880s.

Richard-Ginori
The Doccia Porcelain Manufacturer, of Doccia near Florence, was founded in 1735 by the Marchese Carlo Ginori. The company remained in the hands of the Ginori family until 1896, when it was incorporated with the Società Ceramica Richard of Milan and became Richard-Ginori. Gio Ponti was artistic director from 1923 to 1930 and was succeeded by Giovanni Gariboldi. The company went bankrupt in 2013 and was bought by Gucci.
Ref. V&A, G26

Rie, Lucie (1902–95)
The Liberty's Centenary Exhibition in 1975 featured her stoneware and porcelain.
Ref. V&A

Rörstrand
One of the most famous porcelain manufacturers in Sweden, and in the 1860s one of Sweden's largest industries. Liberty's retailed some of their more innovative designs in the 1950s and 1960s. In 1968 the company merged with English Sewing Cotton Company to form English Calico Ltd, which became Tootal Ltd in 1973.
Ref. V&A, G27

Rossendale Printing Co.
Old-established textile printing company, based in Loveclough, Lancashire. In 1899 it was one of the forty-six textile printing companies that amalgamated to form the Calico Printers' Association Ltd, which was based in Manchester. It is said that at its inception the association accounted for over 80 per cent of Britain's printed fabric output. They were one of the textile printers who supplied Liberty's.
Ref. V&A, C9

Rosso, Elvira Del
Italian textile designer based in Milan, from whom Liberty's purchased designs in the 1950s.
Ref. Buruma

Rosui, Sawada
Japanese artist. Liberty's retailed fans decorated by him.
Ref. V&A, B28

Rousseau, François-Eugène (1827–91)
His family retailed ceramics and glass at a shop on the rue Coquillère in Paris, which he took over in 1855. A follower of fashion, in 1867 he commissioned a dinner service from Felix Bracquemond in a Japanese style, which was an immediate success. He began

to experiment with glass and engaged two of the greatest glass designers of the period, Eugene Michel and Alphonse-Georges Reyen, to work for him. Initially his designs were made by Appert Frères, but he later set up his own glass-making studio. Liberty's sold his crackled glass and continued to retail works from the studio after Rousseau sold it to Ernest-Baptiste Leveille.
Ref. LD

Rowe, Michael
The Liberty's Centenary Exhibition in 1975 featured his silverware.
Ref. V&A

Royal Doulton
Famous china manufacturer of Staffordshire and London. Liberty's were a stockist.

Gordon Russell Ltd
Founded by Sir (Sydney) Gordon Russell (1892–1980), who was one of the leading domestic designers of the twentieth century. The firm's workshop at Broadway (his father had bought the Lygon Arms there in 1904) became a famous furniture producer. Liberty's stocked items from the workshop in the 1950s. Many of the designs produced by the company were by Dick Russell, Gordon's younger brother, who had trained as an architect but took over designing in 1929.

Saul, Isabel (1895–1977)
Designed calendars in the 1930s.
Ref. WA 788/110/2

Scarratt-Rigby, John (1865–1952?)
Set up a textile design studio in Uttoxeter, Staffordshire, in 1887, and designed textiles for Liberty's in the 1880s and 1890s. He produced designs for many of the leading manufacturers of the period, including Baker's and Morton's. He was secretary of the Society of Designers and contributed a number of reviews and articles. Following his divorce (he was married in 1889) he seems to have gone to live in South Africa.

Walter Scherf & Co.
Manufacturer of pewter in Nuremberg, Germany, who produced pieces using the trademark Osiris. The factory, or workshop, was founded by Friedich August Scherf (1839–1922), and his son Walter Scherf (1875–1909) seems to have taken over the factory in 1899. He had previously worked for Orivit. In 1902 the firm developed a new type of pewter, which they called 'Isis'. By 1909 the firm was bankrupt and Walter Scherf took his own life.

Selle, Ferdinand Otto Reinhold (1862–1915)
Founded the porcelain manufacturer Burgau ad Saale Ferdinand Selle in 1901 in Burgau, Jena, Germany. He was a founder member of the Deutscher Werkbund in 1907. After Selle died, his wife continued the business, which closed in 1929.
Ref. V&A, D219

Shand Kydd Ltd
Wallpaper manufacturer established in 1891.
Ref. V&A, D262, 263

Shelley Potteries
See Wileman & Co.

Silver Studio
Design studio established by Arthur Silver (q.v.) in 1880 at Brook Green, Hammersmith. The studio closed in 1963, by which time it had produced over 30,000 designs, mostly for textiles and wallpapers but also for complete interiors, plasterwork, furniture, metalwork, etc. The Silver Studio also acted as agent to some designers.

Silver, Arthur (1853–96)
Born in Reading, where his father was an upholsterer, he studied at the Reading School of Art and was then apprenticed to the designer H.W. Batley (1846–1932). He opened his own studio, the Silver Studio (q.v.), in 1880, which was soon successful. He died suddenly from heart failure on 28 October 1896.

Silver, Harry (1882–1972)
Son of Arthur Silver, he supervised the Silver Studio (q.v.) from 1901 until 1916, when he left and joined the army. He was a gifted designer and certainly from 1905 produced numerous metalwork designs, some of which were used by Liberty's. After the war he chose not to return to the studio (he felt it could not financially support his brother's family and his own), and so opened a garage in north London.

Silver, Reginald 'Rex' (1879–1965)
Son of Arthur Silver, he took control of the Silver Studio (q.v.) along with his brother Harry Silver (q.v.) in 1901 and ran it until it closed in 1963. Initially Rex was the business manager and his brother the artistic director. After the First World War he ran the studio on his own and supplied many of the leading manufacturers in the United Kingdom. He also supplied designs to Macy's and Marshall Field. He died shortly after the studio closed.

Simpson, Ronald D. (1890–1960)
A textile designer and woodworker. Born in Kendal, Cumbria, he joined Morton's, who were based in Carlisle, in 1908 and designed many patterns for them.

SM
Japanese silver mark.
Ref. V&A, B24

Solon, Leon Victor (1872–1957)
Son of Marc Louis Emanuel Solon (1835–1913), a ceramicist who worked for Sèvres, where he specialised in *pâte-sur-pâte* decoration, and who moved to work for Minton in 1870, as Leon was to do from 1900 to 1909. Leon designed textiles, some of his designs being bought by Wardle's and retailed at Liberty's. In 1909 he emigrated to the USA.
Ref. LD

Solven, Pauline
The Liberty's Centenary Exhibition in 1975 featured her glass.
Ref. V&A

Stead McAlpin Ltd
Textile printers and finishers, established in 1835 in Carlisle, who produced many designs by Voysey.

Stevens, Richard S. (1924–97)
A post-war industrial designer, noted as a designer of innovative lighting at Atlas Lighting Ltd between 1954 and 1963. He became industrial design manager for Standard Telephones and Cables Ltd and later for Post Office Telecommunications. He became president of the Society of Industrial Artists and Designers in 1972.
Ref. Calloway

Stewart, Robert (1924–95)
Attended the Glasgow School of Art in the 1940s and was subsequently a teacher there for more than thirty-five years. He was one of the foremost designers of the post-war period. He designed for Liberty's, Donald Brothers and the Edinburgh Tapestry Company amongst others. He later formed his own company to produce printed ceramics.
Ref. V&A, G5, 10, 14

Straub, Marianne (1909–94)
Born in Amriswil, Switzerland, she was the daughter of a textile merchant. She studied art in Zurich and then textile design at Bradford Technical College. In 1937 she joined Helios as head designer and in 1950 she joined Warner's (q.v.). By 1953 she had moved to Great Bardfield in Essex, which was home to a group of artists. She also taught textile design at the Central School of Art and at Hornsey College of Art and later at the Royal College of Art.
Ref. V&A, G11

Sundström, Heljä Liukko (1938–)
Finnish designer who went to work for the Arabia Pottery (q.v.).
Ref. V&A

Sutton, Anne
The Liberty's Centenary Exhibition in 1975 featured her padded knitted and woven love seat.
Ref. V&A

Tadashi, Kamei
Japanese artist who painted fans, together with Sawada Rosui, Masuda Tetsu and Tomimatsu Hirokage.
Ref. V&A, B28

Taylor, William Howson (1876–1935)
His father, Edward R. Taylor, founded the Ruskin Pottery in 1898. William Taylor was a great experimenter with glazes, producing products that were unique. Many have tried to copy the speckled, mottled, lustre and flambé glazes, but without success: Taylor took the recipes to his grave.

James Templeton & Co.
Glasgow-based carpet manufacturer established in 1839 by James Templeton (1802–1883). They became one of the leading carpet manufacturers in Britain and at their peak employed more than 3,000 people. The mill closed in 1979 and the business merged with A.F. Stoddard and Henry Widnell & Stewart to form Stoddard Carpets. Templeton's were one of the manufacturers of designs by Charles Voysey.

Thallon, James (1839–1907)
Trained at the upholsterer Howard & Sons and owned a cabinetmaking business, probably in Dufours Place, Soho, London. He began manufacturing for Liberty's and in about 1887 Liberty's took over his workshop. His son, Thomas (1862–1935), succeeded him as manager of the workshop.
Ref. V&A, B75

Titchmarsh & Goodwin
Of Ipswich, Suffolk. Famous for their reproduction furniture. Supplier to Liberty's in the 1960s.
Ref. WA 1166/220; 221; 222

Tomkinson & Adam
Carpet manufacturers based in Kidderminster, Worcestershire, since 1860. Charles Voysey designed extensively for them.

Trethowan, Harry (1882–1960)
Designed for the 'Poole Pottery', Carter, Stabler and Adams Ltd (q.v.). He was manager of the ceramics and glass department at Heal's and later became managing director of Heal's Wholesale and Export Ltd. He had a huge influence on the Utility ceramics ranges and was a noted author on ceramics.
Ref. V&A, F27

Tsunekichi, Kaji (1803–83)
Japanese cloisonné enamellist in the mid-nineteenth century. With some pupils he established a successful manufacturing operation at Nagoya.
Ref. V&A, B5

Turnbull and Stockdale Ltd
Established by William Turnbull and William Stockdale in 1881 at Ramsbottom in Lancashire. The business rapidly expanded and eventually they were not only textile printers but also weavers. They printed Liberty's fabrics and also designed their own ranges. In 1931 to celebrate their Golden Jubilee they published a book. At the time they had a workforce of over 750, spread over a number of sites. The company was acquired by Sanderson's in 1965.

Varley, Fleetwood C. (1874–1959)
Great-grandson of the watercolour artist John Varley, he was an enameller who joined the Guild of Handicrafts in 1899. Liberty's often used his enamel work in its silver and pewter.

Veazey, David Colin (1868–1956)
A designer of metalwork, born in Whitby in Yorkshire. He won a competition to design a silver tea caddy, organised by Liberty's through *The Studio* magazine. The design was put into production in both silver and pewter – the pewter bearing the signature 'Tramp'. Veazey is an obscure figure but is known to have designed light fittings for Perry & Co. of Grafton Street, London W1, manufacturers of traditional lighting and metalwork. He is thought to have died in Stamford, Lincolnshire, in 1956.
Ref. LS.

Venini, Paolo (1895–1959)
Born in Cusano near Milan, he became acquainted with Giacomo Cappellin, a Venetian who owned an antique shop in Milan. In 1921 they opened a glass factory on the island of Murano, the historic centre of glass making in Venice. Eventually the company became known as Venini & C. and emerged as one of the leading designers on Murano. Venini himself was responsible for many popular designs, including the *fazzoletto* (handkerchief vase), created with Fulvio Bianconi. Liberty's began to sell the glass in the 1950s. Venini's family continued to run the company after he died but it was sold in 1985.

Vigers, Allan Francis (1858–1921)
An architect and designer who is best remembered for his wallpaper and textile designs. He exhibited at the Arts and Crafts Exhibition Society in 1910. At least one of designs is to be found in Wardle's pattern books.
Ref. LD

Voysey, Charles F.A. (1857–1941)
Probably one of the most important designers of the early twentieth century. By training he was an architect, but he began designing wallpapers and fabrics in the late 1880s. He started to design furniture and other domestic items, many of which were retailed by Liberty's.

Walker, Thomas F.
Of 143 Murchison Road, Leyton, E10. Supplier to Liberty's of lacquered brass.
Ref. WA 1166/229; 230

Almeric Walter & Co.
Glass manufacturers of Nancy in France.
Ref. V&A, D253

Walton, George Henry (1867–1933)
Scottish architect and designer. He attended the Glasgow School of Art and was subsequently commissioned to redesign Miss Cranston's tea rooms in Argyle Street in Glasgow. In 1888 he started his own decorating business, which rapidly diversified into designing furniture and stained glass. He also designed textiles for Morton Sundour Fabrics.

J.W. & C. Ward
Woollen and carpet manufacturers of Halifax, Yorkshire, originally at Ellen Royd Mill, Range Bank, in 1874, possibly earlier; later listed as art fabric manufacturers at Brunswick Mills in 1905, and as silk manufacturers at Spring Hall Mills in 1917.

Thomas Wardle & Co.
Founded by Thomas Wardle (1831–1909) in Leek, Staffordshire, they were famous textile dyers and finishers. Aside from printing William Morris's early textile patterns Wardle did extensive work for Liberty's. He also produced textile ranges under his own name and commissioned designs from many of the leading designers of the period.

Warner & Sons
Founded in the late seventeenth century by William Warner, who worked as a scarlet dyer in Spitalfields, London. In 1857 a descendant, Benjamin Warner, bought a card cutting and jacquard business, and later formed a partnership, Warner & Ramm (lasting until 1891), which in 1885 acquired Charles Norris & Co., a prestigious firm which held a royal warrant. The firm became one of the leading textile manufacturers of the period, and it had a long business relationship with Liberty's.
Ref. V&A, D36

Wartha, Vince (1844–1914)
A Hungarian chemist and academic, who was a consultant to the Zsolnay porcelain factory (q.v.). He was probably responsible for developing the eosin glaze. He may also have designed for the Zsolnay factory.
Ref. V&A, D217

Warwick, Matthew
The Liberty's Centenary Exhibition in 1975 featured his woodware.
Ref. V&A

Watcombe Terracotta Clay Company
The designs created by the pottery at Watcombe, Torquay, Devon, were greatly influenced by Christopher Dresser (q.v.). It was taken over by Hexter, Humpherson & Co., the owners of Aller Vale Pottery (q.v.), who were established suppliers to Liberty's.

Waterhouse, Mrs Alfred (1834–1918)
Elizabeth Waterhouse, wife of the architect Alfred Waterhouse and sister of the historian Thomas Hodgkin, started the Yattendon Classes (at Yattendon Court, Berkshire) in around 1890 to teach metalwork skills. She designed many of the pieces, which were usually produced in copper and brass. Liberty's sold some of the work. The classes disbanded in 1914.
Ref. V&A, C27

Watts, Mrs G.F. (1849–1938)
Mary Seton Fraser Tytler married the painter George Frederic Watts in 1886. In 1899 she founded the Compton Potters' Arts Guild (q.v.).

Wedgwood & Sons Ltd
Famous manufacturer of china. Liberty's were a stockist.
Ref. V&A, G23–25

Wedge, James (1939–)
After leaving the Royal College of Art, Wedge designed millinery for the couturier Ronald Patterson. Liberty's gave him a workroom and instead of charging rent their buyers had first refusal for any of his creations. Wedge set up his own shop in Soho in 1962.

West London Antique Company
Supplied designs for a table, c.1960.
Ref. WA 1166/233

Westman, Marianne (1928–)
Swedish designer of ceramics and textiles who is regarded as one of the leading Swedish designers of tableware. She worked for Rorstrand between 1950 and 1971.
Ref. V&A, G27

Whitefriars Glass
See James Powell & Sons.

White Redgrove and Whyte
See Mürrle Bennett.

Whyatt, John
Designed silk scarves in the 1970s.

Wileman & Co.
Traded as Foley Potteries and also Shelley Potteries. Frederick Alfred Rhead became art director in 1896 and in 1899 the journal *Artist* ran an article entitled 'Some Beautiful English Pottery', which was largely devoted to Foley Art Pottery. Liberty's carried the range. In 1910 Percy Shelley, who owned the company, tried to register the name Foley as a trademark but it was also being used by another company, so he changed the name to Shelley. The company ceased to exist in 1966.
Ref. V&A, D221

Willshaw, Arthur
Designed textiles in the 1890s and 1900, which were produced by J.W. & C. Ward of Halifax. Little is known about him, but he seems to have been active from 1875.
Ref. V&A, D26

Wirkkala, Tapio (1915–85)
Finnish sculptor and designer who was a leading figure in post-war design. The scope of his work was immense and ranged over glassware, ceramics and furniture. One of his most famous designs was the Finlandia vodka bottle, used from 1970 till 2000.
Ref. Calloway, p. 193

Wright, John
Textile designer in the 1950s and 1960s. He designed some Coronation souvenirs.
Ref. Buruma

Wyburd, Leonard F. (1866–1960)
Ran the decorating studio at Liberty's from 1883 until he left twenty-two years later. He then established an interior decorating business under his own name. He was a renowned designer of furniture and of interiors.

Wylie & Lochhead
A firm of Glasgow cabinetmakers, founded by Robert Wylie and William Lochhead in 1829. Their furniture was of very high quality and the company was famous across Scotland for their wares. They manufactured furniture in numerous styles, copying details from all the noted designers of the period. M.H. Baillie Scott designed for them. The company was eventually purchased by House of Fraser.

Yattenden
See Mrs Alfred Waterhouse.

Zsolnay
Zsolnay Porcelánmanufaktúra Zrt was founded in 1853 by Miklós Zsolnay (1800–1880) in Pécs, Hungary, to produce stoneware. In 1886 they introduced pyrogranite, a type of ceramic that is resistant to frost and acid, making it very suitable for use as roof tiles. By the First World War Zsolnay was the largest company in Austria-Hungary. Liberty's sold some of their decorative wares, probably designed by Vince Wartha.
Ref. V&A, D217

BIBLIOGRAPHY

Adburgham, Alison, *Liberty's: A Biography of a Shop*, George Allen & Unwin Ltd, London 1975

Anscombe, Isabelle and Gere, Charlotte, *Arts & Crafts in Britain and America*, Van Nostrand Reinhold Company Inc., New York 1978

Amaya, Mario, *Art Nouveau*, Studio Vista, London 1967

Baillie Scott, M.H., and Beresford, A. Edgar, *Houses and Gardens*, Architectural Illustrated, London 1933

Bennett, Daryl, *Liberty's Furniture 1875–1915: The Birth of Modern Interior Design*, Antique Collectors' Club, Woodbridge 2012

Buruma, Anna, *Liberty and Co. in the Fifties and Sixties: A Taste for Design*, Antique Collectors' Club, Woodbridge 2009

Calloway, Stephen (ed.), *The House of Liberty: Masters of Style and Decoration*, Thames and Hudson, London 1992

Gradidge, Roderick, *Dream Homes: The Edwardian Ideal*, Constable, London 1980

Hitchmough, Wendy, *C F A Voysey*, Phaidon Press Ltd 1995

Jackson, Lesley, *20th Century Patter Design: Textile & Wallpaper Pioneers*, Mitchell Beazley, London 2011

Lambourne, Lionel, *Utopian Craftsmen: The Arts and Crafts Movement from the Cotswolds to Chicago*, Astragal Books, London 1980

Levy, Mervyn, *Liberty Style: The Classic Years 1898–1910*, Weidenfeld and Nicholson, London 1986

Luff, David, *Trouble at Mill: A Brief History of the Former Liberty Print Works Site including Textile Printing at Merton Printers Ltd (Libertys) 1965–1982*, Merton Historical Society, Merton 2002

Morley, Christopher, *Dresser's Decorative Design*, ed. Beresford. C. Cargin, Christopher Morley, Salisbury 2010

Morris, Barbara, *Liberty Design 1874–1914*, Pyramid, London 1989

O'Donnell, Anne Stewart, *C.F.A. Voysey*, Pomegranate, San Francisco 2011

Simpson, Duncan, *C.F.A. Voysey*, Lund Humphries, London 1979

Soros, Susan Weber (ed.), *E.W. Godwin: Aesthetic Movement, Architect and Designer*, BGC Yale, 1999

Sumner, Anne, *Tjolöholm: A Woman's Achievement*, Tjolöholm Foundation, Fjärås, Sweden, 2001

Tilbrook, Adrian J., *The Designs of Archibald Knox for Liberty & Co.*, second revised edition, Richard Dennis, Somerset 1995

BOOKS & CATALOGUES

Anna Baruma, *V&A Pattern: Liberty & Co.*, V&A Publishing, London 2012

Victoria and Albert Museum, *Liberty's 1875-1975: An Exhibition to Mark the Firm's Centenary July-October 1975*, Victoria and Albert Museum, London 1975

Clive Wainwright, *Architect - Designers: Pugin to Mackintosh, 5-29 May 1981*, Fine Art Society, London 1981

Arts & Crafts Textiles in Britain, Fine Art Society in association with Francesca Galloway, London n.d.

LIBERTY CATALOGUES

The following are catalogues issued at various times by Liberty's, copies of which are held in the Victoria and Albert Museum Library and in the Westminster City Archives. The Westminster Archives catalogues are listed as additions to the main collection in the Victoria and Albert Museum.

Titles have been taken from the covers of the catalogues. Additional information from the title page is given in brackets when necessary to aid identification. The covers are not counted as pages unless the catalogue is referred to as a leaflet. All the catalogues were issued by the London branch unless stated otherwise.

Victoria and Albert Museum Library

Eastern Art Manufactures and Decorative Objects [1881], 122 pp.

Eastern and European Carpets, Rugs, Matting, Art Fabrics for Furniture and Upholstery [1883], 50 pp.

Catalogue of Liberty's Art Fabrics, with samples of silk, sections on embroideries, handkerchiefs, sashes, fans, jewellery, costumes and pyjamas, [c.1883] 32 pp.

Liberty's Art Furniture [1884], 31 ff.

'Liberty' Art Porcelain Catalogue [1884], 36 pp.

'Liberty' Miscellaneous Catalogue of Eastern and Other Art Objects [c.1884], 28 pp.

Catalogue of a Valuable Collection of Ancient and Modern Eastern Art and Other Embroideries, November 1885, 16 pp.

Eastern Art and Other Embroideries, 1886, 12 pp.

'Liberty' Art (Dress) Fabrics and Personal Specialities [c.1886/7] 24 pp.

'Liberty' Carpet Catalogue [?1887], 48 pp.

'Liberty' Yule-Tide Gifts: Art Novelties for Personal Attire and Home Adornment [1888], 118 pp.

'Liberty' Handbook of Sketches with Prices and Other Information for Artistic and Economic Domestic Decoration and Furniture [1889], 83 ff.

Form and Colour Developments [1890], 174 pp.

Eastern Carpets [c.1890], 20 pp.

Liberty Handbook of Sketches with Price and Other Information for Artistic and Economic Domestic Decoration and Furniture [c.1890], 24 pp.

Yule-Tide Gifts from Sunny Climes [c.1890], 10 pp.

Eastern and Miscellaneous Bric-a-Brac [1891], 30 pp.

Porcelain, Bronzes, and Curios [1891], 42 pp.

A Catalogue of Some of the Valuable and Unique Specimens of Ancient and Modern Eastern and Other Art Embroideries Collected by Messrs Liberty and on View at Chesham House, Feb. 8 to Feb. 13 1892, 40 pp.

Supplementary Exhibits of Modern Turkish Embroideries, 1892, 4 pp., leaflet

British Silk Renaissance: Recent Exclusive Specialities Introduced by Messrs Liberty, 1892, 29 pp.

'Liberty' Yule-Tide Gifts, 1892, 44 pp.

'Liberty' Dress Fabrics at East India House, Silks, Cashmeres, Cottons, Shawls, Embroideries, Chiffons, Jewellery, Fancywork &c. [c.1892], 48 pp.

Jewellery, Handbook Series IV-XI [c.1892-8], Series IV-VI, 4 pp., Series VII and VIII, 8 pp., Series IX, 6 pp., Series X, 12 pp., Series XI, 10 pp.

Evolution in Costume, 1893, 46 pp.

Catalogue of a Loan Exhibition of Embroidery by Indian Women at Chesham House, 1893, 44 pp.

Specimen of Indian Women's Embroidery Lent by Messrs Liberty & Co., 1893, 4 pp., leaflet

'Liberty' Yule-Tide Gifts [c.1893], 40 pp.

Fans, Ancient and Modern, Eastern and Western: A Brief Sketch of Their Origin and Use, 1894, 62 pp.

Catalogue of a Valuable and Unique Collection of Ancient and Modern Eastern and Western Art Embroideries on View at Chesham House, April 1894, 52 pp.

'Liberty' Yule-Tide Gifts, 1894, 40 pp.

'Liberty' Costumes, Mantles and Millinery for Ladies and Children, season 1894-5, 58 pp.

Handbook of Sketches, Part 2 [c.1895], 81 pp.

Artistic Jewellery [1895], 32 pp.

Yule-Tide Gifts Catalogue, 1895-6, 48 pp.

Fans: A Brief Sketch of Their Origin and Use Compiled by Liberty & Co. Ltd, 1896, 24 pp.

History of Feminine Costume [1896], 40 ff.

The 'Liberty' Bazaar Catalogue of Eastern and Western Wares, Quaint, Artistic, and Inexpensive [1896], 66 pp.

Silks [1896], 34 ff.

Cashmeres [1896], 32 pp.

'Liberty' Costumes for Ladies and Children: Spring and Summer Designs, 1896, 48 ff.

The Praise of the Needle [c.1896], 32 pp.

'Liberty' Millinery: Autumn and Winter Designs, 1896-7, 16 ff.

['Liberty' Yule-Tide Gifts, cover missing] [1896-7], 56 pp.

Eastern Antiquities [c.1896-1900], 4 pp.

Curios [c.1896-1900], 4 pp.

Curios, Series XII [c.1896-1900], 4 pp.

'Curio', Series XXIV [c.1896-1900], 6 pp.

'Liberty' Millinery, Series II, Spring and Summer Designs 1897, 16 ff.

Yule-Tide Gifts, 1897, 64 pp.

The Arms of Greece (Particulars of a Unique Collection of Modern Greek Embroideries), 1898, 24 pp.

Chiffoneries and Fantasies: A Catalogue of Miscellaneous Fancy Articles Suitable for Complimentary Presents [1898], 36 ff.

The Liberty-Bazaar: A Permanent Exhibition of the Most Characteristic and Artistic Manufactures of Europe and the Far East [1898], 48 pp.

The Bazaar Catalogue of Quaint, Artistic and Inexpensive Wares [c.1898], 102 pp.

Yule-tide Gifts, 1898, 64 pp.

'Liberty' Millinery, Series V, Autumn and Winter Designs 1898-9, 23 ff.

Exhibition of 'Cymric' Silver-Work, May 1899, 32 pp.

Fancy Dress for Children [1899], 114 pp.

'Liberty' Hats and Bonnets, Series VI, Spring and Summer Designs 1899, 31 ff.

'Liberty' Hats and Bonnets, Series VII, Autumn and Winter Designs 1899, 27 ff.

'Liberty' Yule-Tide Gifts, 1899, 80 pp.

[Cymric Silver, cover missing] [1899 or 1900], 124 pp., including supplement

Hats and Bonnets, Series VIII, Spring and Summer Designs, 1900, 21 ff.

Hats and Bonnets, Series IX, Autumn and Winter Designs, 1900, 21 ff.

The Bazaar: A Catalogue of Quaint, Artistic and Inexpensive Eastern and Western Wares [c.1900], 102 pp.

'Liberty' Yule-Tide Gifts, 1900, 96 pp.

Artistic Novelties [c.1900], 26 pp.

Liberty Handbook of Sketches, Part 2: Reception Rooms, Halls, Dining Rooms, Drawing Rooms, Boudoirs, Morning Rooms, Smoking and Billiard Rooms; also includes part 3 [c.1900], 113 pp.

'Liberty' Costumes, Series XV, Spring and Summer Designs, 1901, 58 ff.

Artistic Novelties: A Catalogue of Miscellaneous Dainty Articles in Silks, Satins, Brocades, &C., Suitable for Complimentary Gifts [c.1901], 24 ff.

[*Liberty Yule-Tide Gifts,* cover missing], 1901, 80 pp.

Hats and Bonnets, Series XI, Autumn and Winter Designs 1901-2, 27 ff.

Revival of a National Industry: Press Opinions on the British Silk Exhibition Held at Hanover Gallery, February 8th to 15th, 1902, 28 pp.

Furniture for Town Flats and Country Houses [1902], 18 pp.

Chiffoneries and Fantasies: An Illustrated Catalogue of Miscellaneous Fancy-Work Suitable for Complimentary Presents [1902], 38 pp.

'Cymric' Gold and Silverwork, Jewellery & 'Tudric' Pewter [1902], 72 pp.

'Liberty' Costumes, Series XVII, Spring and Summer Designs, 1902, 39 ff.

Curios, Nov. and Dec. 1902, Nov. 12 pp., Dec. 14 pp.

'Liberty' Yule-Tide Gifts [1902], 80 pp.

Curios, Jan. 1903, 12 pp.

Founding a National Industry: Irish Carpet Exhibition Held at Grafton Gallery, Saturday March 7 to Friday 13 March 1903, 12 pp.

Founding a National Industry: Irish Carpets, 1903, 30 pp.

Curios, May, July, Sept., Oct.-Dec. 1903, each 12 pp.

Gold and Silver Work in 'Cymric' Designs: 'Tudric' Pewter [1903], 40 pp.

'Cymric' Gold & Silver Work and 'Tudric' Pewter: Yuletide Gifts [?1903], 38 pp.

Liberty Yule-Tide Gifts, 1903-4, 80 pp.

Curios, Jan.-Dec. 1904, each 12 pp.

Book of Garden Ornaments . . . [1904] 36 pp.

Book of Garden Ornaments (to be Obtained of P. L. Carbone, Boston & Harvard Sq. Cambridge), [1904], 36 pp.

Hats and Bonnets, Series XVII, Spring and Summer Designs, 1904, 22 ff.

Liberty Costumes, Series XXI, Spring and Summer Designs, 1904, 55 ff.

Laces, Scarves and Fichus [1904], 24 pp.

Ancient Marble Garden Ornaments, July 1904, 12 pp.

Jura Lace and Muslin Curtains, and Draperies [1904], 14 ff.

Novel Buckles and Hat Pins: Arts & Crafts Ltd. [Liberty's Agents in Shanghai], [c.1904], 44 pp.

Exhibition of Modern Celtic Art at the Grafton Gallery, from 7th to 19th of March Inclusive [1904], 44 pp.

Transfer Designs for Application to Needlework [c.1904], 24 pp.

Yule-Tide Gifts: New Fashions in Jewellery, Silver-Work and Pewter [1904], 40 pp.

[*Dress and Decoration,* cover missing] [1905], 30 pp.

Choice Examples of English Pewter [?1905], 30 pp.

Bric-a-Brac [c.1905], 54 pp.

Bric-a-Brac [c.1905], 48 pp.

Jewellery and Silverwork [1905], 44 pp.

[*Liberty Costumes,* cover missing] [c.1905], 72 ff.

Designs for Needlework [c.1905], 32 pp.

Garden Pottery [c.1905], 24 pp.

Hats and Bonnets, Series XIX, Autumn and Winter Designs 1905-6, 27 ff.

Yule-Tide Gifts, 1905-6, 88 pp.

Curios, Jan., Feb., April and May 1906, each 12 pp.

The Children's Frock Party [1906], 24 pp.

Simple and Durable Furniture at Modest Cost [1906], 16 pp.

Jewellery and Silver Work for Yule-Tide Gifts, 1906, 32 pp.

Novelties for Sports Prizes, Black Jacks and Loving Cups [1906], 12 pp.

Artistic Challenge Cups and Bowls [c.1906], 12 pp.

Hats and Bonnets, Handbook Series XXI [1906], 20 pp.

Lace [c.1906], 16 pp.

Furnishing Fabrics [c.1906], 80 pp.

Curtains [c.1906], 20 pp.

Illustrated Books Selected by Liberty & Co. [c.1906], 28 pp.

Yule-Tide Gifts, 1906, 86 pp.

Curios, Jan., Feb., April, May 1906 and Jan., April, March 1907, each 12 pp., except March 1907 16 pp.

Founding a National Industry: A Special Collection and Exhibition of the Irish Hand-Made Carpets at Liberty & Co's Galleries . . . Monday, May 25th [1907], 8 pp.

Carpets Produced on British Looms [1907], 60 pp.

Furniture [Inexpensive Furniture] [1907], 104 pp.

Oak Panelling [1907], 48 pp.

Garden Pottery: Artistic Forms for Practical Use [1907], 16 pp.

Wedding Gowns and Bridesmaids' Dresses, Series I [1907], 32 pp.

Underclothing, Series V [1907], 24 pp.

Fancy Dress [1907], 68 pp.

Hats and Bonnets Past and Present, Series XXIII [1907], 18 pp.

Artistic Stove Screens [c.1907], 12 pp.

Yule-Tide Gifts, 1907, 124 pp.

Liberty Artistic Fabrics: Autumn and Winter Fashions, 1908, 12 pp.

Lampshades [1908], 16 pp.

White Panelling [1908], 40 pp.

Hats and Bonnets Classical and Fashionable, Series XXVI, 1908, 18 pp.

Picturesque and Fashionable Hats and Bonnets, Series XXVII, 1908, 18 pp.

Picturesque and Fashionable Costumes, Series XXX, 1908, 18 pp.

Robes Liberty Pour Enfants [Paris] [c.1908], 36 pp.

Blouse Suits in the World-Famed Liberty Fabrics [c.1908], 14 pp.

[*Liberty & Co's New Models in Costumes and Blouses Made in the World-Famed Liberty Fabrics,* cover missing] [c.1908], 8 pp.

Shaped Skirts Partly Made [c.1908], 44 pp.

Shaped Skirts Partly Made, [c.1908], 52 pp.

Artistic Jewellery [c.1908], 4 pp.

Bric-a-Brac [c.1908], 56 pp.

Yule-Tide Gifts, 1908, 120 pp.

Picturesque and Fashionable Hats and Bonnets, Series XXIX, 1909, 20 pp.

Picturesque and Fashionable Hats and Bonnets, Series XXVIII, 1909, 18 pp.

Picturesque and Fashionable Costumes, Series XXXI, 1909, 88 pp.

Liberty Special Ties for Dresses and Furnishing [Birmingham], 1909, 32 pp.

Artistic Spoils of the Revolutions in Persia & Turkey, 1909, 12 pp.

Ancient Prayer Rugs from Eastern Palaces and Mosques [1909], 4 pp., leaflet

Select Makes of Eastern Carpets Imported by Liberty & Co. [1909], 48 pp.

Three Styles of Furniture and Decoration [1909], 14 pp.

Upholstered Chairs [1909], 40 pp.

Art in Warfare [1909], 16 pp.

Liberty's Silkworms at Merton Abbey [1909], 4 pp., leaflet

Antiques [1909], 28 pp.

Moonstones [Birmingham] [1909], 20 pp.

Designs for Needlework [?1909], 46 pp.

Designs for Needlework [?1909], 34 pp.

The Growth of Influence [c.1909], 12 pp.

Utensiles Artistiques pour la table [Paris] [c.1909], 12 pp.

Choice and Charming Presents [1909], 40 pp.

Yule-Tide Gifts, 1909, 120 pp.

Chapeaux de campagne [Paris] [c.1910], 12 pp.

Liberty Specialities for Dresses and Furnishing [Birmingham], 1910, 30 pp.

Costumes robes de style et costumes modernes, Series XXXIII [Paris], 1910, 92 pp.

Picturesque Hats and Bonnets, Series XXXI, 1910, 26 pp.

The World-Famed Liberty Fabrics: Spring and Summer Fashions, 1910, 12 pp.

Artistic Carpets Produced on British Looms [1910], 64 pp.

Jewellery and Silverwork [1910], 56 pp.

H.R.H. Printesa Elisaveta of Roumania (A Roumanian Peasant Handicraft) [1910], 40 pp.

Buckinghamshire Lace [c.1910], 38 pp.

Shaped Skirts Partly Made [c.1910], 48 pp.

Tentures [Paris], c.1910, 36 pp.

Liberty's & Co.: Sale of Artistic Fabrics for Dresses and Upholstery [c.1910], 24 pp.

Yule-Tide Gifts, 1910, 120 pp.

Liberty Specialities for Dresses and Furnishing [Birmingham], Autumn and Winter 1910-11, 32 pp.

Designs for Needlework [c.1910-12], 52 pp.

Artistic Flower Bowls and Vases [c.1910-15], 28 pp.

Liberty's Sale of Artistic Fabrics for Dresses and Upholstery [1911], 24 pp.

Log & Coal Boxes and Mirrors [1911], 10 pp.

Liberty's Solid-Oak Panelling [1911], 40 pp.

The Revival of an Old English Craft: English Pewter [1911], 16 pp.

The World-Famed Liberty Fabrics for Dresses and Upholstery: Spring & Summer Fashions, 1911, 12 pp.

Picturesque Hats and Bonnets, Series XXXIII, 1911, 30 pp.

Picturesque Dresses, Series XXXVI, 1911, 92 pp.

Yule-Tide Gifts, 1911-12, 124 pp.

Furniture by Liberty & Co. [c.1911], 96 pp.

English Pewter [c.1911], 20 pp.

Choice and Charming Presents [c.1911], 36 pp.

Reproduction of XII Century Furniture [c.1911], 24 pp.

Children's Hats & Bonnets [c.1911-12], 16 pp.

English Pewter: Useful and Ornamental Wares Founded on Ancient Models [1912], 16 pp.

Liberty Fabrics for Dresses and Upholstery, 1912, 12 pp.

Picturesque Frocks for Children, Series XIII, 1912, 32 pp.

Liberty Furniture and Fabrics [c.1912], 12 pp.

Furniture by Liberty & Co. [c.1912], 42 pp.

Reproduction of Old-English Furniture [c.1912], 32 pp.

Inexpensive Hats [c.1912], 10 pp.

Novelties for Presents [1912], 36 pp.

Picturesque Hats and Bonnets, Series XXXV, 1912, 30 pp.

Liberty Specialists for Furnishing [1912], 16 pp.

Liberty Specialities for Furnishing [1912], 12 pp.

[*English Pewter, no title on cover*] [?1912], 12 pp.

Pottery and Bric-a-Brac [c.1912], 56 pp.

Suggestions for Decorating and Furnishing a Small Dining Room [c.1912], 10 pp.

Blouse Suits in Liberty Fabrics [c.1912], 12 pp.

Picturesque Dresses, Series XXXVII, 1912, 66 pp.

Presents [1912], 112 pp.

Yule-Tide Gifts, 1912, 162 pp.

Inexpensive Hats [c.1912-13], 20 pp.

Inexpensive Hats [Metz & Co., Liberty's Agents In Holland] [c.1912-13], 12 pp.

School Frocks in the Liberty Fabrics [c.1912-13], 12 pp.

Antiques, October 1913, 8 pp.

Liberty Picture Hats, No. 36, Spring 1913, 12 ff.

Picture Hats and Bonnets for Children [c.1913], 12 pp.

Liberty's Silk Scarves [c.1913], 6 ff.

Liberty Jewellery [c.1913], 4 pp.

Yule-Tide Gifts, 1913-14, 16 pp.

Yule-Tide Gifts [Birmingham] 1913-14, 32 pp.

Children's Frocks in Liberty Fabrics [c.1913-14], 24 pp.

Liberty's Choice and Charming Presents [c.1914], 8 pp.

Buckinghamshire Lace [c.1914], 12 pp.

Frocks in Liberty Fabrics [c.1914-15], 28 pp.

Dresses, Series XLII, 1915, 64 pp.

Country Cottages and Their Furnishings [c.1915], 24 pp.

Dresses, Series XLIII, 1915, 60 pp.

Liberty Specialities [Birmingham], 1915, 28 pp.

Choice and Charming Presents [1915], 80 pp.

Small Pieces of Furniture [c.1915], 24 pp.

Lampshades [c.1915], 16 pp.

Yule-Tide Gifts, 1915-16, 82 pp.

Dresses, Series XLIV, 1916, 60 pp.

Blouses [1916], 16 pp.

Yule-Tide Gifts, 1916-17, 64 pp.

Blouses, Autumn and Winter 1916-17, 16 pp.

Dresses, No. 47, Autumn 1917, 48 pp.

Yule-Tide Gifts, 1917-18, 53 pp.

Yule-Tide Gifts, 1918-19, 16 pp.

Liberty Hats & Bonnets, No. 50, Spring 1919, 24 pp.

Liberty Dresses, No. 50, Spring 1919, 48 pp.

Liberty-Frocks for Children, Series L [1919], 18 pp.

Jade Amulets [1919], 28 pp.

Liberty Dresses, No. 51, Autumn 1919, 48 pp.

Yule-Tide Gifts, 1919-20, 32 pp.

Liberty Hats & Bonnets, No. 52, Spring 1920, 24 pp.

Liberty Frocks for Children, Series LII [1920], 16 pp.

Liberty's Jewellery: Some Original Designs in Gold Earrings [c.1920], 4 pp.

New Fashions in Jewellery [c.1920], 4 pp., leaflet

Laces and Chicaneries for Application to Modern Dress [c.1920], 6 pp., folding leaflet

Picture Frocks for Children [c.1920], 16 pp.

Yule-Tide Gifts, 1920-21, 32 pp.

Silk Underclothing, Series XV [c.1920-21], 12 pp.

Liberty Dresses, No. 54, Spring 1921, 48 pp.

Underclothing, Series XVI [c.1921-2], 20 pp.

Liberty Hats and Bonnets, No. 56, Spring 1922, 24 pp.

Liberty Blouses, No. 56, Spring 1922, 20 pp.

Liberty Frocks for Children, Series LVI [1922], 16 pp.

Designs for Needlework [c.1922], 36 pp.

Yule-Tide Gifts, 1922-3, 48 pp.

Liberty Fabrics for Dresses and Furnishing in Designs and Colourings Unobtainable Elsewhere [1923], 4 pp., leaflet with postcard flap

Liberty Dresses and Fabrics [Birmingham], 1923, 24 pp.

Liberty Dresses, No. 58, Spring 1923, 48 pp.

Liberty Blouses, No. 58, Spring 1923, 20 pp.

Liberty Hats and Bonnets, No. 58, Spring 1923, 24 pp.

Liberty Fabrics for Dresses and Furnishing in Designs and Colourings Unobtainable Elsewhere, 1923, 4 pp., leaflet with postcard flap

Liberty Frocks for Children, Series LIX [1923], 16 pp.

Liberty Hats and Bonnets, No. 59, Autumn 1923, 24 pp.

Silverwork [c.1923], 20 pp.

Jewellery [c.1923], 28 pp.

Yule-Tide Gifts, 1923-4, 40 pp.

Liberty 1875-1924 [produced to celebrate Liberty's new shops in Argyll Place and Regent Street], 1924, 26 pp.

Liberty Fabrics in Designs and Colourings Unobtainable Elsewhere [1924], 20 pp.

Liberty Fabrics for Dresses & Furnishing [1924], 8 pp.

Liberty Hats & Bonnets, No. 60, Spring 1924, 24 pp.

Ready-to-Wear Liberty Dresses, Series LX, Spring 1924, 12 pp.

Liberty Frocks For Children, Series LVIII [1924], 16 pp.

Liberty Frocks For Children, Series LX [1924], 16 pp.

Liberty Hats & Bonnets, No. 61, Autumn 1924, 22 pp.

Liberty Dresses, Series LXI, Autumn 1924, 48 pp.

Liberty Dresses and Fabrics [Autumn and Winter Fashions] [Birmingham], 1924, 24 pp.

Liberty Frocks for Children, Series LXI [1924], 16 pp.

Sketch Suggestions for Tudor Fitments and Decorations [c.1924], 16 pp.

Garden Pottery [c.1924], 20 pp.

Liberty Dresses, Series LXII, Spring 1925, 48 pp.

Liberty Hats & Bonnets, No. 62, Spring 1925, 22 pp.

Liberty Over-Blouses and Jumpers, No. 63, Autumn 1925, 20 pp.

Ready-to-Wear Liberty Dresses, Series LXIII, Autumn 1925, 12 pp.

Liberty Dresses, Series LXIII, Autumn 1925, 48 pp.

Ready-to-Wear Liberty Tyrian Silk Jumpers [c.1925], 6 pp., folding leaflet

Silver Work [1925], 16 pp.

English Pewter [c.1925], 12 pp.

Jewellery [c.1925], 18 pp.

Jade Amulets [c.1925], 35 ff.

Chinese Enamel Jewellery [c.1925], 6 pp., folding leaflet

Liberty Lamp Shades [c.1925], 6 pp., folding leaflet

Liberty Frocks for Children, Series LXIII [1925-6], 8 pp.

Liberty & Regent Street by E. Beresford Chancellor [1926], 24 pp.

A Myriad Years of Joy (Ancient Art and Modern Monograms) [1926], 12 pp.

Liberty Over-Blouses and Jumpers, No. 64, Spring 1926, 20 pp.

Ready-to-Wear Liberty Dresses, Series LXIV, Spring 1926, 18 pp.

Liberty Hats, No. 65, Autumn 1926, 24 pp.

Liberty Frocks for Children, Series LXV [1926], 16 pp.

Liberty Silk Shawls [1926], 12 pp.

Liberty Silk Shawls [c.1926], 8 pp.

English Pewter [1926], 12 pp.

Jewels and Amulets [c.1927], 16 pp.

Liberty Stitched Silk Hats [1927], 6 pp.

Liberty Fabrics for Dresses and Furnishing [Birmingham] [1927], 16 pp.

Liberty Down Quilts [1927], 16 pp.

Liberty Stitched Velvet Hats [Birmingham] [1927], 6 pp., folding leaflet

Liberty Frocks for Children, Series LXVII [1927], 16 pp.

Liberty's [Liberty Gifts] [1927], 56 pp.

Liberty's [Liberty's Yule-Tide Gifts] 1927-8, 56 pp.

Liberty Fabrics for Dresses and Furnishing [c.1927-9], 20 pp.

Liberty Hats, No. 69, Spring 1928, 24 pp.

Liberty [Liberty Dresses and Cloaks, Series LXVIII], Spring 1928, 24 pp.

Designs for Needle Work [1928], 24 pp.

Liberty Frocks for Children, Series LXVIII [1928], 16 pp.

Liberty Hats, Series LXIX, Autumn 1928, 24 pp.

[Liberty Dresses and Cloaks, no title on cover, Series LXIX], Autumn 1928, 24 pp.

Liberty Frocks for Children, Series LXIX [1928], 16 pp.

Liberty Cretonnes for Jenners, Princes Street, Edinburgh, Agents for Liberty's [c.1928], 8 pp.

[Liberty Yule-Tide Gifts, no title on cover], 1928-9, 56 pp.

Liberty Hats, Series LXX [1929], 10 pp.

Liberty Cretonnes at James McCutcheon & Co., New York [1929], 8 pp.

Six Styles of Decoration by Liberty & Co. Ltd [1929], 20 pp.

House Decorations: Liberty Colouring Ensures Individuality and Refinement [1929], 24 pp.

Designs for Needlework [c.1929], 24 pp.

Liberty's Spring Catalogue 1930, 24 pp. plus 2 pp. loose

Liberty Hats, Spring 1930, 20 pp.

Liberty Silk Shawls [1930], 12 pp.

Liberty Hats, Autumn 1930, 20 pp.

Liberty Dresses and Cloaks for Ladies and Frocks for Children, Series LXXIII [1930], 40 pp.

Something About Liberty & Co., Regent Street, London [c.1930], 8 pp.

Liberty Dresses Ready-to-Wear [c.1930], 6 pp., folding leaflet

Modern Silver [c.1930], 24 pp.

[Liberty Christmas Gifts, no title on cover], 1930-1, 48 pp.

Embroidery in Perfection by Liberty's [c.1930-5], 8 pp., folding leaflet

Liberty Embroidery Silks [c.1930-5], 6 pp., folding leaflet

Embroidery and Needlework by Liberty's [c.1930-5], 24 pp.

Liberty's Needlework and Its Accessories [c.1930-5], 24 pp.

Liberty Hats, Spring 1931, 20 pp.

Ready-to-Wear Liberty Dresses and Jumpers, Series LXXII [1931], 24 pp.

Liberty Hats, Autumn 1931, 20 pp.

[Untitled catalogue of fabrics, scarves, rugs, etc.] [c.1931], 12 pp.

[Liberty Christmas Gifts, no title on cover], 1931-2, 44 pp.

English Pewter [1932], 32 pp.

Liberty Hats, 1932, 16 pp.

Liberty Dresses and Jumpers for Ladies and Frocks for Children, 1932, 32 pp.

[Liberty Gifts, no title on cover], 1932-3, 40 pp.

Liberty [Liberty Fabrics for Dresses and Furnishing], 1933, 24 pp.

Liberty Hats, 1933, 20 pp.

Liberty Dresses Jumpers and Children's Frocks, Spring and Summer, 1933, 20 pp.

Liberty Coats for all Occasions [c.1933], 4 pp.

Liberty, 1933-4, 20 pp.

Liberty Coats & Wraps, Spring 1934, 6 pp., folding leaflet

Liberty Jumpers, Lingerie and Tea Gowns, Spring and Summer, 1934, 12 pp.

Liberty Hats for Early Autumn Wear, 1934, 12 pp.

The Cultured Pearl [c.1934], 4 pp., leaflet

English Pewter [c.1934], 32 pp.

Liberty's [Liberty Gifts 1934-5], 32 pp.

Liberty Hats for the Spring [c.1935], 6 pp., folding leaflet

Liberty Hats for Immediate Wear [c.1935], 8 pp.

Millinery, Autumn 1935, 16 pp.

Modern Silver and Pewter [c.1935], 6 pp., folding leaflet

Liberty Silver and Pewter [c.1935], 24 pp.

Liberty's Lace, Fans, Petit Point and Amber [c.1935], 6 pp., folding leaflet

She Bought a Liberty Scarf (An Improving Tale) [c.1935], 16 pp.

Liberty & Co. Ltd: Furniture & Decorations [c.1935], 8 pp.

The Year's at the Spring Liberty's, 1936, 30 pp.

Liberty Coats for All Occasions [1936], 12 pp.

Spring 1937, Liberty's, 28 pp.

Gowns by Liberty, 1937, 20 pp.

From Liberty's Children Department [1937], 4 pp., leaflet

Liberty Hats for Immediate Wear [c.1937], 8 pp.

The Renaissance of Merton Abbey [c.1937], 16 pp.

Some Lovely Things at Liberty's [1937-8], 32 pp.

Liberty's Primavera [1938], 16 pp.

Liberty's [1938], 16 pp.

Liberty Hats for Autumn Wear [c.1938], 8 pp.

[Untitled General Catalogue], 1938-9, 16 pp.

[Untitled General Catalogue] [1939], 20 pp.

Now Buy Your Furnishings at Liberty's [c.1940], 8pp plus 2 pp. loose

1945 Before-After Liberty's of Regent Street, 24 pp.

Liberty [c.1945], 6 pp., folding leaflet

[Liberty's Tudor shop, compiled by Ivor Stewart-Liberty, no title on cover], 1949, 24 pp.

Westminster City Archive Collection

Sunshades, Fans and Easter Sun Hats, n.d. [c.1910]

Liberty Chiffoneries, n.d. [c.1914]

Liberty Silk Handkerchiefs, n.d. [c.1920]

Ways of Wearing Liberty Silk Scarves, n.d. [c.1925]

Liberty Dressing Gowns and Motor Rugs, n.d. [c.1930]

Liberty's Lace Fans, Petit Point and Amber, n.d. [c.1935]

She Bought a Liberty Scarf, n.d. [c.1935]

Liberty's from the Inexpensive Dress Department, n.d. [February 1937]

Liberty's: A Few Examples from Our Early Spring Collection, n.d. [March 1937]

Liberty's, Blouses and Suits Folder, n.d. [April 1937]

Liberty's Inexpensive Dresses, n.d. [April 1937]

Liberty's Sale Catalogue 29 December 1937- 29 January 1938

Liberty's Choose Hydrangea Colours This Spring, n.d. [1938]

Decorations and Furnishings by Liberty, n.d. [April 1938]

Day and Evening Coats by Liberty, n.d. [1938-9]

Home Furnishings in 'Moghul' Fabric, n.d. [1937-8]

Liberty Squares and Scarves, n.d. [c.1939]

Liberty's Inexpensive Dresses, Spring/ Summer 1939

Coats, Suits and Jackets [incomplete], n.d. [Spring 1939]

Charming Woollen Frocks at Liberty's, n.d. [October 1939]

Clothes for an English Autumn, n.d. [c.1940]

Now Buy Your Furnishings at Liberty [enclosing a loose page of 'Argram' rugs], n.d. [c.1940]

[Two small catalogues in design of Liberty squares], n.d. [c.1940]

Liberty Blouses, n.d. [1940s]

Spread Your Wings with Scarves from Liberty's, n.d. [1940s-50s]

Happy Christmas at Liberty, n.d. [1950]

What Does Your House Need?, n.d. [1950s]

Smart People Say They Can Never Have Too Many Liberty's Scarves, n.d. [1950s]

Liberty of Regent Street, Spring 1953

Liberty Scarves Are Sheer Temptation, n.d. [1954]

Liberty of London: Christmas 1955

Court Royal Corsetry Comes to Liberty, n.d. [1955]

Liberty Scarves from London Town: A Landmark in Fashion, n.d. [1956]

Liberty Scarves from London Town, n.d. [1956]

A Genius for Presents, n.d. [1956]

Catalogue Supplement of Doll's Clothes and Toys [1956]

Fanfare of Scarves from Liberty, n.d. [1957]

Liberty of London: A House Full of Things [1958]

Handprinted Scarves by Liberty, n.d. [c.1960]

Handprinted Scarves: Legendary Beauty, n.d. [1960]

Handprinted Scarves [William Austin, Corporation Street, Birmingham], n.d. [c.1960]

Make It a Starry-eyed Liberty Christmas, n.d. [1960]

Christmas Magic [cover by Robert Stewart] [1960]

The News is Out at Liberty, Summer 1961

Handprinted Scarves: Flaunt Them Proudly [Georges of Collins Street], n.d. [1961]

Handprinted Scarves [draft catalogue for the American market], n.d. [c.1968]

Silk Scarves by Liberty of London U.S.A., n.d. [1968]

Elegance and Utility 1924-1978: The Work of Susie Cooper R.D.I. [1978]

Mail Order Christmas Catalogue [1984]

Christmas Catalogue [1986]

Catalogue [1987]

Liberty by Post [1998]

Liberty by Post, Winter 1999

Liberty by Post, Christmas Edition 1999

Accessories Catalogue, 2000

Tana Lawn Fabric Collection, 2000

Liberty by Post, Spring 2000

At Liberty, Spring/Summer 2000

At Liberty, Autumn/Winter 2000

Liberty by Post, Winter 2000

Christmas Catalogue, 2000

INDEX

PHOTOGRAPHIC ACKNOWLEDGMENTS

With the exception of those listed here, all the photographs and illustrations in this book either belong to the author or form part of private collections. The publishers have made every effort to contact holders of copyright works. Any copyright holders we have been unable to reach are invited to contact the publishers so that a full acknowledgment may be given in subsequent editions. For permission to reproduce the images on the following pages the publishers would like to thank:

Alessi S.p.A., Crusinallo, Italy: 46, 47

Getty Images: 188/9

Helen Haigh; 137

Photos © Gavin Kingcome: 180/81

www.lacma.org: 36 left (M.2007.211.901), 77 above left (M.2002.28.2), 77 below left (AC1966.196.7), 77 centre right (AC1993.1.14)

The Lakeland Arts Trust: 71 below, 72, 73

Library of Congress: 142

Los Angeles County Museum of Art/©Photo SCALA, Florence: 91 (Gift of Max Palevsky [AC1993.1.15].©2014), 102 above (Gift of Ellen and Max Palevsky ©2014)

Metz & Co.: 187 below left

Museum of Domestic Design & Architecture, Middlesex University: 92, 93, 94, 95, 96, 97

Rumours Decorative Arts (www.rumoursdecorativearts.co.uk): 102 below

Kerry Taylor Auctions (www.kerrytaylorauctions.com): 36 right, 107, 147, 148, 172/3,

174 above

Titus Omega (www.titusomega.com): 50/51, 69 above left, 84 below, 85, 88/9

Tjolöholm Foundation: 114, 115, 116 below (photo Thomas Carlén), 118 left (photo Jenny Nensén), 119 above (photo Helene Fransson), 120 above (photo Jeffrey Jones), 124 (photo Victoria Kvarnström), 125 above (photo Victoria Kvarnström), 126 (photo Helene Fransson), 129

Trustworth Studios: 29, 64, 65, 68, 80,100

V&A Images/Victoria and Albert Museum: 20 left, 48, 58, 106

Roger Viollet/Getty Images: 82 below left

Westminster Archives: Front cover, 4, 13 below left, 14 below right, 18 above, 19 above, 22, 23, 140/41, 158, 161 above left, 162/3, 164/5, 166/7, 168, 169, 170/71, 175, 176, 178/9, 182, 183, 187 above

Windermere Motor Boat Racing Club: 71 above

AUTHOR'S ACKNOWLEDGMENTS

I am deeply grateful for the help and assistance offered by members of the Liberty family, particularly Anthony Blackmore and Richard Stewart-Liberty. I am also very grateful for all the help and assistance offered by the following individuals and institutions: Alessi; Anne Askwith; Helen & Robert Austin; David Breman, Trustworth Studios; The British Library; Geoffrey Curren; John Donovan, Rumours Decorative Arts; Helen Haigh; John Harvey, Titus Omega; Tricia Jameson; Gavin Kingcome; Leeds Public Library; Los Angeles County Museum of Art; Zoe Hendon, Museum of Domestic Design and Architecture; Judith Tankard; Kerry Taylor; Victoria & Albert Museum; Rory Lalwan, City of Westminster Archives; the Director, Maria Sidén, Elisabeth Elfström and Magdalena Kasper and all the staff at Tjolöholms Slott, Sweden.

I would also like to thank the unseen hands at Frances Lincoln who have been, as before, a pure joy to work with: my editor, Jo Christian; Sue Gladstone, picture editor; and the designer, Caroline Clark. And my agent, Catriona Wilson.

Frances Lincoln Limited
74–77 White Lion Street
London N1 9PF
www.franceslincoln.com

Liberty Style
Copyright © Frances Lincoln Limited 2014
Text copyright © Martin Wood 2014
For copyright in the illustrations see opposite

First Frances Lincoln edition 2014

A catalogue record for this book is available from the British Library.
ISBN 978-0-7112-3474-1

Designed by www.carolineclark.co.uk

Printed and bound in China

9 8 7 6 5 4 3 2 1

JACKET Liberty of London amethyst and shocking pink tapestry and silk
chiffon evening dress by Scaasi, 1961.

FRONTISPIECE AND PAGE 216 'Off to shop at Liberty's!' From a Liberty's
catalogue of c.1935.

OPPOSITE CONTENTS PAGE A window display designed by Eric Lucking
for the menswear department, c.1950.

PAGE EDGES AND ENDPAPERS 'Berry', a wallpaper design printed for
Liberty by Essex & Co.